Criminalistics
for the Law Enforcement Officer

Anthony L. Califana, B.S., M.P.S.
Supervising Identification Technician
Westchester County Sheriff's Office, Valhalla, NY
Adjunct Assistant Professor, Iona College, New Rochelle, NY,
and Instructor, Rockland Community College, Suffern, NY

Jerome S. Levkov, Ph.D.
Associate Professor and Chairman of the Department
of Chemistry, Iona College, New Rochelle, NY

Gregg Division

McGraw-Hill Book Company

New York	Mexico
St. Louis	Montreal
Dallas	New Delhi
San Francisco	Panama
Auckland	Paris
Bogotá	São Paulo
Düsseldorf	Singapore
Johannesburg	Sydney
London	Tokyo
Madrid	Toronto

Library of Congress Cataloging in Publication Data

Califana, Anthony L
    Criminalistics for the law enforcement officer.

    Bibliography: p.
    Includes index.
    1. Criminal investigation. I. Levkov, Jerome S., joint author. II. Title.
HV8073.C29   364.12   77-28269
ISBN 0-07-009620-1

To Carol and Dolly

234567890 RDRD 7832109

The editors for this book were Susan Munger and Mary Levai, the designer was Aspen Hollow Art Service, the cover designer was Roberta Rezk, the art supervisor was George T. Resch, and the production supervisor was May Konopka. It was set in Palatino by Progressive Typographers.
Printed and bound by R. R. Donnelley, Inc.

Contents

Preface

This text is intended to serve as an introduction to modern methods used in the detection, investigation, and solution of crimes. It describes all the vital phases of forensic science from a practical and, to an appropriate degree, a theoretical point of view. As such, it is suitable as a text for the police officer or other student of criminalistics. Previous experience in criminalistics or in the physical sciences is not required. Actual case histories are cited throughout the text to illustrate the material. The work will provide a basic knowledge of such subjects as photography, fingerprints and other impressions, ballistics, glass, hair, handwriting and document examination, drugs, and instrumental methods of analysis. These subjects have been carefully selected by the authors on the basis of many years of experience in the field as well as in the classroom.

The courts rely ever-increasingly on scientific evidence. The tools of science are eminently suited to the solution of forensic problems; and newer, more powerful applications of the scientist's arsenal are being made daily. These tools are far removed from the type used by a "Sherlock Holmes" and are often incomprehensible to nonscientists such as police officers, district attorneys or, for that matter, jurors. Many of those involved in the criminal justice system are returning to school to update or increase their knowledge of the criminal justice process. Such updating often includes forensic science.

The chapters are designed to furnish a historical introduction to the topic, the necessary theory, and illustrative case histories. This book may be used in courses with or without an accompanying laboratory session; however, it is not necessary when using this text to have access to specialized equipment or a laboratory.

Our appreciation goes to all those who contributed so freely with photographs, which are a significant part of *Criminalistics for the Law Enforcement Officer*. We would be remiss if we did not acknowledge Frederick Drummond, Department of Laboratories and Research of Westchester County, for his technical assistance with the chapter on blood, as well as Joseph Reich, Firearms Examiner for the Westchester County Sheriff's Office, for his efforts and guidance in the firearms chapter. We would also like to thank James McDonald, New Haven, Connecticut, Police Department, for his critique of the manuscript, and Iona College for its support during the course of this project. Lastly, were it not for the encouragement and understanding of our wives, Carol and Dolly, deprived of our company on many evenings, this book would not have been possible. We owe them our ever-grateful thanks.

"Every contact leaves its trace."

—Edmond Locard (1877–1966),
founder and director of
the Institute of Criminalistics
at the University of Lyons, France,
the first "crime laboratory."

chapter

The Importance of Criminalistics in Police Work

This book describes the many ways in which science helps crime detection. That is what criminalistics is all about.

To anyone interested in modern law enforcement, from students to police officers, an understanding of the basic principles of criminalistics is essential, especially in terms of the practical, day-to-day procedures and routines at the heart of successful investigation.

Such an understanding does not require detailed knowledge of science. In fact, it is the premise of this book that the fundamentals of criminalistics are best understood by seeing them in action in the real world of a law enforcement agency. Of greater concern here are the techniques that prove successful under the press of daily events rather than abstract theories. Accordingly, the reader will find much "how to" advice about sound police work and its relationship to forensic science. These chapters cover the major areas in which the techniques of criminalistics contribute to the identification and apprehension of criminals:

Document examination	Hair	Photography
Voiceprints	Blood	Firearms investigation
Fingerprints	Arson	Impressions as evidence
Glass	Drugs	Preservation and care
	Deception detectors	of evidence

A final chapter deals with testifying in court. This is not, of course, a branch of criminalistics in the formal sense. It is an important aspect of police work, however. No matter how good a case is built by science and police work, the test of all investigation is whether it can be presented effectively in a court of law, so that judge and jury can understand and pass intelligent judgment on the results.

The Frye Decision [*Frye v. United States*, 293 Fed. 1013 (1923)] established the criteria by which a scientific examination is judged to be admissible to a court of law. Recognizing the difficulty in deciding between when it is still experimental and when it is proved, the court stated, " . . . the thing from which the deduction is made must be sufficiently established to have gained general acceptance in the particular field in which it belongs."

The Crime Laboratory

Scientific crime detection is not new. Its principles were most dramatically and eloquently put forth in the late nineteenth century by the famous Sherlock Holmes. Holmes was a storybook character, to be sure, but his creator, Sir Arthur Conan Doyle, gave voice through him to theories of forensic science that have since become realities. Hans Gross, a public prosecutor and judge in Austria, wrote the first scientific monograph on the subject of criminalistics in 1893, and he is credited with being the first to suggest how chemistry, physics, geology, botany, and other sciences could be applied to criminal investigation.

Somewhat later, in France, Edmond Locard translated Gross's ideas into the first crime laboratory for the Bureau de Justice of Lyons. His work met with success, and by the 1920s, many countries had built laboratories solely devoted to criminal investigation. Today, there are hundreds, perhaps the most complete of which is the Federal Bureau of Investigation in Washington, D.C.

Criminalistics today is widely recognized as an exciting and vital field of study. Its role in police work becomes increasingly important, not only because of the remarkable advances in science but also because of changes in the social and legal climate. In 1966 the well-known *Miranda v. Arizona* case was tried by the Supreme Court of the United States. The court ruled that the defendant must be apprised of his or her rights upon being arrested. Among these rights are the right to remain silent and the right to have a lawyer present (to be furnished by the state if the accused is without funds). It has often been said that this decision forced a decreased dependence on confessions for obtaining convictions, as well as an increased need for and reliance on physical evidence for this purpose. Although clear-cut statistics to support or refute this view are hard to obtain, some studies have been made. A review of police cases in the pre- and post-Miranda years in Pittsburgh, Pennsylvania,[1] led to the following observations:

1. There was a significant decline (about 20 percent) in the number of cases in which confessions were obtained.
2. However, confessions are still being obtained in a significant number of cases (in more than one-third of the cases).
3. Of the cases examined, confessions were probably necessary to obtain convictions in about 20 percent.
4. Based on their statistics, they estimate that the Miranda ruling should have resulted in about a 5 percent decrease in the conviction rate.

Although others have indicated a greater impact of the Miranda decision, based on the Pittsburgh study, it appears that the effect of the decision has not been as detrimental to the apprehension and conviction of criminals as is often stated.

Miranda considerations aside, the use of criminalistics to its fullest advantage has not occurred and is not occurring in many criminal investigations. The roots of this deficiency are many—lack of training, lack of understanding of the capabilities of science in this field, and inadequate funds and facilities come to mind immediately.

At the same time, the tools of forensic science have become sharper and more versatile. In this book, for example, you will learn how electron microscopes, gas chromatographs, mass spectrometers, and other remarkable instruments of investigation are able to pinpoint and individualize subtle clues that would have been valueless only a few years ago.

What can criminalistics accomplish? Here are three examples:

In a New England murder case, police found sand in the shoes of a man suspected of committing a murder on a beach. The suspect admitted that he had been walking on a beach, but not the one on which the murder was committed. The police sent the sand to a crime laboratory, which reported the presence of black tourmaline schlorite,

---

[1] R. H. Seeburger and R. S. Wettick, Jr., "*Miranda* in Pittsburgh—A Statistical Study," *Univ. Pittsburgh Law R.*, **29**(1), October 1967.

a substance found only in the sand at the murder scene. Thus the suspect and murder scene were undeniably connected.

The famous Edmond Locard removed particles of a substance from the fingernails of a suspect charged with the murder of his girl friend. The substance turned out to be face powder of the same kind as that used by the victim.

Searching for evidence, a criminalist happened to examine the ear wax of a murder suspect under a microscope. He found tiny seeds, invisible to the naked eye. It turned out that the seeds were a rare type of pollen found only at the scene of the crime. The suspect had flown some 1500 miles from the scene, but he was located and arrested.

Such cases are becoming commonplace as criminalistics plays an increasingly important part in many investigations. A question sometimes arises: Does the criminalist reduce the importance of the police investigator? No. On the contrary, the investigator's role is enhanced because the evidence which he or she recognizes, collects, and preserves becomes more valuable in the hands of a criminalist who knows how to extract its meaning most convincingly.

Indeed, both the technician and the investigator should work together at the scene of the crime. The investigator recognizes the important physical evidence, and the technician handles it with care and skill. The technician comes equipped with all the necessary tools of the trade: evidence bags, identification tags, and the proper forms for labeling. Should the investigator forget photographs, the technician will probably remind her or him. Because of experience the investigator knows where to look for evidence and how to measure its significance. The technician, on the other hand, understands how to handle such things as blood samples, semen, and fabric remnants until they can be brought to the laboratory for analysis. Working together, the investigator and the technician are an effective team.

In order to use evidence to link a suspect to a crime, one almost invariably compares an item discovered at the scene of the crime with an item associated with or found on the suspect. The bit of glass found at the house that was burglarized is only of use if glass that can be compared with it is also found on the suspect. In a like manner, a fingerprint is of little value if the suspect's prints are not on file or the suspect is not apprehended. The evidence may indicate the direction the investigation should take, e.g. a paint chip found on the victim of a hit-and-run accident may reveal the color and make of the vehicle involved.

Among many authorities in the field of law enforcement, there is a widespread belief that criminalistics is just beginning its role in criminal investigation. It has already accomplished much, but its future appears limited only by the imagination, intelligence, and wisdom of its practitioners.

Academically, the study of criminalistics has achieved an impressive status in recent years. It has become a major area of concentration in criminal justice courses at many colleges and universities. A student can now obtain a master of science degree in forensic science (*criminalistics* and *forensic science* are different words for the same field). Some institutions of higher learning now offer the doctorate degree as well.

The following chapters are intended to be an overview that helps the reader understand the aims, purposes, techniques, and methodology of the criminalist's approach to investigation. Upon completion of the book, the reader should have a practical grasp of the subject. Specifically, the reader will be able to recognize evidence, be aware of its potential value, know how to maintain a secure chain of evidence, and understand the kinds of tests that such evidence will be subjected to when processed by a crime laboratory.

chapter

Care and Preservation of Evidence

A bit of paper, a piece of glass, a spot of blood, a spent bullet, a thread of fiber, a strand of human hair—you will see how these things and many others may prove to be crucial evidence in bringing a criminal to justice. Evidence is the raw material of all criminalistics, the basis of the science and art of bringing an investigation to a successful conclusion.

To anyone involved in law enforcement, the primacy of evidence, the need to collect it carefully and to preserve it so that its validity will stand up in court, cannot be overemphasized. This is even truer today than perhaps it was in the past.

Not too long ago, law enforcement officers, district attorneys, and prosecutors considered the obtaining of a signed confession by the suspect to be the strongest link in getting a conviction. In fact, it was so stressed that prosecutors took an active role in making sure that confessions were as free of loopholes as possible in order for them to stand up in court.

The Supreme Court's Miranda ruling has changed this in significant ways. As you may remember, the Miranda ruling guarantees that a suspect be read his or her rights to remain silent and to have the advice and counsel of a lawyer. This has acted as a deterrent to confessions, in most cases because a suspect is most likely to confess when he is first apprehended and is in an overwrought state of mind and emotion.

Whatever the reasons, police all over the country report fewer confessions today than there used to be. As a result, officials are turning more to physical evidence to bring about convictions. This is one of the reasons forensic science has grown rapidly in recent years. It is also the reason that experts in many different scientific disciplines are much more active in law enforcement work than formerly.

This chapter focuses upon a single aspect of evidence: the importance of its careful handling and preservation from the time of its recognition to its introduction in court.

No matter what ingenious (and expensive) scientific techniques have been brought into play to discover and to analyze evidence, the success of an investigation can be measured only by the effectiveness of the evidence in a court of law. That is why so much depends on how evidence is cared for and preserved after it has been found. In this chapter we will cover the care of evidence in the nine crucial steps leading up to its appearance in court.

Step 1: Secure the Crime Scene

The first officer at the crime scene should, as top priority, take swift and sure steps to see that the area is properly secured against any kind of disturbance. The main reason for this precaution is the preservation of evidence.

"Do not touch anything!" should be the order of the day for everyone. Be careful about smudging latent fingerprints or adding fingerprints to surfaces that will be examined later by fingerprint technicians. Unwanted prints add to their burdens because they have to compare them with those of the person who did the ill-advised handling of the evidence. A record of all personnel who entered the crime scene should be kept to facilitate this screening process, should it become necessary.

The first officer should keep a sharp eye out for the possibility that evidence may be moved from its original position at the time of the crime. The officer should make sure that this does not happen, because it causes confusion in reconstructing the events of the crime.

Step 2: Photograph and Sketch the Overall Scene

Pictures should be taken from many different angles of the entire scene. This establishes the relationship of evidence—the murder victim's body, for instance, the overturned chair, the drinks on the table, the bloodied poker on the carpet—to the overall circumstances. It's said in police circles that there can never be too many

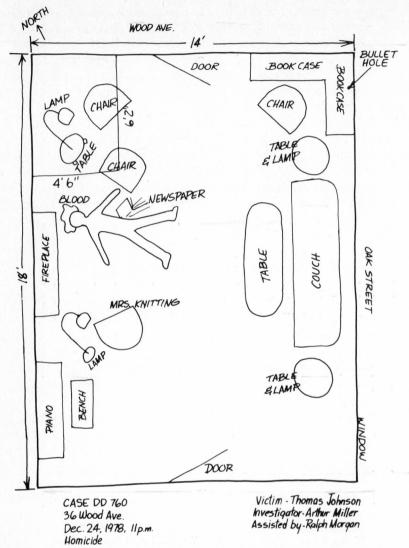

CASE DD 760
36 Wood Ave.
Dec. 24, 1978, 11p.m.
Homicide

Victim - Thomas Johnson
Investigator - Arthur Miller
Assisted by - Ralph Morgan

Figure 2-1   Rough sketch of crime scene; *facing page:* finished sketch of crime scene.

pictures. These photographs, putting the whole scene in perspective, often tell a complete story, which the piece-by-piece examination of the individual segments of evidence then substantiates. A rough sketch of the scene should also be made, including pertinent dimensions, so that the location of the various items can be pinpointed in the photographs (see Fig. 2-1).

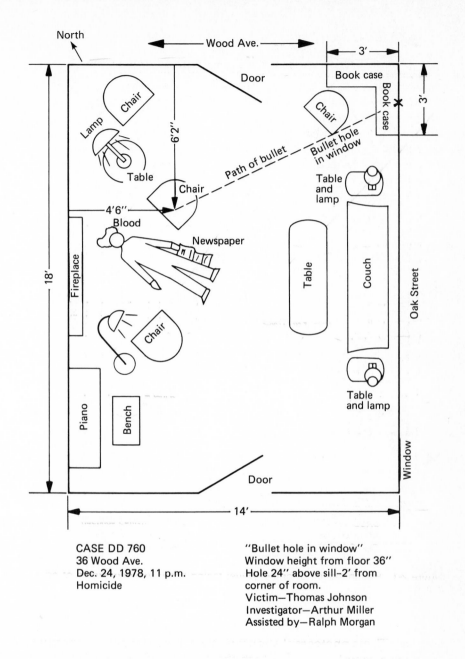

CASE DD 760
36 Wood Ave.
Dec. 24, 1978, 11 p.m.
Homicide

"Bullet hole in window"
Window height from floor 36"
Hole 24" above sill–2' from
corner of room.
Victim—Thomas Johnson
Investigator—Arthur Miller
Assisted by—Ralph Morgan

Step 3: Search for Evidence

It goes without saying that a thorough, systematic search of the scene for all possible evidence must be made. It may be performed by seasoned officers, detectives, investigators, and forensic technicians. The best kind of search results when the forensic technician and the investigator work together. The technician is trained to recognize evidence and knows its potential value. As well as being aware of how easily evidence can be damaged by mishandling, the forensic technician is sensitive to the value of small bits of foreign matter that may, under examination in the crime laboratory, prove of unexpected value. Another plus for having a technician in on the search is that in court, the technician can state that she or he was present when the evidence was found.

Step 4: Take Close-ups

When evidence is found, a close-up photograph should be taken immediately. The picture should show the exact position of the evidence before it is touched. Note its location in the sketch.

Step 5: Mark or Tag All Evidence

The officer finding the evidence should mark the evidence with the necessary identifying data as soon as possible. This is the first step in maintaining the chain of evidence so vital to presenting a good case in court. The mark or identifying label should record the place, the date, the time, and the officer's name (see Fig. 2-2). It's well to remember that often evidence is unacceptable in court because of some officer's failure to identify it properly at the scene of the crime.

Step 6: Place Evidence in a Container

Evidence that cannot be marked or tagged should be placed in a container—a cardboard box, test tube, or evidence bag—with the necessary identification attached.

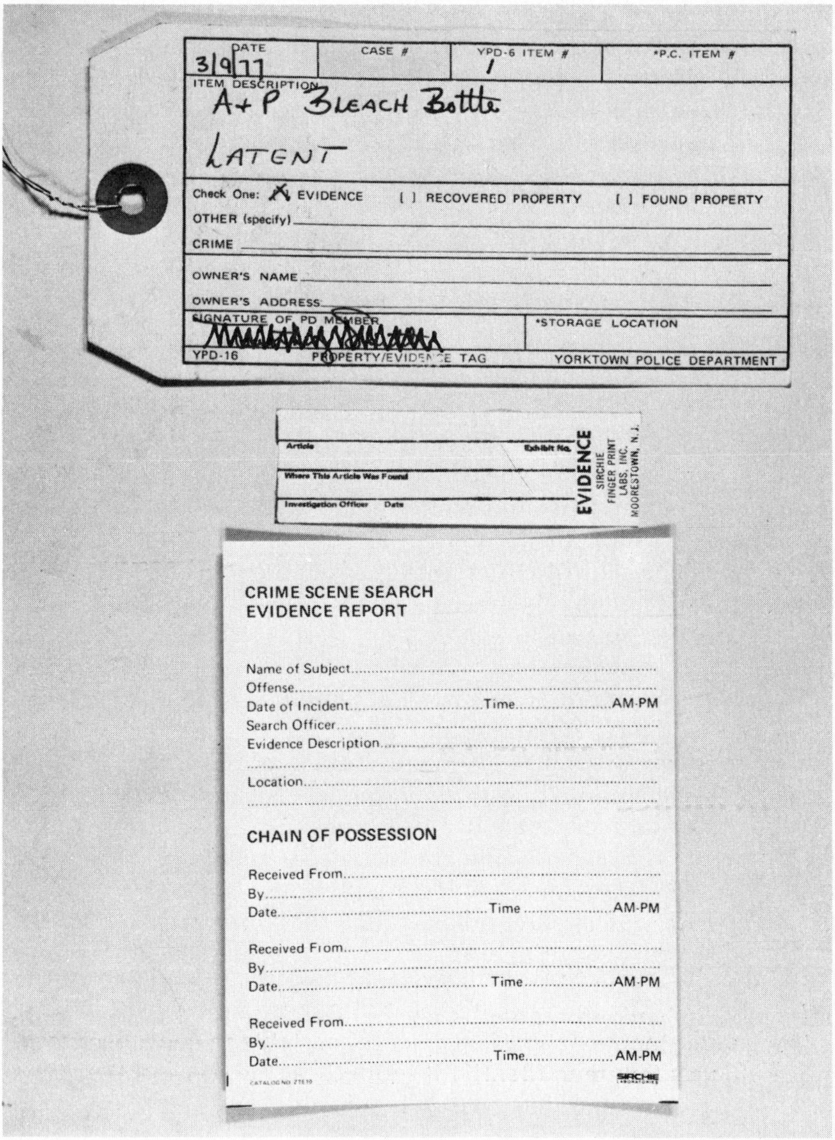

Figure 2-2 Various evidence labels (Courtesy Sirchie Fingerprint Laboratories, Moorestown, NJ).

Step 7: Record in Notebook; Make Official Report

All the details of the crime scene should be included in the officer's notebook and then transcribed in more formal style in the official investigation report. In both, all evidence under consideration, as well as its intended disposition, should be noted. An efficient means of organizing these procedures is given in the crime scene checklist in Fig. 2-3.

Step 8: Send Evidence to the Crime Laboratory

Whenever possible, take evidence to the crime laboratory in person, making sure that it is well protected en route. If you cannot take it, send it by certified or registered mail. An additional word is in order here concerning the care of evidence. Do not forget that foreign matter—even when it is almost microscopic in size—may prove of value in the laboratory. See Fig. 2-4. Items containing blood deserve special measures: Either send them immediately to the laboratory, or place them in separate containers. Never allow blood-stained clothing to be exposed to sun or heat; decomposition of the blood and bacterial contamination will set in.

A word of caution in regard to laboratory examinations: Always have the evidence examined and tested by qualified technicians. This is important because the qualifications of the technicians will certainly be called into question by the defense attorney at the trial. Furthermore, once evidence has been consumed in testing it cannot be retested. So if an incompetent technician gets poor results, that particular piece of evidence is lost for all time.

The Federal Bureau of Investigation (FBI) maintains the highest caliber of forensic experts, but for many reasons local law enforcement agencies cannot always call upon them. For one thing, time is often a factor, necessitating the use of local experts. It is wise to develop a list of experts and specialists who will be available when you need them.

Bloody garments or items containing blood should be taken to a serology laboratory for testing. Bullets, cartridge casings, shotgun shells, clothing containing bullet holes, and firearms should be taken to a qualified firearms examiner.

All latent fingerprint searches should be performed by fingerprint experts. The dusting of objects for revealing fingerprints is done very often by detectives who upon developing a partial fingerprint will feel they are doing a complete, on-the-spot investigation.

Physical evidence, such as glass, soil, clay, and footwear, should be brought to the laboratory for examination and testing.

```
                    LABORATORY CRIME SCENE CHECK LIST
Lab #_____                               Complaint #_____

Offense:_____ Date:_____ Location:_____
Victim(s):_____
Lab Notified By:_____Time:_____ Arrival Time:_____
Person(s) Present:_____

Lab Personnel:_____M.E. Staff:_____ADA:_____

1) PHOTOGRAPHS: Color_____Black & White_____Slides_____4x5_____Aerial_____
                Photographers:_____
                Cameras:_____

2) SKETCH: (Room, Major Furnishings, Location of Body, Physical Evidence, Direction)
           Sketcher:_____ Measurer:_____

3) SCENE: Temperature (interior/exterior):_____/_____Lighting:_____
          Weather Conditions:_____
          Doors/Windows:_____
          Electrical Appliances:_____
          Telephone:_____
          Medications:_____
          Body Description:_____

          Weapon(s):_____

          Vehicle(s):_____

          Other Unusual Conditions:_____


4) SEARCH:
          Personnel:_____
          Method:_____Area:_____
          (Check) Floor____Walls____Ceiling____Doors/Windows____Sinks____Trash____Drawers____
          Outdoors____Entrance____Exit____Other_____

5) PHYSICAL EVIDENCE: (listed on back)        COLLECT STANDARDS!!
          Latent Exams____UV Light_____Casting_____Vacuum_____ Blood Test_____
          Gunshot Residue Test____TMDT____Other_____

6) CRIME SCENE SECURED: Date:_____Time:_____Sealed:_____

7) MORGUE: ME#_____ Fingerprints:_____Photographs:_____
           Identifying Marks/Items:_____
           Wounds:_____
           Other Exams:_____
           Evidence Received:_____
           From:_____To:_____ Date/Time_____

8) CID/CIS: Conference with:_____Date/Time_____

9) SUSPECT:_____ Address:_____D.O.B._____
   Suspect Samples:      (Recovered By/Location/Date/Time)

   a) Photographs_____
   b) Finger/Palm Prints_____
   c) Clothing with shoes_____
   d) Blood & Urine Specimens_____
   e) Fingernail Scrapings_____
   f) Hair Standards_____
   g) Gunshot Residue/TMDT_____

Reporting Investigator:_____ Approving Superior:_____
```

#	Description of Item	Location	Marked	Date/Time	Name
PHYSICAL EVIDENCE COLLECTED: (Improperly Collected Evidence is of Limited or No Value!)					

Figure 2-3 Laboratory crime scene checklist (Courtesy Syracuse, NY, Police Department).

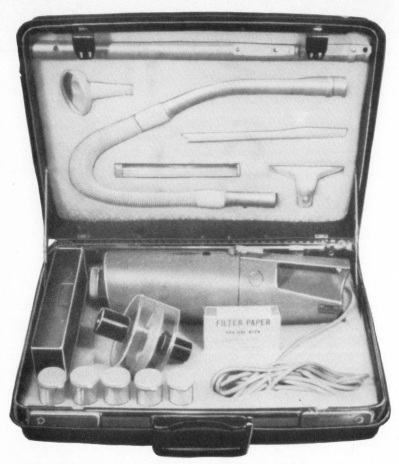

Figure 2-4 Vacuum kit with filter used to search for microscopic evidence (Courtesy Sirchie Fingerprint Laboratories, Moorestown, NJ).

Some laboratories are well equipped to examine hairs and fibers. Hairs and fibers may be either placed in plastic or glass vials or folded in white paper and inserted inside an envelope. (Generally, when two fabrics come in contact with each other or a fabric rubs against a surface, fibers will transfer. Fiber evidence is very small and easily overlooked by investigators.)

Any questionable pills or drugs should be taken to the toxicology or chemistry section of the laboratory for analysis (see Fig. 2-5). If it is necessary to make casts of tool impressions, footprints, or tire impressions, call in an expert who will perform the task efficiently.

Bullets must be removed from a homicide victim in an effort to identify the weapon that fired the bullet. In some localities, the medical examiner may require an investigator to be present during

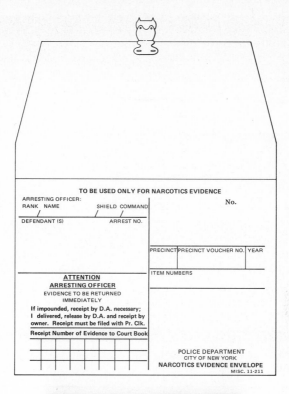

TO BE USED ONLY FOR NARCOTICS EVIDENCE			

ARRESTING OFFICER:
RANK   NAME   SHIELD COMMAND

No.

DEFENDANT (S)   ARREST NO.

PRECINCT	PRECINCT VOUCHER NO.	YEAR

**ATTENTION
ARRESTING OFFICER**
EVIDENCE TO BE RETURNED
IMMEDIATELY

ITEM NUMBERS

If impounded, receipt by D.A. necessary;
I delivered, release by D.A. and receipt by
owner. Receipt must be filed with Pr. Clk.

Receipt Number of Evidence to Court Book

POLICE DEPARTMENT
CITY OF NEW YORK
NARCOTICS EVIDENCE ENVELOPE
MISC. 11-211

Figure 2-5 *Top:* narcotics evidence is placed in a special envelope equipped with a lock; *middle:* these tamperproof bags are used to contain the sealed envelopes; *bottom:* the evidence bag, containing the narcotics evidence, is then sealed (Courtesy New York Police Department Forensic Laboratory).

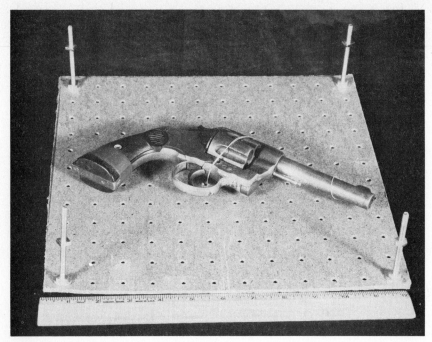

Figure 2-6 Evidence shown fastened to pegboard (Courtesy *Law and Order* magazine, New York, NY).

removal of bullets from the deceased. The medical examiner's report will reveal the fact that the bullet was retrieved from a specific area and turned over to the firearms examiner for identification and testing. The firearms examiner may mark the bullet in the presence of the medical examiner to maintain the chain of evidence. The safekeeping or security of the bullet will be the responsibility of the firearms examiner until it is to be offered into evidence at the trial. Further, the firearms examiner will tender a report as to her or his findings which must be made a part of the file.

With the new disclosure laws, the defense attorney is entitled to review all reports of evidence as well as being able to view the physical evidence before the trial. Some judges have ruled that reports that were made and not submitted to the district attorney or prosecutor may not be brought into evidence at the trial. Defense attorneys are using experts more and more in defense of their clients, which occasionally results in a "battle of the experts."

In view of these circumstances, it cannot be emphasized too strongly that law enforcement officials must keep all receipts for evidence turned over to a laboratory and all reports and results sent back from the laboratory. These may be called up in court.

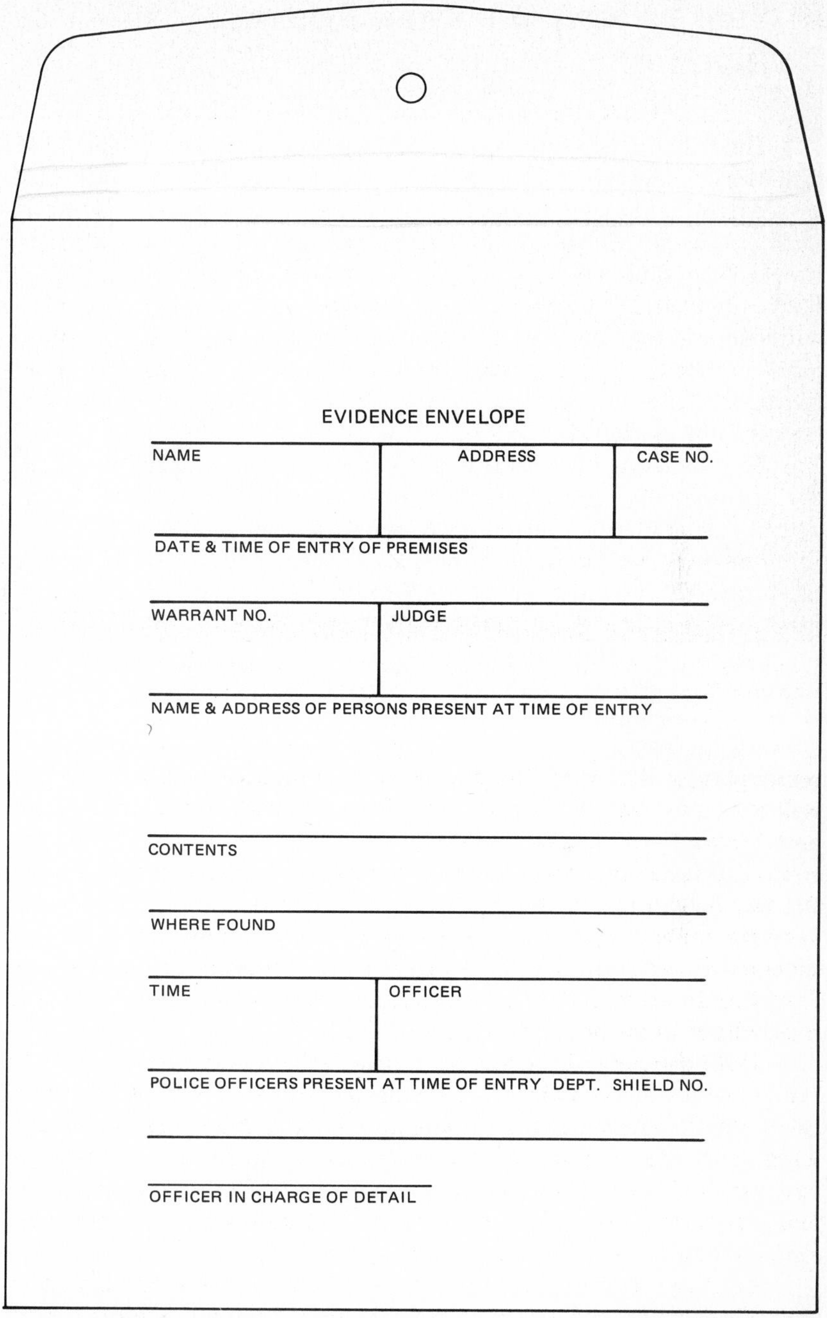

EVIDENCE ENVELOPE

NAME	ADDRESS	CASE NO.

DATE & TIME OF ENTRY OF PREMISES

WARRANT NO.	JUDGE

NAME & ADDRESS OF PERSONS PRESENT AT TIME OF ENTRY

CONTENTS

WHERE FOUND

TIME	OFFICER

POLICE OFFICERS PRESENT AT TIME OF ENTRY   DEPT.   SHIELD NO.

OFFICER IN CHARGE OF DETAIL

Figure 2-7   Search warrant evidence envelop.

Step 9: Keep a Locked Evidence Room

The ideal procedure is for a department or laboratory to maintain a locked evidence room with keys controlled by one individual for securing all evidence until its presentation at a trial. A small department may utilize a locked steel cabinet or maintain a locked drawer in a safe for evidence. If it can be established and proved that evidence had been tampered with or altered in any manner, the evidence will not be accepted by the court. Evidence must be maintained under the strict control or supervision of only authorized individuals. This procedure must be adhered to in order to maintain the chain of evidence.

The handling of evidence is one of the more vital functions of a law enforcement agency performing investigations. It is on the strength of evidence that many convictions are obtained, so its importance must be borne in mind at all times. A detailed outline for handling and transmitting evidence to the laboratory has been developed by the FBI. It is reproduced in Appendix A.

At the presentation of evidence at the trial, it must be proved to the court that evidence had been secured from its discovery, through all testing procedures, until it was offered to the court. The most efficient means of securing evidence is keeping it under lock and key, secure from dust and hands that might defuse its potential in a court of law.

Fingerprinting

This chapter covers the essentials of identifying people by means of their fingerprints—the traces left on objects touched by the human hand. The uniqueness of a fingerprint ranks it among the best type of evidence that a district attorney can use to bring about the conviction of a defendant in a criminal case.

As an important tool in police work, fingerprinting has been the subject of intensive research and study for a long time. It takes years to become an expert. However, reasonable attention to the material in this chapter will provide you with a sound working knowledge of fingerprinting.

To give you an understanding of what fingerprinting is all about, first you will look at how it evolved from early efforts to identify criminals to the present state of the art as a sophisticated technology with many applications in the field of criminalistics. Next, you will examine the coding and classification of fingerprints. This is a most important part of your study, because coding and classification constitute the fundamental principles upon which systems of identification are based. Finally, you come to the "how to" part of your education in fingerprinting. Here you will learn the techniques used by police—how to dust for fingerprints, how to take them, and how to use the various tools needed to do the job in a professional way.

But first, consider how the idea of identifying criminals began and what methods were used as civilization developed.

A Short History of
Fingerprinting

The need to identify criminals was recognized from the earliest days of civilization. "An eye for an eye and a tooth for a tooth" was not only an integral part of the first known criminal code. In the authors' opinion it may have been the first attempt to find a way of spotting lawbreakers by marking their physical appearance. It was made law in the year 2100 B.C. by Hammurabi, King of Babylon.

From that time on, throughout most of the world, criminals have been branded or otherwise distinctively marked so that they could be readily identified. The practice of branding did not die out completely until the twentieth century. Indeed, the Nazis continued a similar practice—tattooing of identification numbers on prisoners' arms—during World War II, long after fingerprinting had become a well-established practice everywhere in the world.

Fingerprints have also been used in court as evidence as far back as the first century. Quintilianus, a Roman lawyer, introduced a bloody print in a murder trial. History reveals that Quintilianus was successful in defending a child accused of killing his father. This case will probably live forever in the realm of criminal justice as the starting point in the history of fingerprinting.

Fingerprints have also long been of use in contracts as a means of legal identification. They appear on contracts of the T'ang Dynasty in eighth-century China and in official papers of fourteenth-century Persia.

History shows, in fact, that people have long recognized that fingerprints may clearly establish an individual's unique identity. By the seventeenth century, scientists began to make progress in observing characteristic patterns and anomalies. Mercello Malpigni, in 1686, was the first to study fingerprints under a microscope, noting the "elevated ridges drawn into loops or spirals." Some 137 years later, Johannes Purkinje, a professor at the University of Breslau, wrote a thesis in which he referred to nine types of patterns found in the fingerprints he studied.

Such scattered observations began to coalesce in the nineteenth century as a number of scientists and others turned their attention to fingerprints as a way of identifying criminals. William Herschel, working in India for the British Foreign Service, did pioneer studies over a period of 20 years and recommended that the British prison system adopt fingerprinting, but his suggestion was rejected. In an article in the prestigious scientific journal *Nature*, Dr. Henry Faulds, a physician working in a hospital in Tokyo, went a step further, suggesting that fingerprints could be traceable and used in the apprehension and conviction of criminals. Finally, a book on the subject was published, bringing a new wave of interest, especially among professionals in police work.

In this period, there was widespread attention being paid to methods of classification and measurement that might enable police to identify criminals with certainty. One of these was called "anthropometry," invented by a Parisian police clerk by the name of Alphonse Bertillon. The Bertillon system was widely adopted by police departments throughout Europe and the United States in the early 1900s. The basic concept of Bertillonage, as the system was called, was that no two individuals would have the same measurements of certain key areas of their bodies. Of course, if different individuals could be shown to have the same measurements, then the Bertillon system would be proved worthless. And that is exactly what happened in a case at the federal prison in Leavenworth, Kansas. It was an extraordinary case in several respects. The two prisoners not only had precisely the same measurements, they also had almost identical names—William West and Will West—and their photographs were exceptionally similar.

A system that could not unfailingly distinguish among all individuals in all cases could not answer the needs of police work, and consequently Bertillonage was dropped in Kansas. Shortly thereafter fingerprinting began to spread in popularity, and Leavenworth was among the first to adopt it.

By this time, many fingerprint systems were available. One of the first cases on record involved fingerprint identification at the scene of a crime that occurred in Argentina in 1892. A police officer named Vucetich identified a bloody fingerprint and proved to the court's satisfaction that the suspect, a woman named Rojas, left the print at the scene. Vucetich was one of the pioneers of fingerprint classification, and a system used in many Spanish-speaking countries bears his name.

The most widely used classification system was developed by Edward Henry in 1896 while he was working as inspector general of police in Nepal, India. The system now used by the Federal Bureau of Investigation contains extensions of the Henry system, but basically it is much the same today as when Henry first proposed it.

Fingerprints play a large role in many areas of society. In 1924, Congress established the Identification Division of the FBI. Its repository contains 180 million fingerprint cards, and new ones pour in, sometimes reaching a rate of 30,000 in one day. See Fig. 3-1.

Fingerprints are taken by arresting agencies for the commission of certain crimes with some variance from one state to another. Arrest fingerprints must be sent to the FBI's national repository in Washington, D.C., and also to the state identification bureau where

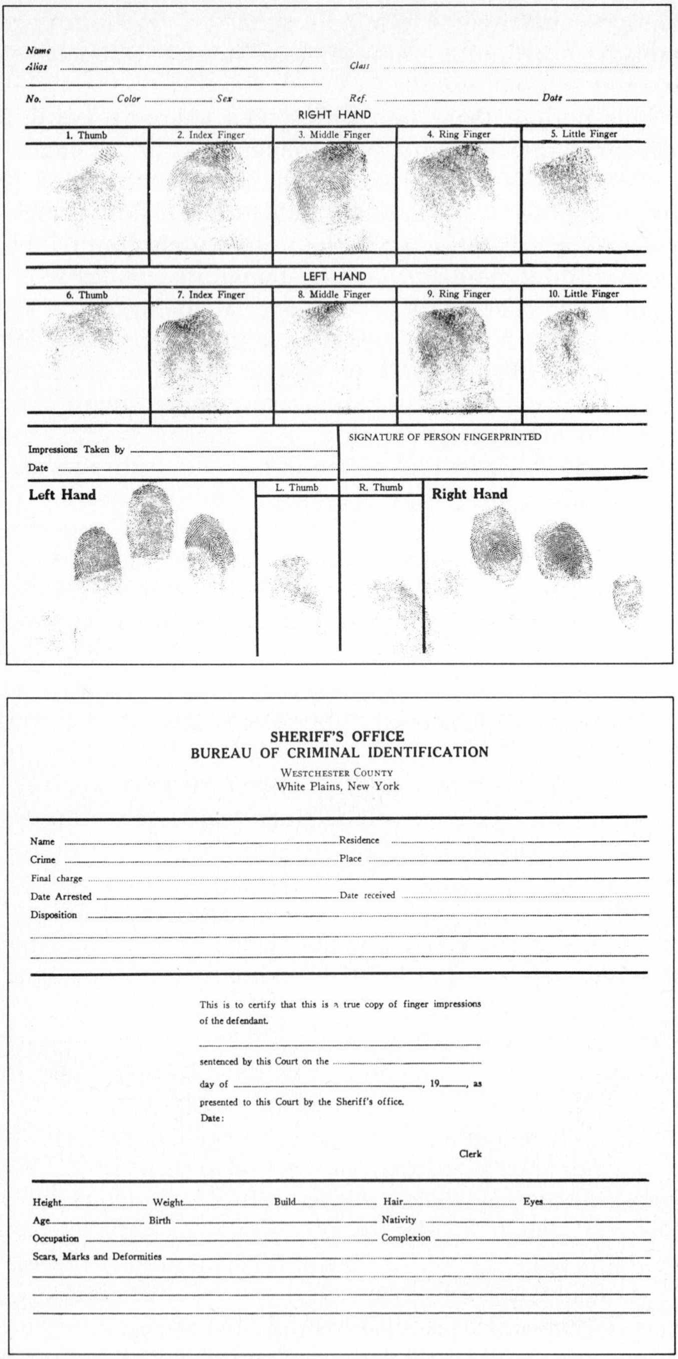

Name
Alias Class

No. Color Sex Ref. Date

RIGHT HAND

1. Thumb	2. Index Finger	3. Middle Finger	4. Ring Finger	5. Little Finger

LEFT HAND

6. Thumb	7. Index Finger	8. Middle Finger	9. Ring Finger	10. Little Finger

Impressions Taken by
Date

SIGNATURE OF PERSON FINGERPRINTED

Left Hand L. Thumb R. Thumb **Right Hand**

SHERIFF'S OFFICE
BUREAU OF CRIMINAL IDENTIFICATION
WESTCHESTER COUNTY
White Plains, New York

Name Residence
Crime Place
Final charge
Date Arrested Date received
Disposition

This is to certify that this is a true copy of finger impressions of the defendant.

sentenced by this Court on the
day of , 19 , as
presented to this Court by the Sheriff's office.
Date:

Clerk

Height Weight Build Hair Eyes
Age Birth Nativity
Occupation Complexion
Scars, Marks and Deformities

Figure 3-1 Fingerprint card.

the crime was committed. Many courts will not allow an arrestee to be released on bail until his or her fingerprints have been searched through the files and a reply received. Although an individual may use a variety of aliases, each arrest will be recorded on his or her "criminal rap sheet."

At present the FBI is testing computers to optically and electronically read fingerprints and record them in memory banks for future comparison. It is hoped that in the not too distant future the entire operation will be performed automatically with only the final comparison being made by a technician.

Now it is time to turn to the heart of these studies—the system of coding and classifying fingerprints.

Coding and Classifying

The method you are going to study has recently been adopted by the National Crime Information Center (NCIC) under the admin-

Figure 3-2   Semiautomatic computerized fingerprint reader (Courtesy Calspan Co., Buffalo, NY).

istration of the FBI. It is compatible with most computers. The Henry system, mentioned earlier, is still the conventional system and is widely used. The NCIC system derives from the Henry system but has the advantage of permitting a layperson to identify a pattern as belonging to a specific finger, whereas the Henry system does not.

Often during an investigation the identity of a suspect must be confirmed by fingerprints. The importance of knowing how to code fingerprints can be readily understood by visualizing the following situation. An individual known as John Doe is wanted by one police department, and all personal descriptive data are sent over the teletype. A department some 100 miles distant has a John Doe in custody whose physical description coincides with that of the wanted individual. Fingerprints of the John Doe in custody are taken. Now it may seem preferable to transmit the full set of fingerprints to the requesting department. This can be done. However, the equipment required to do this is prohibitively expensive. Therefore the classification is sent via Teletype in a matter of seconds. If the coding classification of the John Doe arrested and that of the John Doe wanted agree favorably, it will be a strong indication that they are one and the same person. However, if the coding is in no way similar, the man can be released. A comparison of the actual fingerprints of the John Does will be necessary to confirm the identification.

The NCIC coding, which will be discussed in detail in this chapter, is far simpler and easier to learn than the older Henry system. It is for these reasons that the NCIC coding will be explained.

NCIC Fingerprint Classification Coding

This coding classification is found on the new computerized "rap" sheet, which is received in response to arrest fingerprints submitted to the FBI. The system deals with three basic patterns: arches, loops, and whorls. It also takes into consideration amputated, scarred, or mutilated patterns. The fingers are coded in the following order by finger number as they appear on a fingerprint card:

1 = right thumb
2 = right index finger
3 = right middle finger
4 = right ring finger
5 = right little finger

The left thumb starts with number 6, and the sequence of the left hand is continued until the left little finger is reached—number

10. Two letters or two numerals are used for each finger, as is shown in Table 3-1.

TABLE 3-1: NCIC Fingerprint Classification Coding

Pattern Type	Pattern Subgroup	NCIC Fingerprint Code
Arch	Plain arch	AA
	Tented arch	TT
Loop	Radial loop	Actual ridge count to which 50 must be added; e.g. if the ridge count of a radial loop is 14, 50 must be added to 14 making a total of 64.
	Ulnar loop	Actual ridge count; e.g. if a ridge count is less than 10, use a zero before the count (08).
Whorl	Plain whorl	
	Inner	PI
	Meeting	PM
	Outer	PO
	Central pocket loop whorl	
	Inner	CI
	Meeting	CM
	Outer	CO
	Double-loop whorl	
	Inner	DI
	Meeting	DM
	Outer	DO
	Accidental whorl	
	Inner	XI
	Meeting	XM
	Outer	XO
Missing or amputated finger	Use only if finger is completely amputated or entire first joint of finger is missing.	XX
Scarred or mutilated pattern	Use only if finger cannot be accurately classified.	SR

Fingerprint Ridge Characteristics

The following sketches and descriptions should be helpful as you progress in your study of fingerprints. Each of the drawings depicts an enlarged facsimile of a fingerprint ridge.

Recurve: This gives the appearance of a staple and will be found in loops and whorls.

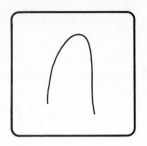

Shoulders of a Recurve: The summit area of the recurve.

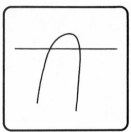

Appendage: A short ending ridge found on the outside of a recurve.

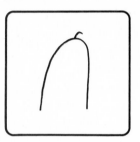

Bifurcation: Two ridges joined.

Divergence: The area where two ridges that had previously run parallel start to separate or part.

The Plain Arch

Fig. 3-3a is an illustration of a fingerprint displaying one of the basic patterns—the plain arch. Note that the ridges start on one side, rise slightly, and flow out the opposite side. This is a clear-cut pattern and easy to identify because it has no focal points (deltas and cores). Many prints, however, are not that simple. The *core* of a loop or whorl will generally be located in the innermost pattern area. A *delta* will either be on one side or the other in loops and on each side of a whorl somewhat below the core. It is always situated at or near the center of a divergence of two lines that surround or tend to surround the pattern area. The delta can be a bifurcation, dot, short ridge, fragment, or point on a ridge.

The Delta Rules

1. The delta may be located at a bifurcation which must open toward the core.

2. When two or more possible bifurcations conform to the definition, the one nearest the core is chosen.

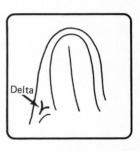

3. When there is a choice between a bifurcation and another type of delta, the bifurcation is chosen provided they are both equally close to the point of divergence.

4. The delta may not be located in the middle of a ridge running between the type lines toward the core but at the end near the core.

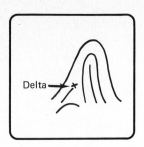

The Core Rules

1. The core is placed upon or within the innermost recurving ridge.

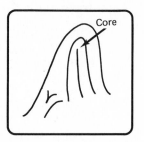

2. When the innermost ridge contains no ending ridge rising as high as the shoulders of the recurve, the core is placed on the shoulder of the recurve farthest from the delta.

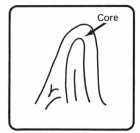

3. When the innermost loop contains an uneven number of rods rising as high as the shoulder, the core is placed upon the center rod whether or not it touches the looping ridge.

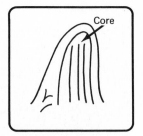

4. When the innermost loop contains an even number of rods rising as high as the shoulder, the core is placed upon the farthest of the two center rods. The two center rods are treated as though they were joined.

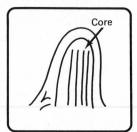

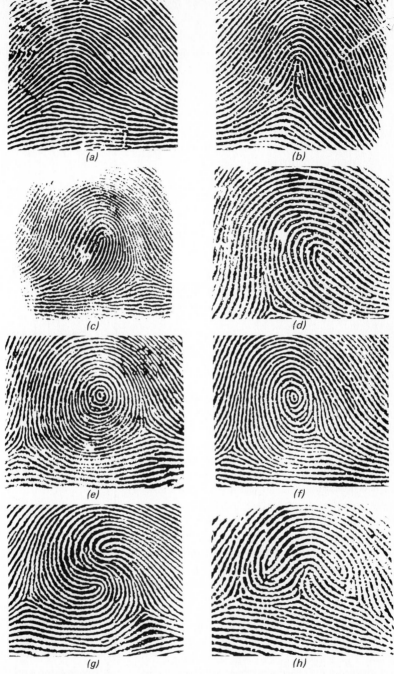

Figure 3-3   (a) Plain arch coded "AA"
                  (b) Tented arch coded "TT"
                  (c) Radial loop of right hand
                       coded "61"
                  (d) Ulnar of right hand coded
                       "14"
                  (e) Plain whorl coded "PO"

(f) Central pocket loop-type
      whorl coded "CO"
(g) Double loop whorl coded
      "DI"
(h) Accidental whorl coded
      "XO"

Loop Patterns

Think of a loop pattern as ridges starting out in one direction, making a U turn, and returning in the direction from which they started. Here are some loops and rules governing their definition:

1. It must contain a sufficient re-curve and its continuance on the delta side until it crosses an imaginary line from delta to core.

2. It must contain a delta.

3. It must have a ridge count of at least 1 that crosses a looping ridge with a white space between the delta and the first ridge count. (See the section on pp. 31–32 dealing with ridge counting.)

4. The recurving ridge must be free of any appendage abutting on its outside at right angles.

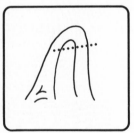

NOTE: The appendage rule of recurves—number 4—is extremely important. It will often affect the definition of the pattern. Consider the recurve as part of the curvature of a balloon and the appendage as a pin. If the appendage is at right angles like a pin, it will break the balloon; but if the appendage lies against it, the balloon will not break. Thus, if an appendage is at right angles on the outside of the recurve, it spoils the recurve; but if it flows off smoothly, it does not.

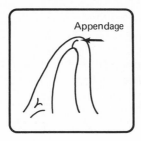

There are two types of loops: radial and ulnar. (These two terms are derived from the names of the two bones of the forearm.) *Ulnar* means that the ridges start on the little finger side, loop around, and come out the same side. *Radial* is just the reverse. The easiest way to distinguish one from the other is to place your hand beside the pattern and see from which side of the hand the ridges start and terminate. Be sure to use your right hand for prints from a right hand, your left for those of a left hand.

Ridge Counting

The ridge count is the total number of ridges touched or crossed by an imaginary line placed between the delta and the core. This line can be seen in the glass of a fingerprint magnifier as an aid to ridge counting. The line is embedded in the glass.

There are three rules for ridge counting:

1. If the imaginary line touches or crosses a bifurcation, it is counted as two ridges.

2. If the imaginary line crosses or touches a small ridge or dot, it is counted as a ridge.

3. For a ridge, dot, or fragment to be counted, it must be as thick as the other ridges.

The Tented Arch

The tented arch differs from the plain arch in that the ridges at the center have a more pointed appearance. There are three basic types of tented arches:

1. Up-thrust type—ridges at the center thrust upward.

2. Angle type—two ridges at the center form an angle.

3. Loop type—it resembles the loop but lacks one of the three essentials of a true loop. (Three essentials of a loop are sufficient recurve, delta, and ridge count across at least one looping ridge.)

Delta Missing

Whorls

There are four different types of whorls: plain whorl, central pocket loop type of whorl, double-loop type of whorl, and accidental type of whorl. Each whorl must have at least two deltas.

The *plain whorl* has at least two deltas and one or more recurving ridges in front of each. (See Fig. 3-3e.) At least one ridge must make a complete circuit, which may be spiral, oval, circular, or any variant of a circle. An imaginary line drawn between the two deltas *must* touch or cross at least one of the recurving ridges within the inner pattern area.

The *central pocket loop* type of whorl has two deltas and at least one ridge making a complete circuit, which may be spiral, oval, circular, or any variant of a circle. (See Fig. 3-3f.) An imaginary line drawn between the two deltas must *not* touch or cross any of the recurving ridges within the inner pattern area. In lieu of a recurve in front of the delta in the inner pattern area, an obstruction at right angles to the line of flow will suffice. The recurving ridges in front of the innermost delta must be free of appendages.

The *double-loop* type of whorl must contain two separate loop formations, two sets of shoulders or recurves, and two deltas. The shoulders of the recurves must be free of any appendages at right angles. (See Fig. 3-3g.)

The *accidental whorl* must contain at least two deltas and may combine any two patterns except the plain arch. (See Fig. 3-3h.)

Tracing of Whorls

All whorl patterns are "traced." Tracing is performed by following the ridge emanating from the lower side or point of the extreme left delta and moving along that ridge until it reaches a point opposite the right delta. If the ridge being traced passes inside the right delta with three or

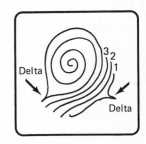

Delta

Delta

more ridges in between or intervening, it is classified as an *inner whorl.*

An outer whorl is determined when the ridge emanating from the extreme left delta is traced to a point opposite the right delta and three ridges or more are found intervening.

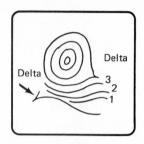

All other tracings of whorls are called "meet whorls." When, for instance, the ridge being traced reaches a point opposite the right delta with no more than two ridges intervening, either inside or outside the right delta, it is a *meet whorl.*

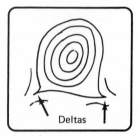

Rules for Tracing Whorls

1. If the traced ridge definitely ends, you must drop down to the next lower ridge and continue tracing.

2. If the ridge being traced bifurcates, you take the lower ridge of the bifurcation and trace along that ridge.

It is well to remember that not all patterns are clear-cut and readily recognized. There are, for instance, loop patterns that closely resemble whorls. Notice in the loop-resembling whorl to the right how each recurve in the left area has an appendage on its outside shoulder, thereby spoiling the recurve.

CROSS-REFERENCING   At the present time, there are no rules for cross-referencing of questionable patterns, but it is good practice to reference all patterns in one category or another, for the sake of thoroughness in classifying.

Latent Prints

A latent fingerprint is one left on an object's surface when it is touched (see Fig. 3-4). The fingerprint is composed of moisture secreted through the pores of the fingers and palms (also the soles of the feet). Most of this moisture is water, salt, proteins, and other matter.

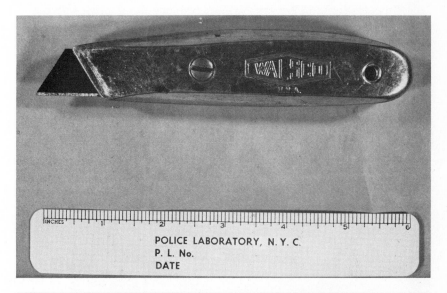

Figure 3-4 *Top:* utility knife found at scene of crime; *bottom:* latent fingerprint developed on knife blade (Courtesy New York Police Department).

A latent print may or may not be visible to the naked eye. Generally, it can be made visible by carefully reflecting light off its surface. At times, a latent print may be photographed in its original state—in grease or a similar substance. Fingerprints that are wet, such as in blood, oil, grease, or soft putty, should never be dusted. A surface suspected of containing latent fingerprints should be dusted with a powder of contrasting color (i.e. on a white or light-colored surface use black powder and on dark-colored surfaces use white or gray powder). See Fig. 3-5.

What equipment will you need for dusting, lifting, and photographing fingerprints? Here's a list of the basic requirements:

2-ounce (oz) [62.2 grams (g)] jar of black fingerprint powder
2-oz jar of white fingerprint powder
Camel's-hair brush for dusting
Magnifier of approximately 5 power
Roll of lifting tape

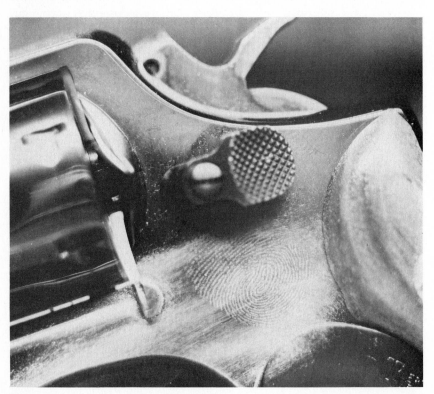

Figure 3-5 Fingerprint on revolver dusted with white powder and photographed with 100-watt lamp using Polaroid P/N 55 film, one second at F8 (Courtesy Bert Blumert, New York, NY).

White cards, size 3 by 5 inches (in)
A camera suitable for photographing fingerprints

NOTE: As a rule, you will find black powder preferable to white because it photographs better in most circumstances. If white powder is used, the ridge lines will appear white. This must be kept in mind when trying to match the latent with the suspect fingerprint.

Experiment in Dusting Prints

Place your fingerprint on a dish of smooth white china. Do not press heavily—a light touch will do. Now, take a small amount of black powder and place it in the cover of the bottle. Dip your brush lightly in the powder, and apply it to the place where you left the print. The print should appear very black. If it does not, run your finger through your hair or against the side of your nose to give it more moisture and try again. Dust very lightly with your brush, making your strokes conform to the pattern formation of the print.

With a little practice, you will be able to make excellent prints.

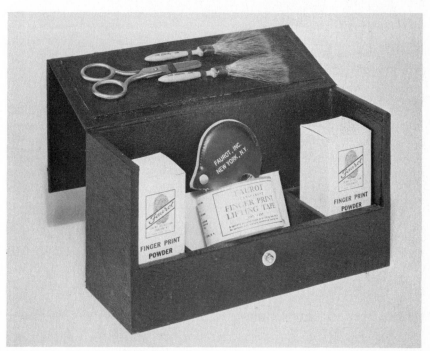

Figure 3-6   Basic field kit for dusting and lifting latent fingerprints (Courtesy Faurot Inc., New York, NY).

Figure 3-7 Complete field kit, including post mortem fingerprinting equipment, ultraviolet powders, assorted dusting powders, lifters, and portable unit for taking fingerprints (Courtesy Faurot, Inc., New York, NY).

Two cautions: *Do not dust too vigorously or you will brush away the latent fingerprint. And always remember to use your powder sparingly.*

Once you are able to bring out your own latent print, take another dish and see what prints you can find on it. As china is a smooth surface, your brushing may disclose the prints of anyone who may have handled the dish. Ordinarily a "fresh latent" will appear very black. If it has a faint grayish or light-black color, the indication is that it is old or the individual who left it had dry skin. Old latents sometimes appear when dusted, but they are usually of little use in police work because normally they turn out to have been left not by a criminal but somebody regularly on the premises.

At the Scene of the Crime

Here is a tip from the experts: A criminal is likely to handle an object exactly the way you would handle it. So, before you start dusting for prints, stop a minute and think about the natural places a criminal might place his or her hands. Even before you do this, however, be sure to question everyone at the scene.

Your first question is, Has anyone touched or moved anything? Next: Has anything been moved from where it is ordinarily kept? Next: Did you see the suspect touch or handle anything?

Now determine the point of entry or "break." This may be a broken window or a forced door. If you find broken glass, pick up each piece by its edges, and place it carefully in an empty box. Glass is an excellent surface on which to find prints because it is smooth and nonporous. Often criminals will pick up a piece of glass to avoid cutting themselves when placing their hands through a broken window to unlock it. Take the pieces with you, so that you can examine them without interference. Any small articles that look as though they might have been touched should also be taken with you. For large surfaces that cannot be moved, it's a good idea to use a large wad of cotton as a dusting applicator and apply the black powder quickly but carefully.

Fingerprint Photography

Once a latent print becomes plainly visible, it should be photographed. Then, if the print does not lift well, you will also have a record of it. Of course, if the object on which the print appears is too large to move, you must take a photograph.

A Polaroid CU5 camera (see Fig. 8-11) is excellent for taking photographs of latent prints, lifted prints, and other small evidence.

Polaroid also makes a positive-negative film that produces not only an instant photograph but also a negative, which can be used for enlarging and for making more prints. The Polaroid CU camera is a "1 to 1"; that is, it makes exact life-size photographs of the subject.

Lifting Fingerprints

Once a satisfactory photograph has been taken, the latent fingerprint may be lifted. Fingerprint lifters come in two types. One is an adhesive, transparent type, and the other is a rubber lifter pad obtainable in either black or white. The rubber lifter type resembles a tire tube patch. Remove the layer of transparent celluloid from the adhesive side. Place the adhesive side over the latent, and rub it gently but firmly with your finger. Peel the lifter from the surface and replace the celluloid cover (see Fig. 3-8).

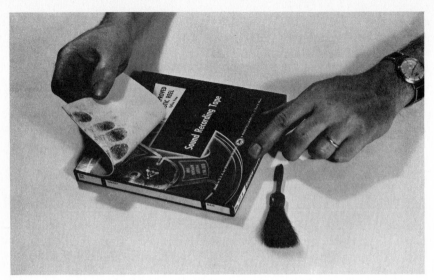

Figure 3-8 Lifting latent fingerprints with rubber lifter.

A latent print will last indefinitely on the rubber lifter. A white rubber lifter is used when black powder has been employed in dusting, and a black lifter is used when white powder is utilized.

The transparent lifting tape comes on a roll similar to Scotch tape with a metal cutting edge for breaking off the tape. When lifting with the transparent tape, you must be very careful, because it is easy to place your own print on the tape. Tear off a piece of tape large enough to cover the latent print you want to lift. Place the adhesive side of the tape over the latent print; rub the back of it gently and firmly, as was suggested with the rubber lifters. Again, peel the adhesive tape from the dusted area and place the adhesive side of the tape onto a clean white 3 by 5 card. This lifted latent fingerprint may likewise be photographed.

When either method of lifting is used, certain identifying information must be placed on the card (preferably on the back) and also on the back of the rubber lifter:

Case number
Date
Location where found
Initials or name of officer lifting print

Fingerprints should be taken of all occupants of the burglarized premises, such as owners, employees, or anyone who has a right to handle the object or surface where the latent was found. Such fingerprints are called "elimination fingerprints." All latent fingerprints should be compared with the elimination fingerprints. The purpose of the elimination prints is to prevent a technician working with what might be called "dead" prints.

Chemical Methods for Developing Latent Fingerprints

Latent fingerprints may be developed on paper or cardboard by a variety of methods such as ninhydrin, silver nitrate, and iodine fuming. Ninhydrin is a chemical that reacts with proteins to give a characteristic color. It is available in a spray can which must be sprayed at the paper at a distance of 8 to 10 in. A latent print can be developed in a matter of minutes by holding the paper near a source of heat such as a 75-watt light bulb. When the prints are prominently visible (a reddish purple color), they should be photographed.

Solid silver nitrate is available from commercial suppliers. A 5% water solution is then prepared. It may be applied to paper or cardboard with a paint brush. After a period of time, when subjected to light, the prints will appear brown. Exposure to sunlight or ultraviolet light will cause the prints to develop very rapidly. When the latents appear, a photograph should be taken immediately and the paper or cardboard placed in a container to prevent its continued exposure to light. If the treated paper is exposed to light for an extended period, it will become such a dark brown that the contrast between the developed print and the paper will be practically nil.

The third method of developing latent prints on paper utilizes iodine crystals. This chemical tends to be absorbed by the organic material in the latent fingerprint. The iodine crystals may be placed in a closed glass container along with the paper and heated gradually. The prints will appear brown. The developed prints must be photographed within minutes after they appear, for they will disappear in a short while. If your first photographs are unsatisfactory, the paper may again be treated with iodine fuming and a second attempt can be made. One can also use an "iodine gun" (Fig. 3-9) to concentrate the fumes on a suspected area. *Caution:* Iodine fumes are corrosive and should not be inhaled.

NOTE: **It is recommended that the chemical testing for latent fingerprints be performed in the crime laboratory.**

X-Ray Photography of Fingerprints

A method employing X-ray photographs has been used successfully to record latent fingerprints left on human skin, e.g. in the

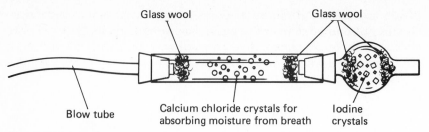

Figure 3-9   Iodine-fuming gun.

case of a strangulation (see Fig. 3-10). This method has also been successful in revealing fingerprints on other materials, e.g. paper, plastics, etc.

Magna-Brush

A popular device being used by many technicians was developed by a former research chemist of Corning Glass, Herbert MacDonell. It is called the Magna-Brush. The novel feature about this

Figure 3-10   (a): Bucky miniature x-ray unit model G (Courtesy Bucky X-Ray International, New York, NY).

tool is that there is little waste of the powders. After a fingerprint is dusted, the powder in the surrounding area may be retrieved and placed in the jar for reuse. The powders may be used on a variety of surfaces, i.e. glass, plastic, wood, painted surfaces, paper, and cardboard.

Taking Fingerprints

Place a small amount of ink about 0.5 in [1.27 centimeters (cm)] in length on the inking surface of the portable kit (see Fig. 3-11). Roll this ink to a fine even texture on the glass or metal surface provided for this purpose. Roll each finger, starting with the right thumb, from one side of the nail to the other, on the inked surface. Now roll the finger in the place provided on the fingerprint card. By rolling a finger from nail to nail you will be sure to obtain the deltas which are located off to the side of a pattern. When inking each finger, place it flat on the inked surface, taking care to obtain the area just *below the first finger joint*. Continue with each succeeding finger until the entire right hand has been taken. Now do the same with the left hand,

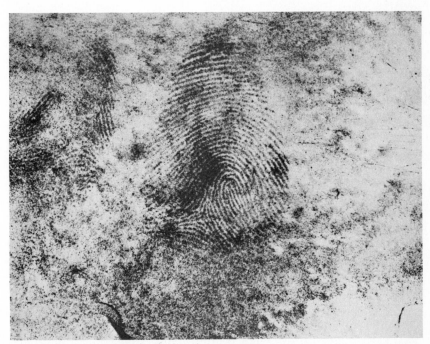

Figure 3-10 (*b*): Radiographic picture of fingerprint on human skin taken with the Bucky miniature X-ray unit Model G (Courtesy Bucky X-Ray International, New York, NY).

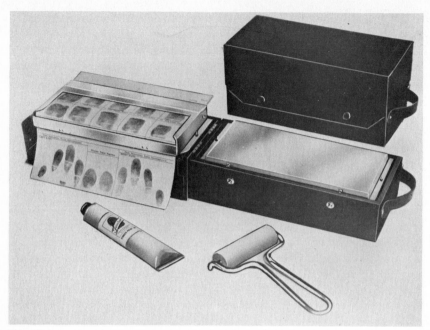

Figure 3-11   Field kit for taking fingerprints (Courtesy Faurot, Inc., New York, NY).

again starting with the thumb and take the remaining fingers of the left hand.

After all ten fingers have been recorded, take the subject's four fingers of the right hand and place them simultaneously in the lower right-hand box of the card marked "right hand."

The same must be done with the four fingers of the left hand: they are placed in the lower left-hand corner of the fingerprint card marked "left hand." Now take each of the subject's thumbs and record them in the areas so designated in the lower center of the card. These impressions taken of the four fingers of each hand simultaneously and the two thumbs are called "flat" impressions because the fingers are not rolled. These flat impressions are used for comparison purposes to determine if the rolled impressions taken of each finger have been recorded in their proper sequence, i.e. number 2, right index finger; number 3, right middle finger; and so on.

When rolling fingers on the "inked surface" of the portable kit and then rolling them on the fingerprint card, do not press too hard. Only a slight pressure is needed—similar to the pressure you would apply if you were to test a freshly painted surface to see if it were dry. Hold each finger firmly when rolling, using your right thumb and right index finger in a clasping fashion around the finger being rolled. You may use your left hand to steady the tip of the finger and

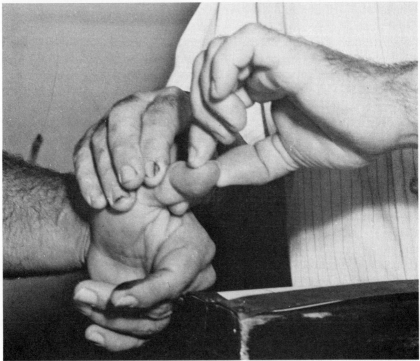

Figure 3-12 Method for taking fingerprints.

to keep it flat during rolling. See Fig. 3-12 for holding the finger and rolling method. The proper method is to roll the thumbs toward the body (right to left), and the fingers should be rolled away from the body (left to right). However, you may roll the fingers in whichever direction is easiest.

Palm Prints

Palm prints are becoming more popular everyday. Some states now specify in their fingerprinting statutes that palm prints may be taken. An identification of a latent print may be made in area of a hand from the tip of the finger, across the finger joints, across the palm almost to the wrist. Contrary to common belief, it is not necessary to obtain the fingerprints from an entire hand; a small area approximately the size of an eraser on a pencil will sometimes suffice.

There are many devices available on the market for taking palm prints. Most utilize a round cylinder to which a piece of paper is attached. Some have two round cylinders, one for inking and the other for recording.

Any round cylinder with a diameter of about 3 in [7.6 cm] and having a width of 5 in [12.7 cm] or more will serve your purpose. An empty can of cleanser or a metal coffee can may be used with a piece of white paper placed around the cylinder with an elastic band on each end to hold the paper to the container. Roll the fingerprint ink to a fine texture; then take the roller and roll it across the entire finger, thumb, and palm. Start at the fingertip, across the finger joint and across the palm. Have the subject hold one hand perfectly flat. Starting with the fingertips pressing at the end of the paper, the cylinder is caused to roll by the pressure of the subject's hand pushing across it.

In this fashion the subject will leave the impression of the fingers and palm on the paper. Do not apply too much pressure to the back of the hand during the recording process. After recording several palm prints, one should be able to record a clear impression of an entire hand. Each paper containing a palm print should include the subject's signature, the date, and the signature of the individual who recorded it. Figure 3-13 shows a photograph of the manner in which the palm is rolled.

A latent fingerprint is used for comparison purposes with those of a suspect, or it may be used for searching in a fingerprint file. Through years of experience it has been found that a useful *modus operandi* (method of operation) fingerprint file will reduce searching for latents to a minimum. A *modus operandi* file that segregates the

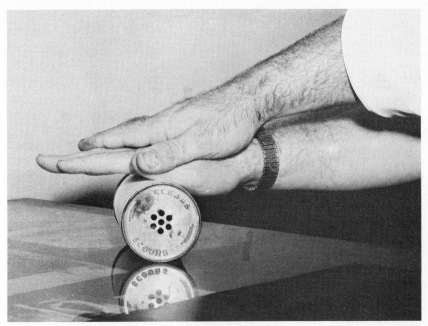

Figure 3-13   Method for rolling a palm print.

fingerprints of burglars in the following categories has been most successful:

> Houses and apartments
> Stores
> Taverns, restaurants, and liquor stores
> Jewelry stores
> Factories
> Public buildings
> Garages and gas stations

Generally a burglar will continue to use one MO (method of operation) throughout her or his career of crime.

Figure 3-14*a* is a photograph of a latent print with the characteristics numbered for comparison purposes. Figure 3-14*b* is a photograph of the rolled impression of the same finger from a fingerprint card taken at the time of arrest, containing corresponding numbers to those in the latent photograph. These photographs are known as comparison charts and are used for court purposes.

Each photograph is an enlargement of the rolled and latent print to almost 4 times its original size. Such is necessary for a layperson to be able to recognize the characteristics. Once you are able to identify

(a)

Figure 3-14 (a) Simulated latent print and (b) rolled fingerprint, with comparison chart of characteristics for court presentation. Numbers indicate the following:

1. bifurcation
2. ending ridge upthrust
3. ending ridge upthrust
4. ending ridge downthrust
5. ending ridge upthrust
6. enclosure, sometimes called "island"
7. bifurcation
8. ending ridge downthrust
9. ending ridge upthrust
10. ending ridge downthrust
11. ending ridge upthrust
12. ending ridge upthrust

the characteristics in a latent print with those in the rolled impression, you can make your own charts. Extreme care must be exercised in charting characteristics on the enlarged photographs. To draw a line to each characteristic, a China marking pencil may be used; or place a dot at each characteristic on both photographs. Such lines or dots may be easily rubbed off in case of error.

Another method of placing charting lines on the photographs is to use a $1/16$ in roll of press tape available in art supply shops. It comes in various colors and has an adhesive side. The numbers may also be placed on the charts by using commercial press-type letters. These will give your chart a professional look.

The characteristics that occur most frequently are shown in Fig. 3-3a through h, and each should be studied carefully.

(b)

The characteristics that occur most frequently and are used for identifying a latent fingerprint with a rolled impression are shown here.

Bifurcation

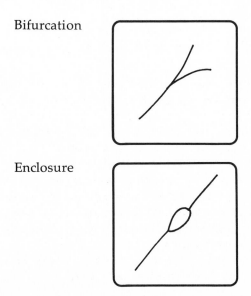

Enclosure

Ending ridge

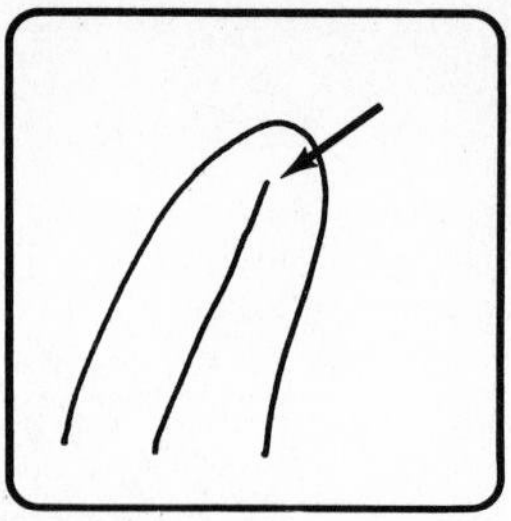

Dot (sometimes called an island)

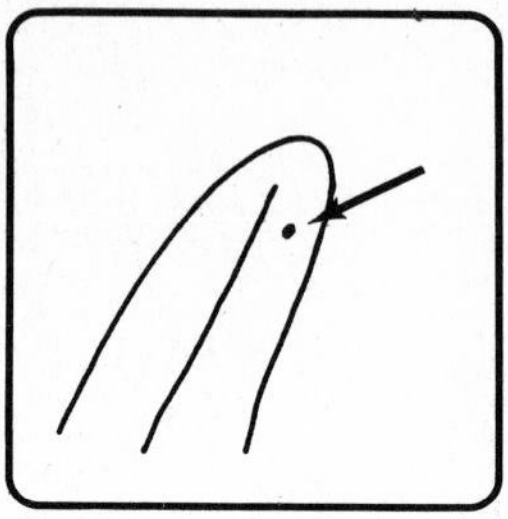

Fork

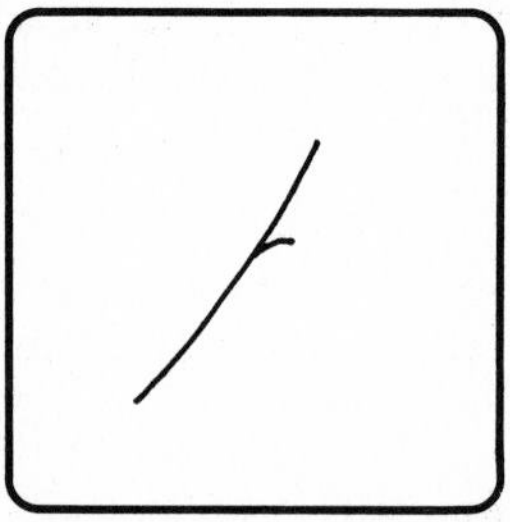

Short ridge

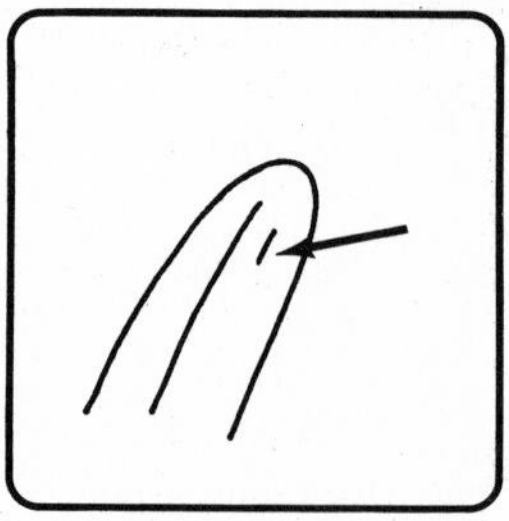

Firearms Investigation

Of the more than 20,000 murders committed every year in the United States, about two-thirds involve firearms—revolvers, rifles, shotguns, semiautomatic pistols, and automatic pistols. For this reason alone, the field of firearms identification (sometimes called forensic ballistics) constitutes a major aspect of law enforcement. It is a field that encompasses not only the weapons themselves but also bullets, cartridge cases, and shotshells.

The Sacco and Vanzetti Case

It was the famous Sacco and Vanzetti case in Massachusetts in 1920 that brought the techniques of firearms identification to widespread attention. This case evoked worldwide controversy because of its political and ethnic implications, and one of the key issues was the identification of the bullets from the victims, and shell casings found at the scene of the murder of a paymaster during an attempted robbery. Both defense and prosecution produced expert witnesses, who gave conflicting testimony about whether the gun found on the defendants had fired the bullets. Sacco and Vanzetti were found guilty, mainly on the strength of the testimony of ballistics experts (prosecution witnesses) that one bullet in one of the victims had been fired by the gun carried by one of the defendants. (Five other bullets recovered from the victims were never matched with any gun.)

Many people have believed that the defendants, Sacco and Vanzetti, were railroaded to the electric chair because of the atmosphere of prejudice against their political beliefs and because of their alien status; they were professed anarchists, and they spoke English with heavy accents. What made the case an international *cause célèbre* was the issue of a fair trial. But the fact is that it was the first trial of any renown in which the issue of firearms identification, with all its technicalities, played a central role. For this reason, the case marks a turning point in the science of criminalistics. From then on, law enforcement officers have been keenly aware, in the course of their investigations of cases involving firearms, that bullets and guns can be matched with a degree of certainty that has increased through the years with improved technology and accumulated knowledge.

Incidentally, in 1961, more than 40 years after the crime occurred, a test bullet fired from the key gun in the Sacco and Vanzetti case was reaffirmed by experts as matching the bullet that condemned the defendants to die. In other words, even in its infancy the science of firearms identification may have served justice well.

The Firearms Examiner

The firearms examiner is a qualified expert who can answer the following kinds of questions in a murder case. These questions are typical of the questions usually asked:

1. Type of weapon, caliber, or gauge of weapon which fired the shot.
2. Distance to the victim at the time of discharge of the weapon.
3. Can bullet be identified?
4. Was the weapon fired recently?
5. Weight of the bullet.
6. Direction of twist and angle (bullet).
7. Was the cartridge case found at the scene from an automatic?
8. Did the individual commit suicide, or was it murder?
9. Width of grooves and lands on the bullet.
10. Number of lands and grooves on the bullet.
11. How many shots were fired?
12. Was the victim shot elsewhere and the body dropped at the scene?

13. Was the fatal bullet fired from the weapon found at the scene?
14. Type of bullet—jacketed, semijacketed, or unjacketed—hollow point, soft point, or wad cutter.

Naturally the degree of certainty with which these questions can be answered depends upon the circumstances of the particular case. In order to fully appreciate the procedures used in arriving at answers to these questions, one must understand the characteristics of handguns, such as their method of manufacture and how they operate, as well as the characteristics of their ammunition. See Fig. 4-1.

Most problems in this area of law enforcement are concerned with the matching of a particular bullet found at the scene of a crime with the particular gun from which it was fired. A gun barrel imprints the bullets traveling through it with a distinctive pattern of scratches or striations. If the police want to know whether a bullet or cartridge case was fired from a particular gun, they compare it with test bullets and cartridge cases fired from the same gun.

Such bullet comparisons are possible because of the way gun barrels are made. A barrel is machined from a solid blank of steel. It is drilled, bored, and reamed to a specific caliber. Rifling tools cut spiral grooves (generally in the neighborhood of $1/4000$ in deep) into the barrel's bore in order to impart a gyroscopic stability to the bullet after it leaves the muzzle. (See Fig. 4-2.) Were it not for this rotational spiraling motion, the bullet would flop end over end shortly after leaving the muzzle. The portions of the bored barrel are termed the "lands" of the barrel. The distance between two opposing lands determines the caliber of the weapon after grooves are cut into the barrel. Actually the caliber of the bullet is slightly larger than the caliber or measurement of the bore. Were this not so, there would be few, if any, rifling marks (striae from the lands and grooves) on a fired bullet, and loss of energy because of gas passing by the sides of the bullet would also occur. The number of lands and grooves may vary from two lands and two grooves to as much as twenty lands and grooves, depending on the manufacturer (Fig. 4-3). The width of the lands and grooves, the angle of twist as well as its direction, i.e. whether it twists to the right or to the left as the bullet enters the barrel, are also identifying class characteristics.

The grooves in the bore are cut with hard metal tools which will have various imperfections in their cutting edges when worn. These will leave many fine patterns of striations in the bore.

As they are used, these imperfections on the tools will change through wear; and though many barrels are "rifled" in succession with the same tool, there will always be an individual variation in markings. No two barrels, though of the same manufacturer and processed in sequence, will leave the exact same pattern of striation

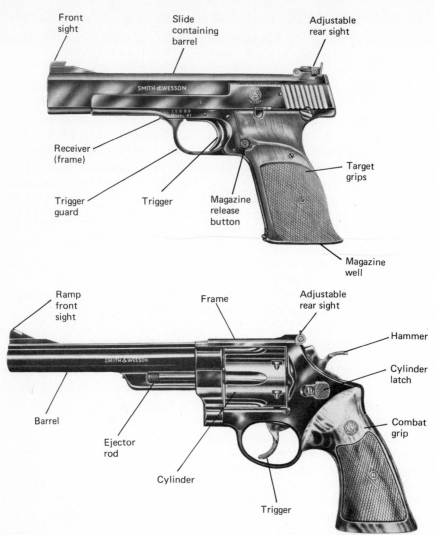

Figure 4-1 *Top:* .22 automatic; *bottom:* .44 magnum (Courtesy Smith & Wesson, Springfield, MA).

on the bullet. This is why bullets may be compared and identified as to the gun from which they were fired. As many as 500 firings from the same weapon will not cause significant major alterations of a bore, which would prevent identification of a bullet. This statement must be modified if the weapon is not cleaned or becomes rusty or pitted between firings. If the barrel is rusted, dirty, or pitted, the striae will be much more pronounced than if it had been properly maintained. As a result of the explosion of its powder charge, the bullet is propelled into the barrel. As the bullet spins through the bore, it is marked by

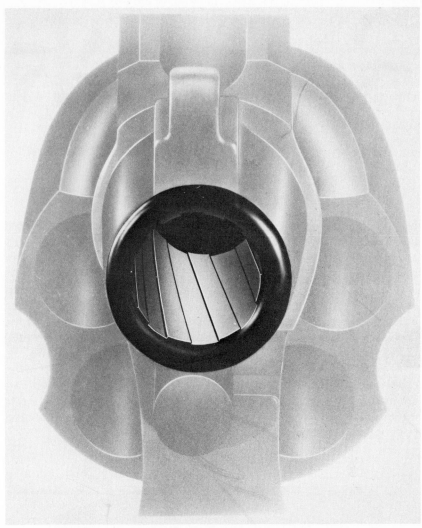

Figure 4-2   Rifled barrel with eight grooves (Courtesy Charter Arms, Stratford, CT).

a particular pattern of striae imparted from the lands and grooves
of the rifled barrel (Figs. 4-4 and 4-5).

Cartridges

Figure 4-6 illustrates the component parts of a typical cartridge.
A bullet may be semijacketed or totally jacketed in copper, steel,

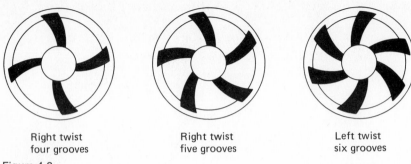

Right twist
four grooves

Right twist
five grooves

Left twist
six grooves

Figure 4-3

brass, cupronickel, or gilded metal (see Fig. 4-7). Generally a jacketed bullet will have a lead core. Some of the types of bullets commonly encountered are soft-point, hollow-point, flat-nose, wad cutter, or round nose. See Fig. 4-9.

Many bullets (especially lead type) will contain characteristic cannelures. These are circumferential grooves near the base of the bullet used for holding lubrication (see Fig. 4-8). Lubrication of the bore is necessary to prevent friction and bore leading. Crimping marks may also be visible on the bullet as well as on its casing.

Today's cartridges contain a variety of elements in their powder charge, some of which are trade secrets. The following ingredients are usually present in most modern cartridge primers (in addition to the nitrocellulose and/or nitroglycerin which are the principle components of the powder charge):

Base   Cannelure   Cannelure   Groove   Nose
                           for
                           lubrication

Figure 4-4   Spent bullet.

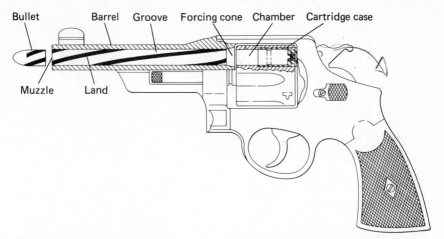

Figure 4-5   Diagram of revolver showing distance the bullet must travel from the chamber through the forcing cone before it engages in rifling.

Oxidizers: barium nitrate
                lead nitrate
                potassium nitrate
                sodium nitrate
                lead peroxide

Fuels: antimony sulfide
                calcium silicide
                aluminum

Abrasive: ground glass used for rimfire only

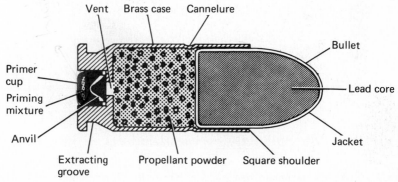

Figure 4-6   Component parts of a cartridge (Courtesy Am. Inst. of Applied Science).

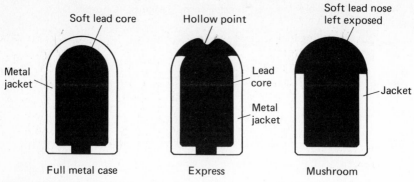

Figure 4-7 Diagram of jacketed bullet types (Courtesy American Institute of Applied Science, Syracuse, NY).

Discharging the Cartridge

Pulling the trigger releases the hammer, causing it to fall forward. Either the hammer contains a firing pin, or it strikes a firing pin contained in the weapon (Fig. 4-10). In either case, the firing pin is driven into the primer cap, leaving an impression upon it. In the majority of cartridges (with the exception of rimfire), an anvil in the primer cup initiates a flash in the primer compound, which then ignites the powder. The burning of the powder creates combustion and gases, causing pressure and expansion of the cartridge in all directions. This may cause the cartridge case to be impressed with useful identifying marks associating it with a particular weapon. These may be from the breech of the weapon (also caused by the recoil of the case against the breechface as the bullet is ejected) and from the firing chamber walls as the shell is pressed against it (Fig. 4-12 and 4-13).

When a cartridge case is found at the crime scene, an examination will sometimes disclose whether it is from an automatic weapon

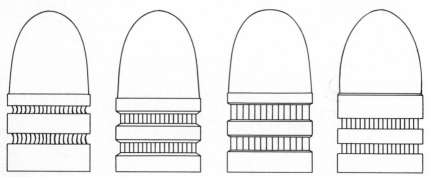

Figure 4-8 Bullet cannelure designs (Courtesy American Institute of Applied Science, Syracuse, NY).

Figure 4-9   Types of cartridges (Courtesy Olin-Winchester, New Haven, CT).

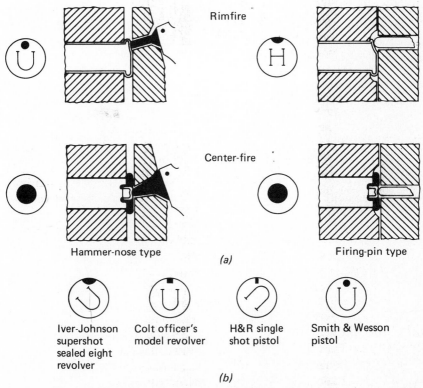

Figure 4-10   *Top and center:* diagrammatic illustrations of the operation of a firing pin; *bottom:* the difference in firing-pin impressions left on rimfire cartridges by four makes of .22 arms.

Figure 4-11   Difference of rim for automatic and revolver. Center cartridge is from an automatic. Note groove for the extractor.

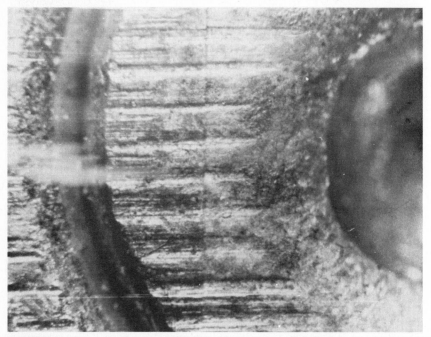

Figure 4-12   Breechface markings of .38 revolver. Semicircle on right is crater made by firing pin. Left: test casing. Right: evidence casing (Courtesy Joseph Reich).

Figure 4-13　Shotgun breech block (Courtesy American Institute of Applied Science, Syracuse, NY).

which utilizes a cartridge extractor (see Fig. 4-11). The mark of an extractor from an automatic will be found on the cartridge rim edge, as will an ejector mark on the case head. See Fig. 4-14a through d. Such markings are common but not always distinctive. On occasion the type of automatic has been determined by the relationship of the ejector mark to the extractor mark. Another possibility is that magazine marks may be found on a cartridge which could be identified when the magazine is found (Fig. 4-15). If the cartridges have been removed and replaced on more than one occasion in a magazine, more than one mark may be found. (*Note:* It may be possible to determine, from the location of the recovered cartridge cases and a knowledge

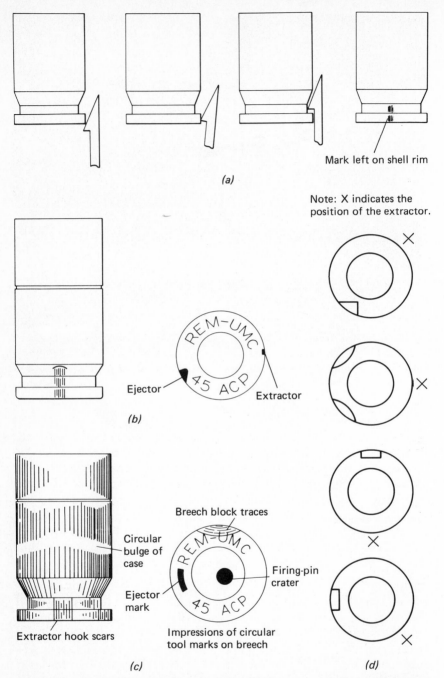

Mark left on shell rim

(a)

Note: X indicates the position of the extractor.

Ejector   Extractor

(b)

Breech block traces

Circular bulge of case

Firing-pin crater

Ejector mark

Extractor hook scars

Impressions of circular tool marks on breech

(c)

(d)

Figure 4-14   (a) Extractor engaging shell rim; (b) extractor and ejector marks, cartridge fired in Colt .45 automatic pistol; (c) cartridge fired in Thompson machine gun; (d) relative positions of extractor (x) and ejector traces found on casings from four different automatic weapons.

Figure 4-15 Marking on cartridge casing made by turret bolt from .44 magnum Ruger rifle, viewed through split screen of comparison microscope. Left half is test, right half is evidence (James McDonald).

of the weapon that fired them, from where the weapon was fired. This rests on the fact that automatic weapons discharge their cartridge casings at characteristic angles and for certain known distances.) The primer cup is generally composed of a soft metal such as copper, and the firing pin characteristic can be identified by the shape of its impression. Round, half-round, triangular, rectangular, or wedge-shaped are characteristic forms of firing pins on rimfire cartridges. Most firing pins may be slightly off center or contain individual unique wear marks that can be identified upon magnification (Fig. 4-10). Occasionally, reloads have been found at a crime scene, and this will be apparent from the unusual number of markings on a cartridge case.

The velocity or speed of a bullet varies with its manufacturer and ranges anywhere from several hundred feet per second to upward of 4000 feet/second (ft/s) [1219.2 meters/second (m/s)] for high-speed rifle bullets. It is dependent upon the amount of powder, the powder grain size, the amount of graphite coating on the powder, the bullet weight, its shape and design, and the barrel length through which it is fired.

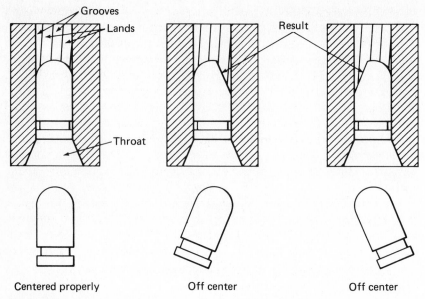

Figure 4-16   Result of bullet entering forcing cone off center (Courtesy American Institute of Applied Science, Syracuse, NY). Center and right-hand figures exaggerated.

Trigger Pull

Of importance in some cases is the amount of trigger pull pressure needed to discharge a weapon. There have been cases where a child as young as 3 years is supposed to have pulled a trigger and fired the fatal shot. It was up to the investigators to determine whether this was possible. The following list shows some typical trigger pull pressures:

22 rifle—4 to 6 pounds (lb) [1.8 to 2.7 kilograms (kg)] except target models
Military rifle—4 to 7 lb [1.8 to 3.2 kg]
Revolver, single-action—$3^{1}/_{2}$ to $5^{1}/_{2}$ lb [1.6 to 2.5 kg], except target models
Revolver, double-action—10 to 15 lb [2.3 to 6.9 kg]
Semiautomatic pistol—$4^{1}/_{2}$ to $6^{1}/_{2}$ lb [2.0 to 2.9 kg], except target models
Shotgun—4 to 6 lb [1.8 to 2.7 kg]

Investigating for Firearms

As the technology of firearms identification developed, the responsibility of law enforcement officers to conduct rigorous and disciplined investigation of the murder scene became even greater than it had been. Care had to be taken of bullets and weapons found at the scene of the crime because they would play an important role in the outcome of the case. A review of the steps a police officer should take when she or he first appears on the scene of a murder is in order.

The first action taken by an officer at a murder scene is to call the department immediately, by the quickest, surest means—radio, walkie-talkie, or telephone. The next step is to *secure the area*. This means to allow no one to touch or move anything, least of all the victim. No one should be allowed to leave the scene. The area should be roped off, and all entrances and exits to the immediate locale blocked.

Figure 2-3 shows the crime scene checklist used by the Syracuse, New York, Police Department. It is as complete and thorough a guide to good law enforcement procedure at the scene of a murder (or, for that matter, any crime) as you are likely to find. Take time to study it carefully.

An Orderly Investigation

The most important first move in any investigation is to notify the following agencies: medical examiner or coroner, district attorney or prosecutor, the forensic laboratory, and the investigators. This, of course, follows the immediate notification of your own police department.

Photographic History

Another important step is the photographic "history," or record, of the murder scene, with close-ups of wounds, weapons, and all possible evidence. Every effort should be made to have the photographs portray the scene exactly as it was at the time of the crime. The room should be photographed from every angle. Both color and black-and-white film should be used. If a professional police photographer is not available, an officer can use a Polaroid or Instamatic camera to provide a minimum of coverage.

Sketches should be made at the same time, showing dimensions of the room, location of furniture, windows, doors, and the relationship of important objects to the body (that is, chairs, bureaus, cartridge cases, spent bullets, etc.).

Gathering Evidence

If the crime was committed outdoors and multiple shots were fired, a good deal of searching will be required to locate stray bullets, particularly if the area is grassy or has cinders or soil. If the surrounding surface is concrete, stone, or brick, bullets may have ricocheted. Be on the lookout for what may appear to be fresh marks where a bullet may have struck. Should bullets be found in wood, plaster, floor tile, or some other surface, they should be photographed before removal. The surrounding area of the bullet should be cut out and removed with the bullet intact.

Evidence, such as bullets or cartridge casings, should be placed in a container after the place where they are found is photographed, and marked for identification with case number, date and time found, location, and name and initials of the officer finding it. In addition, the officer should mark the bullet or cartridge with his or her initials. *The bullet is marked on its base and the cartridge casing on the inside mouth of the casing.* If the evidence is turned over to a laboratory, a receipt must be obtained, the same procedure as is followed with other evidence. A word of caution to police officers: If you are ever called upon to testify, do not use your notebook, as once it is taken out in court, it may be subjected to all types of questioning by the defense counsel.

Use caution in handling a weapon, to prevent it being accidently discharged and to preserve latent fingerprints, blood stains, and other tangible evidence such as hairs. A revolver or automatic may be picked up by the grip, with a handkerchief, to prevent smudging of fingerprints, or it may be picked up by placing a string through the trigger guard.

The handgun should be placed in a box with a tag containing the necessary identifying data previously mentioned. Generally, after the weapon has been unloaded, the forensic technician or criminalist will search for latent fingerprints, for it has been found that a limited amount of dusting powder will not harm dry bloodstains. In unloading a revolver, one should make note of the position of fired and unfired cartridges.

If fingerprints are found, they should be photographed and lifting tape should be placed over the latent fingerprint and left intact. It is suggested that lifting tape remain intact so the weapon may be produced at the trial with the fingerprint visible. After the weapon has been examined for fingerprints, the next step is to search for human hairs or fibers. More often than not, in a contact shot against the head, hairs, blood, and tissue are found around the weapon's muzzle because of backsplash. Finally, dried blood should be carefully scraped from the weapon and tests conducted for blood grouping. Whenever any evidence is turned over to a forensic laboratory, a receipt should be obtained to maintain the chain of evidence. All such receipts should be kept in the case file.

If a weapon with a serial number is found at the scene, more than likely it was stolen. When the serial number is filed off, there are processes that may be tried to bring about its restoration. It is highly unlikely that robbers or murderers would leave a gun at the scene with its serial number registered to themselves. Most guns found at crime scenes are unregistered.

The majority of police departments maintain an unidentified bullet file from previous homicides that can be used for future comparison purposes, should the same weapon be used in more than one homicide. Some of the class characteristics of bullets and cartridge casings that will be useful in such a file follow:

Bullet	Cartridge Casing or Shell
Weight	Manufacturer's headstamp
Diameter or caliber	Firing pin marking
Number of grooves and lands (width and depth)	Caliber or gauge
	Breechface markings
Jacketed or not (and type)	Extractor markings
Twist direction	Ejector markings
Angle or twist	Revolver or automatic
Manufacturer	Clip or magazine marks

One of the first steps taken in examination of a bullet is to obtain its weight in grains [437.5 grains = 28.3 grams (g) = 1 ounce (oz)]. The weight helps determine the caliber along with other distinctive designs, such as shape of base, nose, cannelures, etc., as well as the possible manufacturer. Depending on the condition of the barrel, the number of lands and grooves and their direction of twist may be determined from the recovered bullet.

Foreign matter such as particles of sand, plaster, glass, paint, wood, and wire screening has been found on spent bullets. Figure 4-17 shows the weave of a piece of cloth impressed upon a bullet on contact. Rarely is a bullet found in perfect shape unless lodged in a soft area of skin. However, a small area of a groove may render sufficient striae to effect an identification. There are many reasons why insufficient markings might be found on a bullet: the bullet might have been fired from a barrel much larger than the caliber of the bullet; the bullet might have been fired from a starter pistol, a Saturday Night Special, or possibly a homemade device such as a zip gun or a weapon with a smooth bore; the bullet might have been badly deformed.

Additional identifying characteristics may be found on a bullet when, for example, in a revolver the cylinder and barrel do not line

Figure 4-17   Wad cutter bullet generally used for competitive shooting. Note woven impression on side of bullet and piece of cloth that made this impression. Because of improper loading, bullet struck cloth sideways (Courtesy Brian Downey).

up properly, thus deforming the bullet as it passes from the chamber into the breach (Fig. 4-16). If the bore is too large, there will be a lack of sharpness to the land and groove impressions. If the weapon is not in good condition, the bullet may travel a short distance in the barrel, resisting the directional twist of the lands before engaging them properly. This produces fanlike marks at the head of each land impression known as skid marks (Fig. 4-18).

As mentioned above, a small area of the bullet may be sufficient for a comparative examination to be made. A comparison microscope is used. This device might have made the solution of the Sacco and Vanzetti case more clear-cut and final. The comparison microscope was developed principally by Philip Gravelle, John Fisher, and C. Waite in conjunction with Col. Calvin Goddard. With this instrument, two bullets or cartridges can be examined simultaneously. It actually consists of two single microscopes mounted side to side with an optical coupling device that enables one to view what is mounted on their examination stages simultaneously. (Fig. 4-19).

The evidence bullet—whether found at the crime scene or removed from the victim's body—is compared with a test bullet ob-

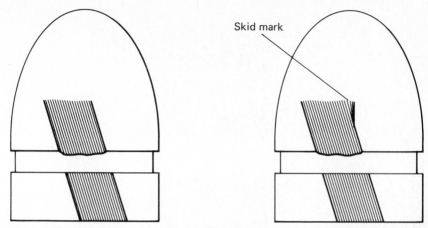

Figure 4-18   The bullet on the left was fired from a single shot target gun. There are no skid marks. The one on the right was shot from a revolver. Note the skid mark at the upper right of the land trace (Courtesy American Institute of Applied Science, Syracuse, NY).

tained from the suspect's weapon (Fig. 4-20). Each bullet or cartridge is mounted on a mechanical stage. Both specimens face the same direction. One bullet or cartridge case will be turned until an area containing prominent striae is found. Then the other bullet or cartridge case will be rotated in search of the same area of similar markings. The markings will never be exactly alike, but the similarities will offset the dissimilarities. Many comparison microscopes are fitted with a Polaroid camera for obtaining instant photographs, and others are equipped with the conventional type of camera. At one time 8- by 10-in enlargements of the identifying striae were used in court, making it possible to place an enlarged photograph of each specimen over the other to show the matching striae. This practice has been discontinued because of the limited depth of focus (sharpness) of microphotographs, which aroused doubts in jurors' minds. Some markings or striae were in focus, and others were not.

As we have seen, the firearms examiner compares the unknown or evidence bullet from the murder victim with a test bullet from the suspected weapon.

Test bullets may be obtained by discharging a weapon into either an 18-in² [116.1-centimeter² (cm²)] box about 5 ft [1.5 m] in length containing cotton or a water tank of larger size. In using a water tank, the bullet may be located very quickly by glancing into the tank, although not much searching is required to find a bullet in a cotton test box. Cotton does have one added disadvantage: it tends to polish off some of the fine striations as the bullet passes through it, particularly with lead bullets. See Fig. 4-21.

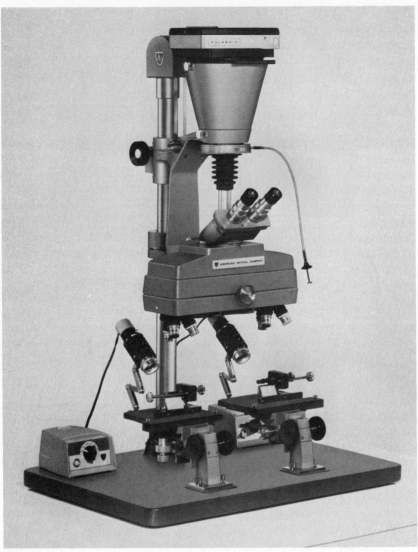

Figure 4-19   Forensic comparison microscope (Courtesy American Optical Corp., Southbridge, MA).

Examining the Body

In some jurisdictions, the medical examiner or coroner will insist that an investigator of the local police, a state police officer, a sheriff's deputy, or a representative of the prosecutor's office witness the autopsy.

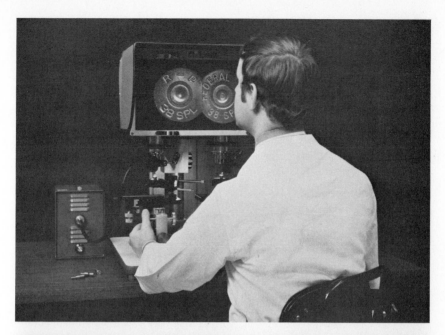

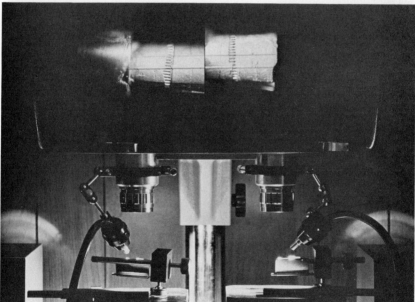

Figure 4-20   *Top:* visual identification of cartridge head stamp area and firing pin impression viewed under CP-6 comparison projector; *bottom:* CP-6 showing lands and grooves on a spent bullet (Courtesy Unitron Instruments, Inc., Woodbury, NY).

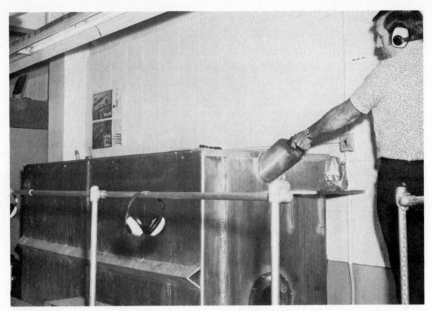

Figure 4-21 Test firing in water tank (Courtesy New York Police Department Forensic Laboratory).

It is possible for a bullet to enter the chest and be found in the lower abdomen. Sometimes bullets do enter and exit from a body (Fig. 4-22). The exit wound may not appear much different from the entrance wound. Deflection of a bullet can be caused by it striking bone, cartilage, or muscle. The taking of x-rays of the body will eliminate guesswork and will disclose the exact location of the bullet(s). Such action will eliminate probing for a bullet.

Since some bullets are made of lead, a metal softer than that used in surgical instruments, they can be easily marred. If there is any probing, identifying characteristics or striations may be obliterated. In any event, the bullet must be removed with extreme care. Once removed, it too should be placed in a marked container with the necessary identifying data—case number, date found, location, name of doctor finding same, and officer receiving the bullet. The bullet may be marked with a metal scribe on the base; or, if that is too distorted, a secondary area such as the nose may be used. The evidence bullet should be marked by the person recovering it—police officer, doctor, or medical examiner. If the bullet is turned over to a forensic laboratory or firearms examiner, a receipt should be obtained and made a part of the file. The ideal situation is when the firearms examiner is present at the autopsy, observes the removal of the bullet, and receives it from the medical examiner.

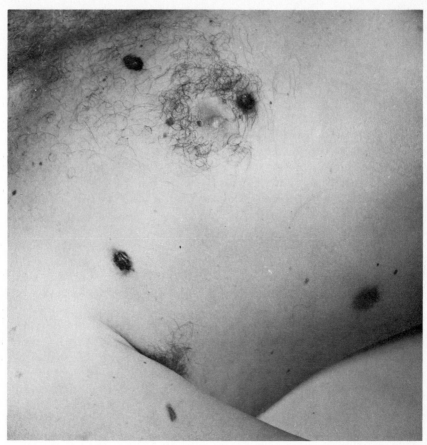

Figure 4-22 Multiple bullet wounds. Top three are entrance holes and lower wound is an exit hole. Note tattooing on skin and bullet crease on arm.

Clothing

Examine the area of clothing surrounding a suspect bullet hole for powder residue. If powder is present or there is a seared or singed wound with powder soot or smudging, the weapon was fired at or near a contact position. The victim's clothing should be placed in separate containers, unless they are wet or damp with blood. The clothing should be marked for identification. Wet, bloody clothing should be hung up to dry by natural processes and not subjected to forced heat or other unnatural drying. An important reason for placing the victim's clothing in separate containers is to preserve and facilitate the search for foreign matter such as hairs, fibers, and glass by the laboratory technicians and to prevent contamination of areas of clothing for future examination and chemical testing. The path of the bullet will be revealed by an examination of the outer clothing and underclothes. Sometimes a bullet may leave a grazing mark on the arm before entering the body, thus indicating the position of the arm at the time of firing.

Cases of Suicide

Extreme caution should be the rule in an investigation of a suspected suicide case. A seemingly open-and-shut case of suicide may turn out to be murder at a later date. A few washings of the hands by the individual who committed the shooting will remove all traces of residue left from discharging a weapon. Testing a person's hands early in an investigation for having fired a weapon may eliminate him or her as a suspect in the future if the case proves to be a homicide. (See neutron activation analysis and atomic absorption spectrometry in Chap. 15.) Also, careless handling of clothing will dislodge some particles of powder from a powder pattern that could reveal the distance from which the weapon was fired. This distance is an important factor, and one that must be verified, particularly in cases appearing to be suicides.

Gunpowder or gunshot residue patterns vary with the length of the barrel. The cartridge from a 2-in barrel will leave a larger pattern than the same cartridge fired from a 6-in barrel from the same distance. Other factors that affect the powder pattern are wind conditions and the cartridge powder charge. The powder pattern, or "tattooing" or "stippling," as it has come to be called, is caused by a combination of partially burned and unburned powder granules that are discharged and blown out of the muzzle along with the bullet (Fig. 4-23).

Once the weapon and the cartridge type have been determined, test patterns can be conducted until a comparative pattern is obtained. (See Fig. 4-24.) Generally, the assumption can be made that the weapon may leave a visible pattern when fired from a distance of under 2½ ft [0.76 m]. Nonvisible patterns can be developed by chemical or other means from a distance of up to 5 ft [1.5 m].

A careful examination of the skin surrounding the wound will reveal particles of powder when the weapon was fired at a close range. Often the unburned powder will pass through the victim's garments and be observed on the skin. One can easily examine a garment to see if there is singeing or burning around the entrance hole.

Other tests may be performed in many instances to determine the approximate distance of discharge. One test is called the "Walker test"; it uses "fixed," or desensitized, chemically treated, photographic paper. The test will generally prove positive unless the weapon was discharged at too great a distance to leave residue. The success will also depend on the manner in which the clothing was

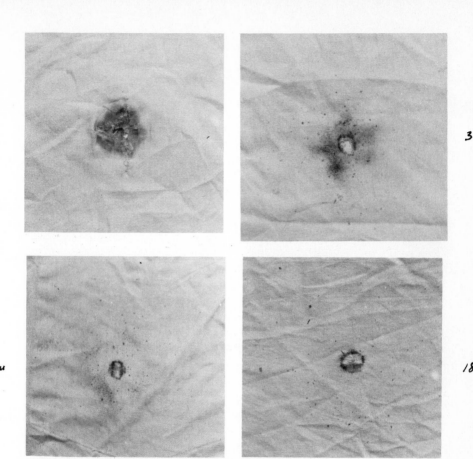

3"

8"

18"

Figure 4-23 Gunshot residue powder patterns, .38 special revolver, 4-in barrel, Remington lead cartridge. *Top left:* contact shot; *Top right:* 3 in; *bottom left:* 8 in; *bottom right:* 18 in (Courtesy Joseph Reich). Note: The black ring around the hole in all but the contact shot photograph is "bullet wipe," due to grease wiped off bullet as it passed through cloth, not because of deposited powder.

handled before testing. If the clothing was shaken to any extent, such action would likely dislodge some but not all powder residue. On the other hand, if the garment containing the bullet hole was carefully placed in a cardboard box, plastic bag, or some other container, most of the residue will remain intact. The distance from point of discharge to a wound is always an important factor in a questionable suicide. Unless the weapon was discharged at a considerable distance by some remote-control device, a powder pattern should be present. Certainly, if no powder pattern is present, the weapon was discharged at a distance of 3 ft or more. Such testing is also important in cases of self-defense. A word of caution is necessary: If the clothing

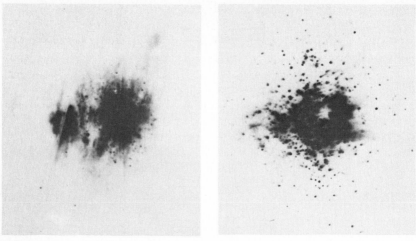

Figure 4-24 *Left:* Powder pattern on clothing of deceased; *right:* test powder pattern. Note similarity of two patterns (Courtesy Joseph Reich).

contains wet blood, it must be dried before being tested. If it is not dried, the only result will be a sheet of "bloody photography paper."

Preparing Test Paper for Walker Test

1. Photography paper is desensitized, or fixed, by placing it in "hypo" or fixer for approximately 10 minutes (min) with some agitation. The paper is next washed under running water for approximately three-quarters of an hour after which it must be dried. This action removes the silver halides and leaves only a gelatin-coated paper.

2. The paper is treated with 0.5% solution of sulfanilic acid for 10 min and dried.

3. The dried paper is now treated with 0.5% solution of alpha naphthylamine (*note:* care must be exercised as this is a known carcinogen) in methyl alcohol and again dried.

4. The gelatin side of the paper is placed in contact with the area of the garment where the bullet hole is located. The garment is pressed from the opposite side with a hot iron for approximately 2 min using a pressing cloth dampened with 25% acetic acid in distilled water.

5. Orange-red specks appearing on the paper represent the pattern of either burned or unburned residue of powder particles. The approximate distance from which the weapon was discharged can be determined by test firing until a similar pattern is obtained. The color reaction on the paper indicates the presence of nitrites. It is possible to detect powder residue after a year's lapse of time when the clothing has been carefully preserved. A color photograph should be taken of any positive reaction in the form of orange-reddish specks, for they will probably fade and become almost invisible after a time. A photograph of the test again maintains the chain of evidence.

Infrared or x-ray photography will also reveal gun powder residue on dark clothing.

One method of testing for gunpowder residue on the hands utilizes a cotton swabbing technique. The swabbings are subjected to neutron activation analysis (see Chap. 15). The individual performing the test must wear plastic or rubber gloves in order to prevent any contamination of the testing area.

Each swab is saturated with 5% nitric acid and then rubbed on the area of the hand, i.e. two swabs for the back of the hand and two for the palm. The swabs are then placed in a marked polyethylene container. Both hands are tested in this manner.

Two cotton swabs containing only nitric acid are used as a control to verify that the acid and cotton are uncontaminated. It was found that cotton swabs with wood shafts contained contaminants. So it is recommended that only cotton swabs with plastic shafts be used. A number of state police departments supply kits for such testing in murder or questionable suicide cases only. They, in turn, send the samples to the U.S. Treasury Department's National Office Laboratory in Washington, D.C. Commercial kits for swabbing are available from a number of supply houses.

Shotgun Cases

Shotguns are often used in both suicides and homicides. This fact can be readily determined when the body is viewed because a shotgun at close range produces a large wound, to say the least. A shotgun discharged at a contact position will cause massive destruction to a body area.

There are no rifling marks in a shotgun barrel; the bore is smooth and completely devoid of lands and grooves. A shotshell contains a large quantity of lead shot varying in size, so it is impossible to find any identifying marks on the small pellets. Many times the gauge can be determined by the diameter of the wad or the wad base. The plastic wad is found inside a shotshell. Its purpose is to keep the shot charge together for a reasonable distance after it leaves the muzzle.

Many times, the plastic wad will be found inside a wound when the shotgun is fired at a reasonably close range. In one particular holdup, where the payroll had been placed in envelopes in a shoe box, the shotgun wad was found inside the victim's chest, along with particles of the paper money. Evidently, the victim had crouched with the box in front of his chest in an effort to protect himself.

In the investigation of a crime involving a shotgun, it is worth remembering that the wad from a shotshell may travel as far as 22 ft [6.7 m] or more from the point of discharge.

Determining a Bullet's Direction of Travel (Trajectory)

Generally, one needs two points of contact to determine the path of a bullet from the weapon to its final resting place. For example, a bullet fired through a window lodges in a wall. One can then estimate its direction of origin by drawing a straight line between these points. Knowledge of the weapons and cartridge characteristics as well as some elementary physics can aid in estimating the distance the projectile might have traveled. If the bullet has embedded itself to some depth (for example, in a wall, a mattress, or other item of furniture), one can estimate its trajectory from the direction of its path in the item. The situation is complicated by the fact that bullets tend to be deflected from a straight-line path when they strike something.

Doctors K. K. S. Pillay and William Hester of the Pennsylvania State University have performed some research in identifying the direction of travel of bullets fired from handguns. Their testing has been limited to shots fired indoors at a distance of up to 40 ft [12.2 m]. The procedure involved moistened strips of filter paper being placed first in contact with suspected areas in circular patterns at various distances from the target, and then in a polyethylene container. The container was then subjected to neutron activation analysis (see Chap. 15). Their research was based on identification of the elements barium, antimony, copper, and gold being present in greater amounts in the direction of the bullet's path because the bullet sheds minute amounts of these metals as it travels from weapon to target.

Erased Serial Numbers

When a number is stamped into metal, the molecular structure of the metal under the impression is changed. When the serial number has been filed off such a metal, quite often it is possible to restore the serial numbers to a point where they can be photographed. This will be possible if, as is often the case, the number has been filed off only until it is no longer visible but not far enough to remove the altered area under the impression. First the area is polished with a fine emery paper or cloth. Then it is cleaned with an organic solvent like acetone or benzene. Next it is swabbed with cotton saturated with the following chemicals:

80 cc of concentrated hydrochloric acid
30 cc of distilled water
25 cc of ethyl alcohol
5 g of cupric chloride

The action of these chemicals is to dissolve the metal. However, the metal that was under the serial number will dissolve at a rate different from the rest of the metal. If the rates of dissolving are sufficiently different, the number will become visible (Fig. 4-25).

The swabbing may have to be performed for as much as 1 hour (h) or possibly longer. If the numbers appear, a photograph must be taken immediately, after which the chemical action must be stopped by washing with water, drying, and oiling. These chemicals will work with steel. Other reagents must be used for copper, aluminum, lead, and any alloys.

An electrolytic method uses the following reagents: sulfuric acid, gelatin, and copper sulfate. The area must be first polished with emery cloth and then swabbed with the above reagents in conjunction with approximately 6 volts (V) of electricity. At times the number may appear in a matter of minutes.

The Paraffin Test

A test used for many years to determine whether a person had fired a handgun was the paraffin test, which uses the reagents di-

Figure 4-25 *Above:* obliterated serial number; *right:* partially restored serial number (Courtesy New York Police Department).

phenylamine and diphenylbenzidine. This test was developed in 1933 by Theodore Gonzales of Mexico. It was based on nitrate and/or nitrite particles being deposited on the hand by gases from a discharged cartridge.

This method of testing has been largely discontinued today because a positive reaction will occur if a person has had contact with substances such as fertilizer, tobacco, cosmetics, and such vegetables as peas, beans, and alfalfa. These substances contain the same chemicals being tested. The test has been not recognized in New York State courts since 1950 by reason of its being too inconclusive. The test remains important because the paraffin may be used for testing by neutron activation analysis. A kit for this purpose was developed by Dr. K. K. S. Pillay at the Department of Nuclear Engineering, Pennsylvania State University, University Park, PA.

The most important area of the hands for testing is the connecting skin between the thumb and index finger. This area is the most susceptible to gases leaving residue of nitrates and nitrites when a weapon is discharged. Actually little equipment is needed for the test:

Rubber or plastic gloves
Two nylon brushes
Two containers for the wax
Two plastic bags or containers for the cast of each hand
Diphenylamine
Sulfuric acid
Distilled water

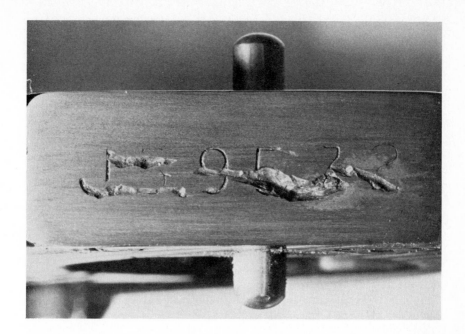

Procedure

1. Rubber or plastic gloves must be worn by the person applying the paraffin.
2. Paraffin must be free of contamination and heated to about 120°F [48.9°C] or until liquefied. The container of paraffin must be free of contamination. (Pillay actually developed a special mixture to be used instead of paraffin.)
3. Two separate nylon paint brushes—approximately 1 in [25.4 millimeters (mm)] in size—must be rinsed in distilled water before using. A separate brush and container must be used for each hand to avoid contamination from one hand to the other.
4. The paraffin may be painted on the hand to a depth of approximately 1/8 in [3.2 mm].
5. When the paraffin has dried, each cast is removed and placed in a marked container indicating from which hand it had been taken along with the initials of the officer or technician who made the cast. Whatever residue was contained on the hands will be transferred to the paraffin. Only these five steps are necessary when testing of the paraffin is to be done by neutron activation analysis (NAA). The paraffin lift is removed, placed in a special plastic bag, and subjected to NAA.

Should one wish to perform the original diphenylamine testing, the following chemical reagents should be used:

Diphenylamine solution
0.5 g diphenylamine
100 cc concentrated sulfuric acid
20 cc distilled water

As soon as the paraffin is removed from the hand, the above solution must be applied. If the testing produces a purplish-blue color, this is a positive reaction, the intensity of color being a measure of the amount of powder residue.

The most promising modern test appears to be a combination of x-ray fluorescence spectroscopy and scanning electron microscopy[1] (Chap. 15). The former is used to detect the lead, barium, and antimony that are present as a result of the discharge of the weapon. Use of scanning electron microscopy enables one to establish that these elements were produced by powder discharge from a firearm: tests have shown that when this is the case, these elements are found combined in particles of *a rather specific shape* whereas when they are due to sources other than the discharge of a firearm, no such particles are found.

Cleaning Old Guns

Often a rusted revolver, automatic, or shotgun may be found from which an examiner will wish to conduct tests. Before any tests can be performed, the weapon must be cleaned and the rust removed. The procedure follows:

1. Field-strip the weapon (disassemble).
2. Place the rusted parts in ultrasonic cleaner commonly used by jewelers along with 2% acetic acid (photographic stop bath). White vinegar may be substituted for the acid with an equal amount of water.
3. The rusted parts should remain in the solution for an hour or more when the rust can be seen no more. Next, the parts should be rinsed in acetone.
4. Wipe clean with a cloth, stiff toothbrush, or very fine steel wool to remove any remaining residue.

[1] LEAA News Release, August 18, 1976.

Generally, during the above process the finish of the metal is removed, and all parts should be lightly oiled.

Trace Metal Detection Test

By using a method known as TMD (trace metal detection), sometimes it is possible to determine whether a person has handled anything of metal—a steel firearm, for instance. The chemical reagent 8-hydroxyquinoline is used in the testing. The reagent is obtainable in spray cans (Sirchie Laboratories). A hand suspected of having fired a weapon is sprayed and then examined under ultraviolet (UV) light. The color appearing under the UV light varies with the type of metal. Occasionally an outline of the metal configuration or outline of that part of the weapon held with the fingers and palm can be seen.

It would take a comprehensive volume to cover adequately all the areas of firearms identification. This is not the purpose of the chapter. The authors' intent is to give the student an overview of the subject so that, when confronted with a situation involving firearms identification, he or she will know the proper steps to take.

chapter

Glass

Glass plays such a large role in every aspect of living that the investigator must pay close attention to it at the scene of a crime. Often a shattered window, a broken bottle, or a smashed headlight contributes important evidence. In searching suspects and crime scenes, investigators are alert to the value of glass as evidence. Police work includes a thorough study of its characteristics. It is an example of that type of microscopic evidence which may be easily transferred to the clothes of the criminal and just as easily go unnoticed by him or her.

Glass appears to be a solid, but technically it is a "supercooled liquid," that is, a noncrystalline mixture of the oxides of silicon, calcium, and soda lime. This distinguishes it from true solids which are crystalline in structure. There are hundreds of different kinds of glass being manufactured today, from ordinary window glass to that designed for the windows of spaceships. Spaceship glass can withstand heat up to 900°C. Lenses, mirrors, prisms, and photographic filters use highly developed glasses of many kinds. In most police work, however, the glass involved is the ordinary variety, not very complex in composition or structure. Glass most often found at the scene of a crime is limited to the following types:

Window glass
Plate glass
Safety glass (in car windows, for instance)

Headlight lenses
Bottles
Eyeglasses
Tempered glass
Watch crystal glass

At the Scene of the Crime

Glass is one of the best surfaces for obtaining fingerprints, and all glass connected with the crime should be examined first for latent prints. The point of entry or "break" is the place to start the search. Often a burglar will break a window or door pane and pick out pieces in order to reach in and unfasten the lock, leaving prints on the fragment—usually on both sides, a thumb on one side, an index or middle finger on the other.

Note: Always handle glass fragments carefully; wear gloves and handle them by their edges. The fragments should be placed in a box and brought to the police laboratory without delay.

What an Investigator Needs to Know about Glass

Impact

When glass is struck by an object, it bends to the maximum of its flexibility or elasticity, at which point it fractures. The statement is often made that glass fractures not from compression but from tension created by force. That is, as the glass bends, the side that is struck is under compression while the opposite side is being stretched and is in tension. When it reaches its tensile limit, it fractures. These considerations determine the characteristic appearances of broken glass. If a projectile has sufficient force, it will pass through the glass, making a cone-shaped (referred to as crater-type, cuplike, or funnellike) hole. The larger side of the cone will be on the exit side.

When an object strikes glass with mild force, generally it will cause a recognizable pattern of cracking; or it may cause the entire glass to fracture, fragment, or shatter. This will vary according to the nature of the glass involved. The fractures or cracks are known as radial (or primary) concentric (or secondary) (Fig. 5-1). A cross section of such fractures will have marks known as conchoidal striations (sometimes referred to as rib marks or stress lines) (Fig. 5-2). Hackle marks will be found generally on the edge of a cross section. As two pieces of glass rub together at the corners, small pieces flake off, producing the hackle marks. Hackle marks are irregular indentations on the edge of glass. The radial fractures are caused first and radiate in what might be called a starlike design, similar to the spokes of a wheel hub. They form first on the side opposite to the force and tend to be more prominent on that side. The concentric fractures intersect the radial cracks in a sort of circular fashion. Some authors refer to these as spiral fractures because they tend to produce a circular effect or concentric lines of fracture.

As stated above, the sides of the radial and concentric fractured pieces of glass will have conchoidal striation "lines." In radial cracks they will be perpendicular (at right angles) to the exit side and parallel to the entry side, whereas the opposite is true for concentric fractures (Fig. 5-3). The pattern of these markings makes it possible to reconstruct the glass, and on occasion this is done. Reconstruction may be performed by fitting together all pieces of glass jigsaw style

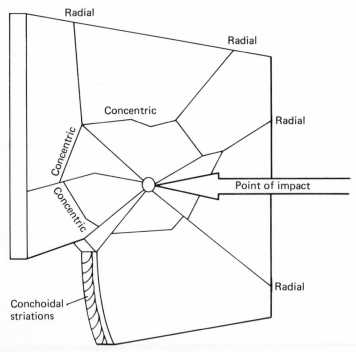

Figure 5-1 Simulated radial and concentric glass fractures.

Conchoidal striations   Hackle marks

Figure 5-2 Side view of glass sheet showing conchoidal striations and hackle marks caused by chips.

on a large piece of cardboard or table and then taping them together to form the original shape. The tiny fragments of glass that fly backward on the same side from which the breaking force originated cause the hackle marks previously mentioned. These particles will be so small that the individual who broke the glass will not be aware of their presence unless by chance she or he receives a cut and notices the bleeding.

An officer or investigator will want to distinguish which side of the glass faced the outside and which the inside. This can usually be determined by examining the glass for putty or paint-color residue around the edges. An examination of the surrounding area of the window or door frame will disclose the colors used on each side of the glass. In addition, the outside of the window will have rain spots apparent in the glass after a time and will be more soiled than the inside of the glass. The exception will occur when the glass has been recently washed before any rain has fallen.

The ultimate in glass evidence is when a piece of glass will fit jigsaw style into its original position. Even though tiny fragments along the edges of the radial and concentric cracks are missing, the feel of the fit will be quite evident. Such occurrences are not too common but are as convincing as are matching fingerprints for proof that two pieces came from the same source. In a case of a hit-and-run injury, a fragment of glass had to be surgically removed from a youth. It was clearly shown by matching the glass that the suspect vehicle had struck the young man. In another case, the skull of a homicide victim contained fragments from a glass bottle with which he had been struck. Particles of glass found on the suspect's clothing compared favorably with that found in the victim's skull.

A bullet and other projectiles, when shot with sufficient force, will pierce glass with a clean, round hole which is craterlike in cross section, the larger end being opposite the side of impact. If the bullet is spent, however, it is more likely to break the entire window. A

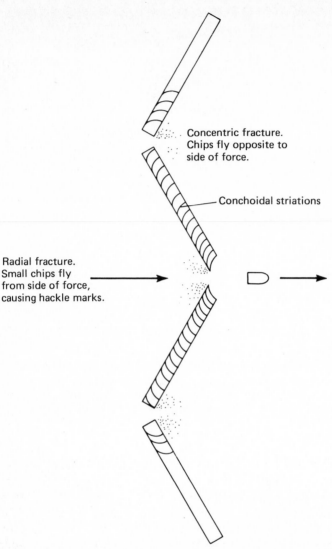

Concentric fracture. Chips fly opposite to side of force.

Conchoidal striations

Radial fracture. Small chips fly from side of force, causing hackle marks.

Figure 5-3 Bullet with sufficient force will fracture glass, causing a radial and concentric pattern. Flaking, or glass fragments (not shown), occurs on exit side of glass, producing a cone shape. This flaking is much larger than the minute chips causing hackle marks.

weapon fired at close range will also break an entire window because of the pressure of the gases leaving the barrel. There will also be a residue of powder that can be identified on the glass as a confirming fact of the closeness of the firing.

Generally, it is possible to determine the order of fire of bullets by reason of the fact that the radial cracks of the second bullet will terminate when reaching the radial cracks caused by the first shot. See Fig. 5-4.

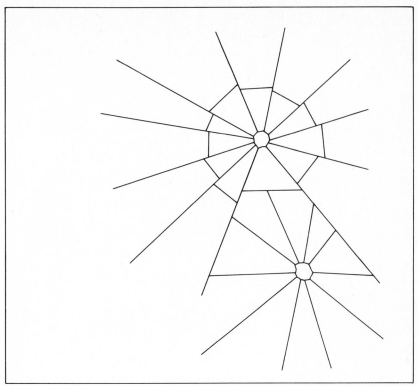

Figure 5-4   Multiple glass fracture. Simulated effect of two bullets. The top fracture was from the first bullet fired. Fractures of the second bullet terminate upon reaching fractures of the first bullet.

The angle of fire may also be determined by the shape of the hole. A bullet fired at an angle will create a somewhat elliptical hole. The entry side of the hole will be somewhat smoother than the exit side, where considerably more flaking will be apparent. The entry side is an important factor in determining whether the shots were fired from inside or outside an automobile. Very often a bullet fired at safety glass commonly used in autos will cause overall fragmentation.

Common Forms of Glass

Safety glass is two pieces of glass cemented together or joined in the center by a transparent adhesive plastic. Before the advent of safety glass, mesh wire (similar to what is commonly referred to as chicken wire) was embedded in the glass during manufacturing. When such glass was struck, it would crack; but most of it would be held by the wire, so it did not shatter.

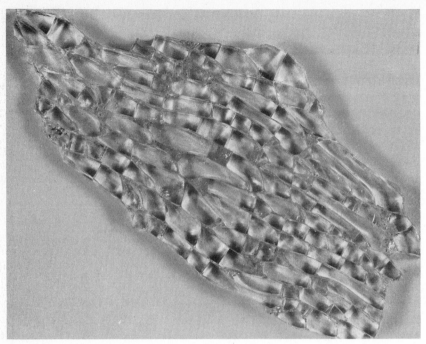

Figure 5-5 Fragmentation of tempered glass.

Tempered glass is used in storm doors, shower doors, and some car windows. Tempered glass is made stronger than ordinary glass by heat treatment, which introduces controlled compressive stress on its surface. This glass will not shatter into pointed fractures, but will become fragmented in a more or less mosaic pattern with little or no sharp edges. Testing has proved that a 38-caliber slug will cause the complete fragmentation of a tempered window in a vehicle at 12 ft [3.7 m]. Fig. 5-5.

Plate glass is found in store-front windows, doors, and display cases. It is a thick glass that will take more force to break than common ordinary window glass. Many years ago a burglar removed a round circle of plate glass from the window of a jewelry store. He reached in and helped himself to all the jewelry within reach. On capture he boasted that no one would ever learn his secret for removing the perfect circle of glass with no other fracturing occurring. One theory is that a diamond glass cutter could have been used with some sort of a metal can used as a guide. Then a sharp blow to the circled area would cause the glass to fall out. A rubber suction cup could have been used to prevent the glass from falling to the pavement.

Colored lenses used in sunglasses, camera lenses, and filters are produced by adding metal compounds while the glass is in the molten state, which impart a color to the glass. Colored lenses are the easiest type of glass to identify by comparison methods or chemical testing, because of the elements used in production. Some of the metals used in colored glass manufacture are chromium, cobalt, copper, and antimony. The latest development in the lens area has been the manufacture of photochromic lenses that automatically darken in sunlight and brighten indoors or in dense shade. These are becoming more popular every day and eventually will be found at a crime scene.

Cars do not carry as much glass as they used to—taillights, back-up lights, and such are now made of plastic. Windows and headlights are still glass, and they help investigators in many automobile-connected crimes.

Bottle glass is very common and is generally green, brown, or colorless. This does not mean that bottle glass is difficult to distinguish. The late criminologist P. L. Kirk and G. W. Roche studied fifty samples of brown glass from beer bottles, and all but two were distinguishable by refractive index and density differences. These properties will be discussed shortly.

Glass and Heat

Glass subjected to intense heat, as in a fire, will crack overall in wavy lines and generally will fall toward the fire side. An explanation of this might be that when the oxygen is consumed in an area, it more or less creates a vacuum, causing the glass to fall toward the fire side. An explosion will literally blow the glass out of its framework and shatter it over the surrounding sidewalk and street.

Over the years, there has been great advancement in heat-resistant glass and glass ceramics. One of the first of this type was Pyrex or, technically, borosilicate glass. This glass becomes soft and will flow at approximately 800°C, whereas window glass will flow at about 600°C. Such glass contains a greater amount of silica. Corning has produced 96 percent silica glass under the trademark VYCOR that resists extreme heat shock and temperatures up to 900°C.

A Hypothetical Case

You may wonder if some of the foregoing material is not getting far afield of criminalistics. Consider the following case. It is hypothetical but not unrealistic.

Glass fragments of Pyrex are found on a kitchen floor, the scene of an alleged accidental death. The husband states that his wife fell and struck her head against a corner of an open dishwasher. A fragment of heat resistant glass is found embedded in her head. He explains the Pyrex fragments by stating that the coffee glass percolator broke over the stove while being heated. An experiment with this type of vessel will disclose that upon fracturing over a hot flame, it merely fractures and all the water pours out. There is no flying debris. This would certainly tend to disprove his statements and tend to prove that she was struck with the percolator.

Identifying Glass Samples

Glass samples are identified generally on a comparative, rather than an absolute, basis. The known piece of glass, being the control, is compared with the unknown from the crime scene. Two pieces of glass may be examined and tested for similarities in properties by various methods. Density and refractive index are important approaches. Other approaches include physical matching of the pieces, measurement of the curvature (as in eyeglass lenses), and analysis of the composition using neutron activation analysis or emission spectrometry (see Chap. 15). Density and refractive index are constant physical properties of a glass sample. Within certain limits the only variance will be in other samples of glass of a different origin. In other words, two fragments from the same origin should have similar density and refractive indices.

Density

"Density" is defined as the mass (or weight) of an object divided by the volume it occupies. The principle of density (buoyancy) was discovered by Archimedes about 300 b.c. It has been applied to the identification of glass in more modern times since it is a constant characteristic of the glass which may readily be compared with other samples of glass. The comparison rests on the fact that when a substance (e.g. glass) is placed in a liquid having the same density as that of the substance, the substance will remain suspended in the liquid, neither rising or falling.

In practice, a density gradient tube of 10 to 18 in [25.4 to 45.7 cm] in length is prepared by carefully adding liquids of different densities. Usually mixtures of bromoform and bromobenzene are used because this combination enables one to cover the normal range of glass densities, 2.2 to 2.89 grams/milliliter (g/ml). Thus a series of liquid layers are produced. The most dense will be at the bottom of the gradient tube and the lightest at the top. The evidence piece and the standard are carefully added to the tube. It should be emphasized that the investigator must be able to distinguish between the evidence piece and the standard by their physical appearance so that there is no chance of them becoming mixed up after being placed in the tube. If the two pieces do not float at the same level, this is taken to mean they are from different sources. If they do float at the same level, they may come from the same source. Further proof of this may be obtained by heating the tube about 10°C. Since increasing its temperature decreases the density of the liquid, both pieces will sink. If they again come to rest at the same level, they are presumed to have the same density and to have a common origin.

The Refractive Index

A second test for similarities in two pieces of glass is that of refractive index. Light travels faster through air than through glass or any other transparent substance including water. When light strikes a piece of glass at any angle, its velocity is reduced. The beam of light passing through the glass is bent, whereas the same light bypassing the glass is not bent or refracted and has a greater velocity. The difference, or ratio, between the velocity of light in a vacuum and its velocity through glass determines the degree of refraction and is known as refractive index. To illustrate the principle, place a pencil in a glass of water and observe how the pencil appears bent. Of course, it is the light that is refracted and not the pencil. The refractive index of glass depends upon its composition. If two pieces of glass come from different sources, they should have different compositions and therefore different indices of refraction. To repeat: when two pieces of glass have the same density and refractive index, the assumption can be made that they originated from the same piece.

INDEXING WITH A MICROSCOPE Refractive index is usually determined by an immersion method. One places the fragment in the well of a special glass slide. Enough liquid of known refractive index is added to cover the particle of glass. The slide is placed in the microscope, and the edge of the glass is brought into focus. An outline or white halo will be observed along the edge of the glass. This is known as the Becke line. Glass containing hackle marks or rough edges will not yield a good Becke line. In focusing the microscope upward, if the line moves toward the glass fragment, it has a higher refractive index than that of the liquid. The liquid is then removed, and one of higher refractive index is added. The process is repeated until the refractive indices of the liquid and the glass fragment are the same, as indicated by the absence of the Becke line. Differences in the order of 0.001 refractive index units can be detected. The uniformity obtainable with today's methods of mass production often

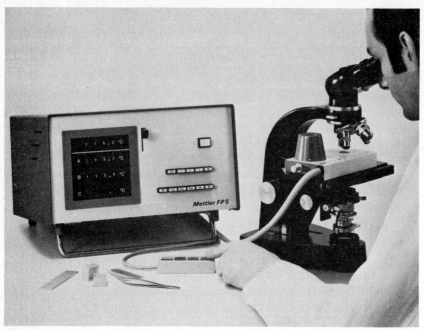

Figure 5-6 Mettler hot-stage microscope (Courtesy Mettler Instrument Corp., Hightstown, NJ).

results in headlights made by different manufacturers having variations even smaller than this, making this method useless to discriminate between them.

Refractive index may also be determined by using a microscope with a heating stage (see Fig. 5-6). This is probably the most popular means used today. A particle of glass is placed in liquid of known refractive index on a microscope slide. The particle of glass may be as small as the tip of a needle. The liquid must be one whose refractive index decreases as its temperature increases and also must be slightly higher than the highest possible index of the glass. The temperature of the heating stage is gradually increased. When the outline of the glass fragment disappears, the temperature is recorded. At this point, the refractive index of the liquid and the glass are the same. Reference tables will show the refractive index of different liquids at various temperatures, thus enabling the refractive index of the glass to be determined. This is faster and much more sensitive than the Becke line method. It permits measurements of differences in refractive index as small as about 0.00004 refractive index units.[1]

[1] P. R. DeForest and S. M. Ojena, *J. Forens. Sci. Soc.* **12:** 315, 1972.

Spectographic Analysis

For many years the spectrograph was used to identify glass particles. In this method the glass under examination is made to burn at a high temperature. The elements in the glass thus emit different colors or wavelengths of light. These wavelengths are recorded on photographic film, and a comparison is made of the film from each of the two samples. (See emission spectrograph in Chap. 15.) The disadvantage of this method is that it destroys the glass and therefore may not be the best approach in cases to be settled in court.

NOTE: Neutron activation analysis is also used in identifying glass fragments. This will also be discussed in Chap. 15.

X-ray fluorescence Spectroscopy (Chap. 15) provides another sensitive, nondestructive method for determining the composition of glass samples for comparison purposes.

Checklist

Procedures for examining glass by the police investigator include:

1. Determine type of glass.

    a. Window   f. Bottle
    b. Plate   g. Lead crystal
    c. Safety   h. Colored glass
    d. Tempered   i. Automobile headlight
    e. Heat-resistant glass   j. Corrective lens

2. Search for latent fingers.
3. Glass broken from inside or outside?
4. Thickness determined by a micrometer.
5. Was weapon fired at close distance, as indicated by powder residue found on the surface of glass?
6. Surface characteristics—glass design or casting pattern, curvature.
7. Was glass fracture caused by fire?
8. Approximate size of projectile and angle of penetration.
9. Number of bullet holes and order of fire.
10. Blood spots or splatters enabling blood typing or grouping.
11. Glass bottle used in assault may contain victim's hairs.

12. Rain spots and/or dirt will show exposed side of window.

13. Putty and paint will also assist in determining outside and inside of a window.

14. Glass fragments will enable comparison testing with known or control samples.

15. Testing by
    a. Refractive index
    b. Density
    c. Spectrographic analysis
    d. Neutron activation analysis
    e. Microscopic comparison
    f. Dispersive power—this is related to the refractive index. It is actually determined by measurement of the refractive index at each of three different wavelengths of light. This is another characteristic property of a piece of glass that may be used for comparison purposes.
    g. Examination with ultraviolet light for fluorescence.

Hair and Fibers

Hair and fibers are often referred to as *transfer evidence* and more often than not confirm Locard's statement that " . . . every contact leaves its trace." Many crimes involve direct physical contact between victim and perpetrator. In a rape or assault there may be a struggle—the victim grabbing or scratching at the assailant, the assailant forcibly restraining the victim. Whenever such contact is involved, there is almost invariably an inadvertent transfer of microscopic evidence. Body hairs, head hairs, pubic hairs, and clothing fibers are the most common examples. They may fall at the scene of a crime or be embedded on a weapon. They are all the more valuable because they pass unnoticed by the criminal.

A single hair under the fingernail of a suspect helped lead to a conviction in a recent murder case. In murder, rape, and assault, it is always important to search the scene for hair—it may well be the only physical evidence obtainable. Often, however, finding hair requires the most painstaking investigation.

NOTE: The possibility of finding fibers from clothing should not be overlooked. Like hair, fibers can provide evidence linking a suspect to a crime. Hairs and fibers are elusive, and criminals are not likely to stop and look for them, even if they should think to do so.

In a recently solved murder case in Westchester County, hairs found inside a hat discarded by the murderer were used to eliminate a number of suspects.

Searching the Scene

Clothing of both victim and suspects should be closely examined for hair. Be sure that the clothing is not placed in contact with any other garment, for this may result in cross contamination. Photographs of the area where the clothing was found should be taken before anything is touched or moved. Each article should be placed in an evidence bag or box and marked for identification with the following information:

1. Case number
2. Date and time found
3. Location
4. Name of officer who found evidence
5. Officer's initials or signature

When the clothing is examined, each evidence bag should be emptied over a large table covered with white paper. Another method is to place the clothing on a hanger and shake it so that the hair will fall to the table. Sometimes police use a vacuum cleaner with a filter attachment for retrieving hair from clothing, but, of course, this picks up lint and other residue as well. However, in some cases, where the hair is found may be critical, e.g., was it on the left sleeve or right pant leg? etc.

In rape cases, a doctor or a nurse should use a comb to find foreign hairs in the pubic area (Fig. 6-1). Hair evidence often plays a crucial role in sex crimes, and good police work demands absolute thoroughness and care in its collection. Note the attention to detail in the following report:

> Strands of hair from the clothes of subject were found to correspond with those of the victim, as did also a loose pubic hair which was found on the penis of subject. Under the foreskin the doctor found a small clump of mucus which on examination was found to consist of small tangled scraps of wool, most being dyed in bright colors. These colors showed complete correspondence

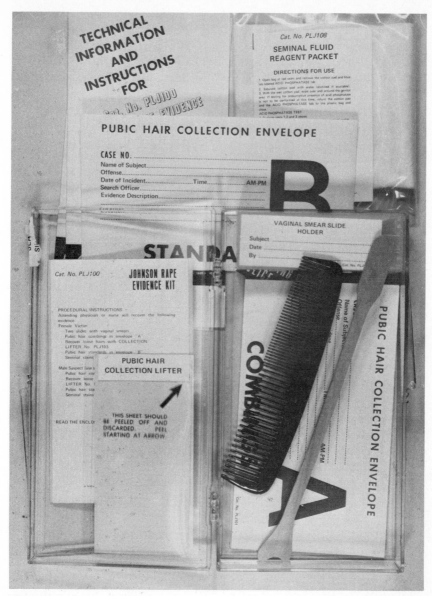

Figure 6-1   Johnson rape kit (Courtesy Sirchie Fingerprint Laboratories, Moorestown, NJ).

with the woolen sheepskin bed cover which was lying on the bed at the time of the crime.[1]

[1] Arne Svenson and Otto Wendell, *Techniques of Crime Scene Investigation,* American Elsevier, New York, 1965, p. 145.

What to Look For

A cursory examination of hair will disclose little other than color. But the laboratory criminalist or technician finds much to be studied in a step-by-step, scientific procedure. Here is what the criminalist looks for:

1. Human or animal (and what kind of animal)
2. Color
3. Other characteristics
   a. Straight or curly
   b. Natural or artificial wave
   c. Kinky
   d. Dyed or bleached
   e. Tapered ends
   f. Square end
   g. Burned
   h. Crushed
   i. Singed
   j. Stretched
4. Growth since dyeing
5. Naturally fallen out or pulled out
6. Specific area of body origin
   a. Scalp
   b. Eyebrows
   c. Eyelashes
   d. Beard or mustache
   e. Pubic
   f. Arms, legs, chest, back
   g. Ears
   h. Nose
   i. Axillary (armpit)
7. Race
   a. Negroid
   b. Caucasian
   c. Mongoloid (Oriental, Eskimo, American Indian)
   d. Mixed race
8. Foreign substances
   a. Blood
   b. Sweat
   c. Tears
   d. Ear wax
   e. Semen
   f. Vaginal secretions
   g. Flour
   h. Sawdust
   i. Paint
   j. Grease (automotive)
   k. Metal filings
9. Microscopic identifying characteristics
   a. Cuticle
   b. Cortex
   c. Medulla

In any homicide case, a cardinal rule followed by the medical examiner is to obtain samples of hair from the scalp, arms, underarms, legs, and pubic area. Approximately one dozen hairs from each area of the body are sufficient for an examination. To ensure that a good representative sampling is obtained, not all the hairs should be taken from the same spot. Take samples of scalp hair, for instance, from the sides, back, and front.

Hair samples should be placed in a stoppered vial or test tube; if these are not available, fold them in a white paper, place in an envelope, and seal. Vacuum sweepings should be placed in an evidence bag. Most medical examiners will remove hair samples with tweezers, in order to obtain strands with shaft and root. Some authorities do recommend cutting hair samples with a scissors. Combing is another method for obtaining samples. Extreme care should be used in handling evidence to avoid contamination, crushing, or other distortion.

The medical examiner does not need permission to obtain hair samples from a deceased individual, but permission is needed from a living individual. The proper procedure is to obtain written permission or, if necessary, a court order. Hair samples should be obtained by a pathologist, medical examiner, physician, or nurse, not by an investigator or police officer.

TIP: Always take more than enough hair for thorough study. Too little can hinder the examination in the laboratory.

It is customary for the medical examiner or coroner to remove any foreign substance found under each fingernail of a deceased. The matter is placed in a small plastic box or envelope and identified as to the finger from which it was taken. There is always the possibility of finding a portion of a hair under a fingernail in cases of rape, assault, or homicide, or when any kind of struggle has taken place.

Important Characteristics of Hair

Hair originates in the outer layer of skin called the epidermis and is composed in large measure of proteins, the most common of which is keratin. Keratin is a major element of human fingernails and toenails and also of claws, horns, and feathers of many animals.

Hairs have three phases in their growing cycle: anagen (growing follicle), catagen (retrogressive stage), and telogen (inactive and nongrowing). *Telogen* is the term commonly used to describe naturally fallen hair.

Human hair is constantly falling out and being replaced, the growth cycle ranging from 18 months to 7 years depending somewhat on its location. The factors controlling the growth cycle are not known, but unquestionably they relate to an individual's physical condition and genetic makeup.

The average rate of growth for hair from the scalp is about 0.1 in [2.5 mm] per week, or 0.36 to 0.5 mm per day. Hair varies in diameter from $1/150$ to $1/500$ in and will weigh between 500 and 800 micrograms (μg) (20 millionths of an ounce), depending upon its length and thickness.

Hair resists decomposition for hundreds of years. Witness the following. Recent analysis of the hair of an unidentified mummy confirmed that the mummy was none other than Queen Tiy, the grandmother of King Tut. She died sometime around 1400 B.C.

Examination with a microscope reveals three general parts of a hair: the root (enclosed in a follicle), the shaft, and the tip. (See Figs. 6-2 and 6-4.) The shape and length of the tip will vary from one area of the body to another; but all hair, when it first starts to grow, has a pointed tip.

The old belief that hair grows after death is a fallacy. However, after death the skin becomes dry, and this causes a man's beard to stand out, which is probably the basis for the belief. On two occasions, one of the authors was present at the morgue after the disinterment of two bodies. Neither body showed growth of the beard, although both had been dead for a period of 4 to 6 months.

The shaft, which is most useful for purposes of comparison, contains three concentric parts (see Figs. 6-3 and 6-4):

1. Cuticle, outside covering resembling roof shingles
2. Cortex, the middle layer
3. Medulla, the centermost canal, sometimes called the "core"

Cuticle

The cuticle is covered with scales of various shapes or forms depending on species. Each scale ending points toward the tip of the hair. The thickness of the cuticle is approximately 0.5 micrometer (μm) (20 millionths of an inch). In human hair the cuticle scales overlap more so than in most animals. The cuticle scales are generally distinguishable from one animal species to another (see Fig. 6-6). It is a most helpful feature in ascertaining whether a hair is human or animal.

The scanning electron microscope can reveal the individuality of the cuticle pattern of human hair (see Fig. 6-7). Since it is usually

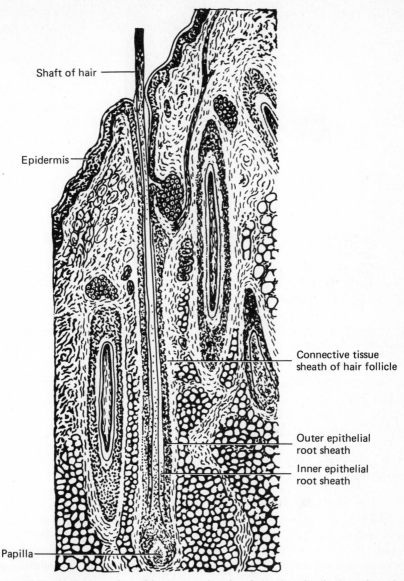

Shaft of hair

Epidermis

Connective tissue
sheath of hair follicle

Outer epithelial
root sheath

Inner epithelial
root sheath

Papilla

Figure 6-2 Vertical section of human scalp, showing a longitudinal section of a hair and its follicle.

difficult to see with the ordinary light microscope, the cuticle is often made visible by making a cast of it. This is done by pressing the hair into softened (by heat) vinyl or semi-hardened nail polish lacquer. After the hair is removed, the impressions made by the scales are easily seen.

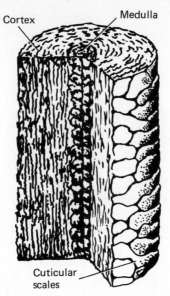

Figure 6-3   Structure of hair.

Cortex

Most human hair derives its color from the cortex. Some hairs contain fusi (air pockets) among the cortical cells. The cortex is composed of melanin granules of two kinds—eumelanin (brownish black) and phaemelanin (yellow-red)—which determine its color. Gray or white hair has little of this material and many air pockets.

Medulla

The medulla, the innermost core of a strand of hair, is found most often in thick hair, in the center section, not at the root or tip. In humans the medulla is often absent or not continuous. Occasionally, a person with gray hair will have a two-tone color in the medulla. Gray or white hair will be somewhat transparent with no medulla or cortex visible (see Fig. 6-5).

Examining Hair

Scalp hair generally has more characteristics (i.e. cuticle, cortex, and medulla) than hair from any other part of the body. Long, straight hair can come from only the scalp and from no other part of

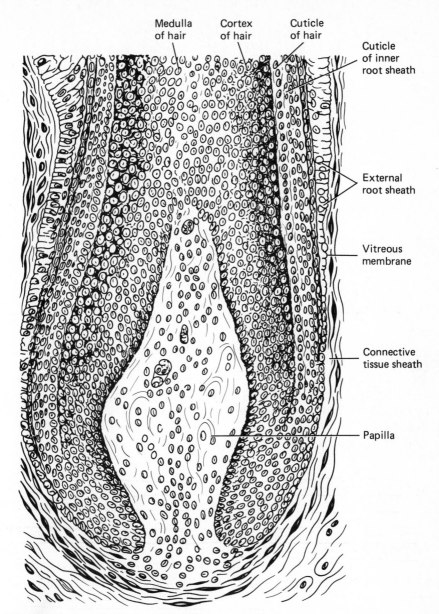

Figure 6-4   Longitudinal section of lower end of hair root.

the body. The average individual has more than 100,000 scalp hairs. An individual scalp hair ordinarily has a constant diameter with little or no variation. Hair on the elderly will have a weaker pigmentation, and sometimes color is completely absent. As one grows older, one's hair has a tendency to get thinner in diameter.

Baldness is quite common among males and is considered to be

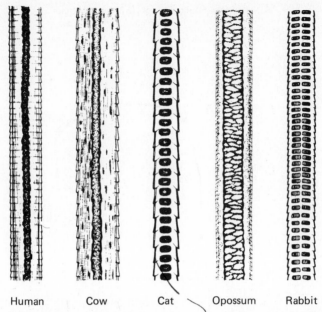

Human   Cow   Cat   Opossum   Rabbit

Figure 6-5   Comparison of human, cow, cat, opposum, and rabbit hairs (medullas).

hereditary. On one occasion, one of the authors saw a completely bald young female. She had died in a fire. She appeared to resemble a store mannequin, and everyone assumed that her hair had been burned to the scalp. Later it was learned that she had worn a wig, and the cause of her baldness at the young age of 20 was never determined.

Hair from the eyebrows and eyelashes is much thicker than hair from the head and usually will have long, tapering ends as well as thicker medullas (Fig. 6-8). Hair from the eyebrows, eyelashes, and nostrils is generally stiff and thick, tapering to a point averaging 0.25 to 0.5 in [6.3 to 12.7 mm] in length. Hair from the chest, arms, back, and legs is thinner and softer.

At one time, hair with long, tapering ends was identifiable with the female sex, but this is not true today because males also wear their hair long. Female scalp hairs often have a much thinner diameter than the male hairs.

Pubic and underarm hairs (axillary) are coarser, more wiry, and curlier than those found on other areas of the body (Fig. 6-8). Variations in the cross sections of hair (oval, circular, triangular) from different parts of the body, as well as from different races, have been reported. Intraindividual differences seem so great as to make generalizations unreliable. Forensic technicians ordinarily encounter only scalp and pubic hairs in an investigation. Rarely do they see hairs

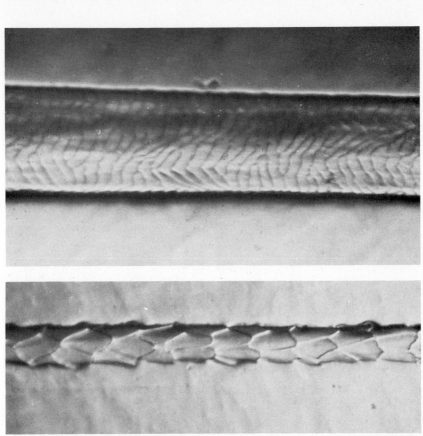

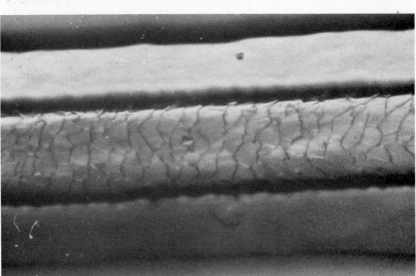

Figure 6-6   Scales of various animal hairs viewed under a microscope. *Top:* rabbit; *middle:* mouse; *bottom:* raccoon.

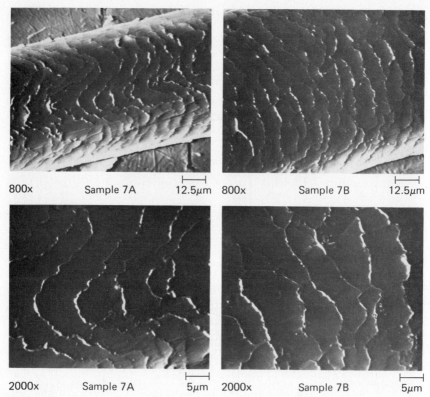

800x Sample 7A 12.5μm 800x Sample 7B 12.5μm

2000x Sample 7A 5μm 2000x Sample 7B 5μm

Figure 6-7 Photograph of two hairs taken with scanning electron microscope (the symbol μm stands for micrometer, which equals one millionth of a meter). 7A was taken from under the carriage of a car; 7B was taken from victim. Both 7A and 7B seem to have characteristics of human hair. 7B is 50 percent larger in diameter than 7A. In general, 7A has a more fractured appearance than 7B. A spectral (x-ray) scan shows both samples to have approximately the same sulfur and chlorine content, 3.0 and 0.6 percent respectively (Courtesy Applied Research Laboratories, Sunland, CA).

from other areas of the body. Pubic or underarm hair that has a square end when seen under a microscope will indicate recent cutting. A pointed end will be a strong indication that it has never been cut. Continuous rubbing of hairs against clothing tends to cause the ends to fray.

Years ago, races could be definitely determined by an examination of hair, but intermarriages make identification less certain these days. Caucasians have the highest number of colors—red, brown, blonde, and black. Chinese, Japanese, Mongols, and American Indians have straight black hair.

At times, it is possible to determine how long since the hair was last dyed by measuring the new growth that does not contain dye.

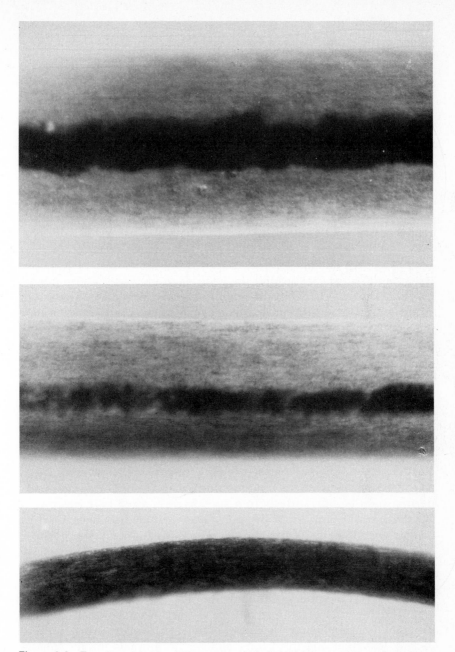

Figure 6-8 *Top:* beard hair; *middle:* male pubic hair; *bottom:* male scalp hair.

The length of time since the last cutting can be approximated by a microscopic examination of the end of a hair. Hair that has been cut a day or two before examination will have a somewhat square end. When four or five days have elapsed since cutting, the end may appear quite jagged, possibly due to friction and wear or the flaking off of scales.

A microscopic examination of hair will reveal if the hair had fallen out naturally or was cut, bent, crushed, broken, pulled out, dyed, or burned (Fig. 6-9). It will also show any foreign matter adhering to its surface.

A hair that has been recently pulled out will ordinarily contain particles of skin adhering to the root, but hair that has fallen out naturally will not. Also, hair that has been pulled out will have a moist root, generally fuller than the root of a hair that has fallen out naturally.

A freshly pulled hair will contain what appears to be a white, transparent substance around the root when viewed under a microscope. Hair that has been subjected to extreme tension (pulling) will stretch, thus affecting the diameter. A minute examination of hair may reveal such matter as blood, sand, soil, grease, chalk, dust, paint, semen, and many other identifiable substances. At times, it is possible to determine, with some degree of accuracy, the individual's occupation or some specific area where he or she spends a lot of time, when a particular residue is found on a hair—flour, for instance, on a baker, sawdust from wood sawings on a carpenter or millwork hand, grease on an automotive mechanic, and metal filings on a machinist.

After an initial examination, hair may be cleansed with ether or alcohol, thus enabling better viewing under a microscope. There have been cases where a bludgeoning weapon contained hairs adhering to its bloody surface. In a suicide case, a red hair was found adhering to the muzzle of the gun. The weapon had been fired in contact with the side of the temple, where the hairs are short. Thus, hair provided almost incontrovertible proof of the weapon used.

There is nothing that resembles human hair (Fig. 6-10). It is much different from that of the majority of animals, with the exception of certain members of the ape family.

The medulla of animal hair may vary from one-half to two-thirds of the diameter of the strand of hair. In humans the medulla is usually less than one-third the diameter. In animals the medulla is generally made up of a series of cells or segments, which is not the case with humans. Further, animal hair gets its color primarily from the medulla.

An efficient crime laboratory will have a large collection of sample hairs, particularly of animal species. This is necessary when a hair is found at a crime scene to determine whether it is human or

Figure 6-9 *Top:* Human hair cut with razor; *middle:* human hair hit with blunt in-strument; *bottom:* torn human hair.

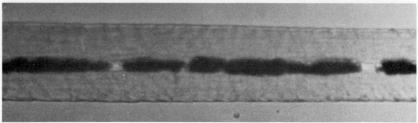

Figure 6-10 Medullas of various animal hairs. *Top:* horse; *bottom:* cow; *facing page—top:* rabbit; *middle:* cat; *bottom,* human (straight).

animal and which species of animal. It helps to simplify the comparison of hairs. There have been instances of hair found on clothing that belonged to a pig, cow, skunk, or horse, because these hairs are used in brushes.

Other Methods of Laboratory Analysis

Density

A tentative identification of two similar hairs may be performed by comparing the density of each. The hairs should be washed in alcohol and ether or acetone, and dried before being placed in the gradient tubes. (See Chap. 5 on glass.) The density of hair is between 1.310 and 1.390. When using a large gradient tube containing layers of liquids of varying densities, e.g. nitrobenzene or bromobenzene, the hair will be suspended when reaching a density common to its own. If two hairs suspend at the same level, they have a common density. Each tube should be allowed to settle for 24 hours before the hairs are placed in it. After the hairs have been in the liquid for 24 hours, readings may be taken.

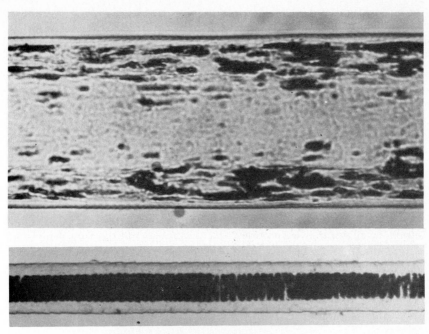

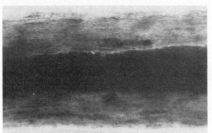

Neutron Activation Analysis

One of the most recent advances in forensic science is neutron activation analysis, which has made it possible to identify approximately fourteen different trace elements in a single hair a little over 1 in [25.4 mm] long. The elements are identified not only qualitatively, but quantitatively as well.[2] NAA, as it has come to be known, has disclosed arsenic, bromine, antimony, argon, copper, silver, gold, manganese, mercury, iridium, selenium, sodium, lanthanum, strontium, and zinc in a human hair. One of the most advantageous aspects of NAA is that it generally does not destroy the sample. Spectrographic analysis of hair, a common former method, destroys the sample (see Chap. 15).

In a murder case, a young girl's fingernail contained a single

[2] R. Dybcynski and K. Boboli, "Forensic and Environmental Aspects of Neutron Activation Analysis of Single Human Hairs," *J. Radioanalytical Chem.*, **31**: 267–289, 1976.

strand of hair. NAA was accepted in court as establishing a link between the hair and the suspect. It has been estimated that the likelihood of two hairs, each from different individuals, having the same concentration of nine different elements is about one in a million.

An interesting sidelight: An NAA examination was performed on hairs from Napoleon Bonaparte, revealing that they contained 13 times the normal amount of arsenic. This brings up the possibility that Napoleon's suspicions about being poisoned may have been correct. It is also possible, of course, that the arsenic may have come from the soil of Napoleon's several graves. A metallic element, arsenic will remain in hair and bones indefinitely. Agencies such as the Bureau of Alcohol, Tobacco, and Firearms will perform NAA for police.

Recently one of our students was involved in an investigation of a vehicular homicide involving a woman walking her dog. The hairs found on the suspect's vehicle, when analyzed by NAA, compared favorably with those of the victims. A plea of guilty brought the case to an abrupt end.

Pyrolysis gas chromatography is presently being investigated as a means of identifying elements in hair and fibers (Fig. 6-11). When hair is pyrolyzed (heated to a destructive temperature), a vapor is given off that can be analyzed and identified upon separation (Chap. 15). This is still very much in the experimental stage with respect to hair analysis.

Blood Grouping from Hair

There is research being conducted in some laboratories for determining the blood grouping from hair. This is much more difficult than typing from blood and does not appear to be as reliable.

Fibers

Fibers can be divided into three classes depending on their source: animal, e.g. wool; vegetable, e.g. kemp and cotton; and synthetic, e.g. rayon, nylon, acetate, and dacron. The animal fibers possess the same characteristics described in the section on hair since they are, in fact, animal hairs. Through microscopic examination vegetable fibers are distinguishable because they have no scales or medullas, but do have a readily observable cellular structure. (See Fig. 6-12.) Their reaction with a variety of stains is also characteristic.

The synthetic fibers do not possess scales, medullas, or an internal cellular structure. Synthetic fibers, possessing little structure, are more difficult to distinguish solely on this basis of appearance. (See

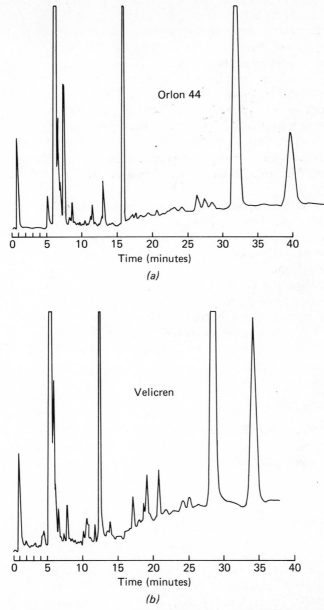

Figure 6-11 Pyrolysis gas chromatograms of (a) Orlon and (b) Velicren. The time at which the various peaks appear as well as their relative heights permit one to distinguish between various substances (Courtesy Varian Associates, Palo Alto, CA).

Fig. 6-13.) A variety of chemical and optical tests are employed. For example, viscous fibers are insoluble in acetone, but cellulose acetate fibers are readily soluble. Measurements of refractive index and ob-

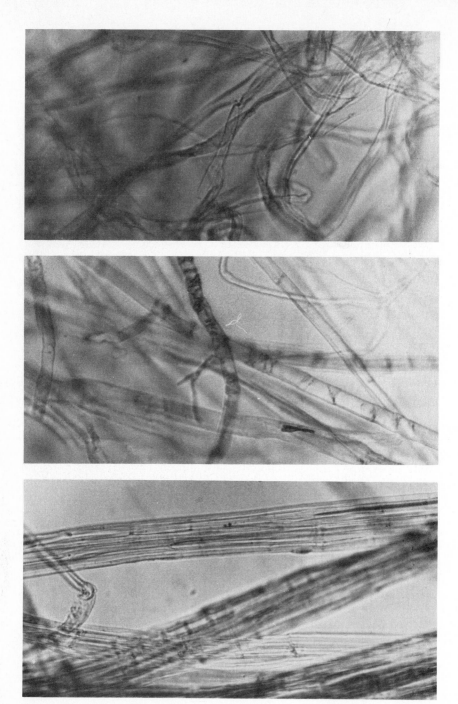

Figure 6-12   Various fiber materials. *Top:* cotton; *middle:* linen; *bottom:* hemp.

Figure 6-13 *Top:* fiber, synthetic—75 percent acrylic, 25 percent polyester; *bottom:* silk fibers.

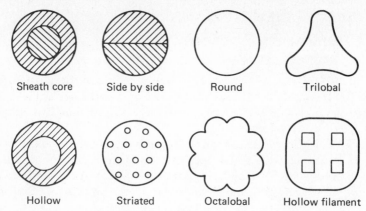

Sheath core   Side by side   Round   Trilobal

Hollow   Striated   Octalobal   Hollow filament

Figure 6-14   Cross-section of synthetic fibers.

servation with polarized light reveal characteristic differences. Although the synthetic fibers do not possess the natural cellular structure associated with "organic" fibers, they can have (and often are engineered to have) unique and readily observable structures (Fig. 6-14). Various chemicals are added to give desirable properties or color: titanium dioxide is a delustering agent; copper and manganese salts are used as antioxidants for better heat and light durability. These additives can readily be identified by instrumental analysis.

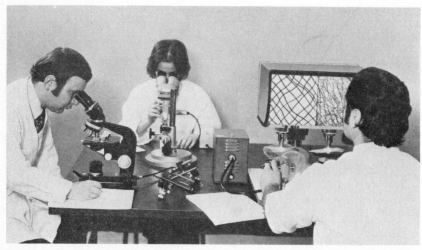

Figure 6-15   Comparison of weaves of different fibers (Courtesy Unitron Instruments, Inc., Woodbury, NY).

The Importance of Hair and Fibers to the Criminalist

Crimes of violence, as you have seen, require the most careful search for all possible bits and strands of hair and fiber as clues that may prove of crucial importance. A strand of hair may link suspect and victim in telling ways.

The area of hair identification has advanced considerably in the past few years because of the applications of modern scientific techniques. However, a human hair cannot yet be uniquely identified as belonging to one individual. Nonetheless, the authors feel that such will be possible in the not too distant future.

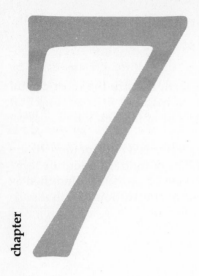

chapter

Blood and Body Secretions: The Biochemistry of Criminalistics

In crimes of violence, in hit-and-run accidents, and in some burglaries, blood and body secretions are routinely encountered as vital evidence. Laboratory analysis of blood, bloodstains, semen, vaginal secretions, saliva, mucous, and other body fluids may reveal much information useful to investigators. It can help link a suspect to the crime, for instance, and provide strong evidence leading to positive identifications of persons involved.

This chapter deals with the investigator's role in the handling of blood and other body fluids at the scene of the crime. The basics of forensic serology and immunohematology are also presented here on the ground that familiarity with the principles of forensic biochemistry is essential to sound police work.

At the Scene

As a law enforcement officer or crime laboratory technician, you may be called upon to be first in line for the procurement of physical evidence at the scene of a serious crime where blood has been shed or body secretions left behind. It then becomes your responsibility to obtain, identify, safeguard, and transfer this evidence in a legally and scientifically acceptable way.

Blood and body secretions are altered by extremes in temperature, bacterial contamination, aging, and moisture. Mishandling by a person at the scene can make even a simple blood grouping procedure on a fresh, wet blood specimen a worthless exercise and may necessitate the use of a more complicated (and less reliable) technique. Sometimes bacterial contamination of a specimen can prove even more detrimental to a case than not having found the article at all. Some bacterial contaminants can give erroneous results upon testing, and a wrongly blood grouped piece of evidence can only serve to confuse the investigation and wreak havoc with a prosecutor's case.

What, then, should be done to guard against the mishandling of biological specimens? Here are basic guidelines:

On-the-Scene Guidelines

1. Any wet or damp articles of clothing should be air dried at room temperature before packaging or storage (Fig. 7-1). If this is impossible, the article should be immediately removed to the laboratory.
2. Articles should be placed in individual packages (preferably plastic bags) to prevent mislabeling and cross contamination. This is especially important when articles must be packaged while still wet or when there is the possibility of more than one blood group being present (two or more persons bleeding).

Figure 7-1   To avoid putrefaction, moist, blood-stained fabrics must be dried out before wrapping. Do not dry by artificial means, such as by an electric heater.

3. Descriptive tags should be placed on the bags and the bags sealed. Tags should contain all pertinent information (what, where, how, when, and by whom), as is the case with all physical evidence.

4. Proceed to the forensic laboratory as soon as possible to obtain the best results.

5. If the evidence must be stored for a short period, refrigerate the specimen at approximately 40°F [4.4°C], but do not freeze.

6. Liquid blood or body secretion specimens should be placed in test tubes or plastic boxes, sealed, and immediately delivered to the local laboratory. There is the possibility that a great deal of information can be obtained from this liquid specimen which could not be as reliably obtained from a specimen which has dried.

7. Make sure that whenever evidence is transferred, a legally acceptable receipt is obtained from whoever accepts the articles (date, time, description of evidence, case numbers, and a signature of the person receiving the specimens should be included).

8. If there is ever any doubt on how to handle or collect a specimen, by all means contact the laboratory for assistance.

At the Laboratory

Once the bloodstained or secretion-stained evidence has been properly delivered to the laboratory, the law enforcement officer's responsibility is over. The laboratory technician's work then begins. First, a full description of the evidence must be written. Then the article is photographed, examined for fingerprints, hairs, fibers, or any other trace evidence which might, at a later date, become an important clue to the investigation.

Definitions

The laboratory work mainly concerns two branches of biology: forensic serology and immunohematology. *Serology* is the study of the liquid portion of the blood—blood serum. Blood consists of two main parts: the liquid (serum) portion (which is actually straw-colored) and the red and white blood cells (billions of these) which are suspended in the serum. The red blood cells give blood its characteristic red color. *Immunohematology* is the study of antigen-antibody reactions as they relate to the solid or cellular matter of the blood, especially the red blood cells, which primarily carry oxygen through the body.

Antibodies are chemical substances produced by the body in response to an invading foreign substance, and they are found in the blood serum. The foreign substance is called the "antigen." An antibody reacts only with its antigen, much like a key is made to fit one specific lock.

Medical science applies this knowledge with the use of innoculations to develop an immunity against diseases. Disease-causing organisms are killed and injected into a patient's body in order to produce antibodies that would provide protection from infections upon later contact with that disease. Antigens and antibodies are always described together. Something cannot be labeled an antigen if it does not have the ability to stimulate antibody production in an individual's body, and something cannot be labeled an antibody if its production is not initiated by an antigen.

Is It Blood?

Once the preliminary examinations are made, work starts on any suspicious stains to determine if that reddish or brown stain is actually blood and not red paint, rust, wood stain, wine, cherry soda, or whatever. Common tests performed in this area are usually called "nonspecific chemical tests." They rely upon testing the stain with several chemicals and observing a distinct color change. The most common of these tests are the "benzidine" and "reduced phenolphthalein" procedures. Several cross reactions have been noted with these tests, and care must be exercised in their use; but they are quite accurate as screening tests for blood when used by experienced personnel with proper scientific controls.

Is It Human?—The Precipitin Test

Once the possibility of the stain's not being blood has been ruled out, work can then proceed to the next step—the determination of species of origin. While at first glance this might appear odd, a great many times a bloodstain on an automobile bumper involved in a hit-and-run accident actually comes from a dog, cat, or other animal; or a bloodstain found in the trunk of a car after hunting season turns out to be from a deer or rabbit. Therefore this step of the examination of a stain cannot be omitted.

For this test a serological (antigen-antibody) technique is used. A saline (salt water) extract of any dried blood serum present in the stain must be used. A small amount of saline is added to the article in question. If the article is a piece of material, a section is cut and placed in a test tube, and several drops of saline are added. The material is soaked in the saline for several hours. If the article in question is a weapon, car seat, floor, etc., the technique, of course, must be modified. An eyedropper is used (a serologist calls it a "pipette") with a small amount of saline. This saline is rinsed onto the stain and back into the dropper several times, which tends to loosen and dissolve the specimen. This mixture of saline, serum, and blood cells is then placed in a test tube and spun in a centrifuge which separates the solid matter (the blood cells) from the liquid (which is saline and blood serum). This saline-serum extract can now be tested with testing serum or antiserum.

Testing serum or antiserum is produced either in the laboratory or commercially by innoculating laboratory animals such as rabbits or goats with purified substances for which the test is made. The animal's body recognizes the injected substance as being a foreign intruder. Immediately the animal's immunity (disease-fighting) system begins producing antibodies to seek out, and mark for destruction, these foreign substances. These antibodies can stay in the animal's bloodstream for extended periods.

A small amount of the animal's blood is then removed, and its blood serum (which contains the antibodies) is methodically purified so that, finally, it contains only the antibody to the original substance which was injected. This antiserum containing the known antibody can now be used to test for, and identify, an unknown substance in a stain (Fig. 7-2).

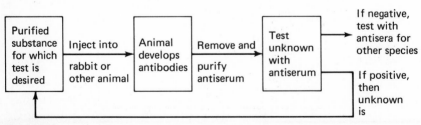

Figure 7-2

To give a common example: rabbits are injected with human blood serum, which causes the rabbits to have an immune response and develop antibodies directed against human blood serum. Some of the rabbit's blood is removed; the serum is then purified so it will contain only those antibodies to human blood serum. This antiserum is then used in tests to determine if an unknown stain contains human blood serum (a positive reaction) or the blood serum of another species (such as pig, horse, etc.) with which the antiserum will not react.

Here is how it is done. A tray of gelatin has two parallel rows of small holes punched in it. In one row of holes is placed a series of saline-serum extracts of the stained weapons or clothes for which tests must be conducted to determine species of origin. In the opposite row of holes is placed the antiserum from the rabbits. The extracts and antiserum both "diffuse" or migrate toward each other through the gelatin and meet somewhere in the middle of the two rows of holes. When they meet, a nonsoluble solid (precipitate) is produced. It can be seen as a white, hazy band in the gelatin. Only then can the serologist say with certainty that the extract is from a stain of human origin. If there is no reaction, it might then be profitable to test the extract with antiserums to other species.

Since the above procedure works with rabbits and humans, it can also work for rabbits and dogs, dogs and goats, goats and sheep, etc. Some species combinations do not react quite as well as others, and sometimes species cross reactions occur; but the basic procedure for antiserum production and testing is the same. In most well-equipped serology laboratories, at least a dozen or more different species of origin can be identified. See Fig. 7-3.

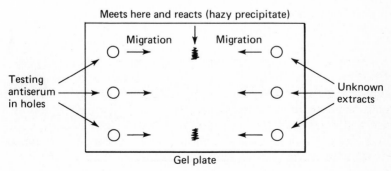

Figure 7-3

What Blood Group Is It?—The A-B-O System

The next step, now that the stain is known to be human blood, is to discover the blood group systems to which the specimen belongs. A blood group system is a family of related blood group factors (chemical substances) present in the red blood cells. More than a dozen of these "families" have been identified to date, and the discovery of more seems likely. The first and most important blood group system is the A-B-O system. The A-B-O system is the most obvious of these systems, its antigens being found on red blood cells and other body tissues. Its relative strength of reaction is high, its stability in terms of adverse conditions is good, and its clinical importance (transfusionwise) is critical. The classical "cross matching" of blood for transfusion purposes, which is done to prevent incompatible or mismatched blood (which could cause extensive damage or even death to a recipient), covers this A-B-O system.

Everyone (with very, very few exceptions) belongs to one of the A-B-O blood groups. The system basically contains only two chemical components or antigens, A and B. These two antigens can be statistically combined in four different ways. If a person's red blood cell has only one antigen, say A, the person is described as belonging to blood group A. If only the B antigen is present, the person is described as belonging to blood group B. If both A and B antigens are present, the subject is group AB. And if the person has neither A nor B antigens, then she or he is blood group O. There are A-B-O system "subgroups" known, but they are of little concern here.

Antigen Which Red Blood Cell Contains	Blood Group Assigned
A	A
B	B
A and B	AB
None	O

Starting from birth, antibodies to any blood group antigens that are not indigenous to that individual's red blood cells are developed in the blood serum. For example, people belonging to blood group A would have antibodies to B antigen (anti-B) in their blood serum since B substance is "foreign" to an A body. Conversely, people of blood group B would have antibodies to A substance (anti-A). Individuals who have both A and B antigens on their red blood cells would not produce antibodies to either A or B substance, while persons who are group O have neither A nor B antigens indigenous to their bodies and would produce antibodies to both A and B substance.

Blood Group Antigen on Red Cells	Antibody in Serum
A	Anti-B
B	Anti-A
AB	None
O	Anti-A and anti-B

Determining the A-B-O blood group of an individual is a two-step process. First, it must be determined which antigen (A, B, both, or neither) is on the red blood cell. Second, it must be determined which, if any, corresponding antibodies are present in the blood serum. This red cell (or "forward") grouping using red cell antigens and serum (or "reverse") grouping using the serum antibodies are always done on specimens of liquid (whole) blood.

Approximate Percentages of A-B-O Blood Factors in General Population	
Group O	45%
Group A	37%
Group B	14%
Group AB	4%

Sometimes on dried bloodstains only one or the other (but not both) of the red cell and serum grouping is feasible because of the quantity of stain, age, or contamination of the stain. It should be immediately apparent that any blood grouping using dried stains has more variables and is less reliable than the grouping of fresh, liquid blood.

The same blood grouping procedures that are used in a hospital blood bank cannot be used, without modification, to determine the blood group of dried stains. Several excellent red cell grouping techniques have been adapted from standard blood bank techniques, namely, the absorption-elution and absorption-inhibition procedures. One test, the Lattes crust test, is used strictly for dried stains. An excellent serum grouping technique is also available using dried serum—the isoagglutinin procedure. Two or more results confirming one another, using different techniques, lend much credence to later testimony in a court of law.

Other Blood Factors

The rather widespread use of the above dried-stain techniques for blood group systems other than the A-B-O system has been investigated. While some encouraging results have been obtained, a great deal of work remains to be done on these other systems. The work is slow mainly because of the inherent problems of instability, contamination, and cross reactivity of certain antiserums. The Rh system, especially the Rh factor (the "positive" or "negative" usually tacked onto the blood group on your dog-tags or blood donor card), the M-N-S, system and certain of the more stable blood enzymes using electrophoretic techniques seem to hold the greatest promise for the future of forensic blood grouping. Research is currently underway which shows promise of eventually enabling the investigator to identify, from a bloodstain, what allergies or diseases an individual may have had. This depends upon the same type of immunological reactions described above.[1]

Other Bloodstain Characteristics

Aging of a bloodstain is determined primarily by two factors: drying time (from liquid to dry states) and color change of dried stains from red to brown or even black. These are, at best, highly subjective observations. Drying times are dependent upon temperature, humidity, air flow above the stain, porosity of the surface covered by the stain, and even barometric pressure. Usually, few or none of these variables are known to the investigator. Drying times can range from a few minutes (for a small stain at a high temperature, large and porous surface area, and low humidity) to many hours or even a day or more (for a large, thick stain at low temperatures, nonporous surface, and high humidity).

Freshly dried stains appear bright red for up to several days before a gradual darkening will make them appear red-brown, then brown, and finally black. These color changes tend to be affected by temperature, with the stain tending to darken faster (or even discolor) with rising temperatures. These differing shades of brown during the aging process are very difficult for a trained serologist to

---

[1] L. A. King, D. J. Werrett, and P. H. Whitehead, "Anti-body Profiling of Bloodstains," *Forens. Sci.*, **8**, 1976.

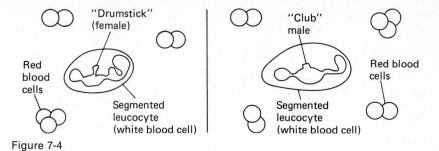

Figure 7-4

differentiate and close to impossible for the untrained investigator, except in the most general fashion.

Sexing of individuals from certain white blood cells (and other tissues) has been done for many years in clinical laboratories on freshly drawn blood specimens (or scrapings from the inner cheeks). A great deal of reliability has been observed in these tests. The theory is to observe what is known as sex chromatin in a certain percentage of leucocytes (white blood cells). These "Barr bodies" (after the discoverer) or "drumsticks" and "clubs" are sometimes difficult to determine, even in fresh blood. (Fig. 7-4.) But it must be emphasized that these determinations are from freshly taken specimens and not dried stains. Blood and other biological substances undergo drastic changes during the drying process and are usually so deformed as to render a microscopic examination worthless (except in highly controlled laboratory experiments). Much work must yet be completed in this area before this procedure becomes widespread.

Ishizu and Noguchi claim success in determining the sex of an individual from dried stains as old as 2 years.[2] Their technique involves observing fluorescence of treated leucocytes in the stains of males.

Direction and impact force of bloodstains on surfaces have been increasingly studied. Certain factors have been readily accepted, while others have been rightly disputed. The subject is not usually one for the casual observer. The following diagrams may be of some help in understanding the basic concepts of stain patterns (Fig. 7-4). It must always be remembered that both landing surface characteristics (smooth like glass or rough like cement) and original velocity of the airborne blood have great bearing on what the final stain will look like (Fig. 7-5). Test patterns should be made on similar surfaces for comparison.

[2] Hideo Ishizu, "Studies on Sex Identification of Human Blood and Blood Stains," *Japanese Journal of Legal Medicine,* **27** (3): 168–181, May 1973.

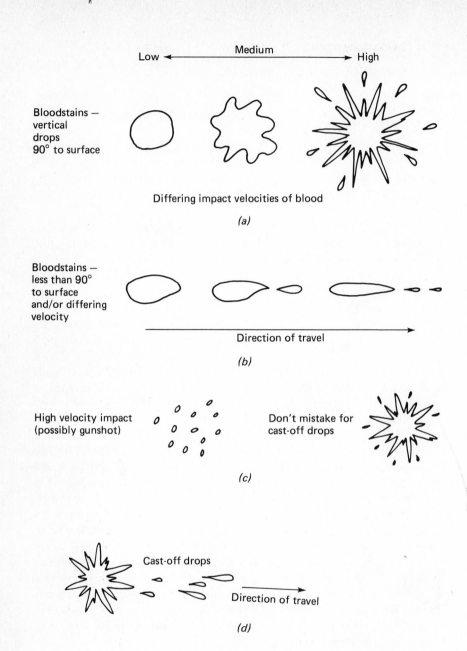

Low ←——— Medium ———→ High

Bloodstains —
vertical
drops
90° to surface

Differing impact velocities of blood

(a)

Bloodstains —
less than 90°
to surface
and/or differing
velocity

Direction of travel

(b)

High velocity impact
(possibly gunshot)

Don't mistake for
cast-off drops

(c)

Cast-off drops

Direction of travel

(d)

Never make a determination on a particular area of a pattern taken out of context of the total stain area.

Figure 7-5

Blood Group Antigens in Body Secretions

The same A-B-O chemical components or antigens that an individual might possess on his or her red blood cells are present in a water-soluble form in the body secretions of approximately 80 percent of the populace. These soluble antigens can be present in relatively high quantities in saliva, seminal fluid, vaginal secretions, and nasal secretions. Lesser quantities sometimes can be detected in perspiration, tears, and urine.

The search for these body secretion antigens uses techniques similar to those employed for the grouping of dried red blood cells, although certain limitations apply. The technique most used in this area, at present, is the absorption-inhibition procedure adapted for a quantitative approach. This technique gives information as to not only what antigen(s) is present, but to what extent (relatively speaking) it is present. The more sensitive absorption-elution technique recently has been recruited for work in this area, but has demonstrated the ability for false positive reactions and should be used (at least for the present) only in conjunction with the more classical absorption-inhibition technique.

Care must always be exercised in the interpretation of a test result and in the conclusions reached. While neat (uncontaminated) nasal secretions or saliva might routinely be encountered, vaginal secretions and seminal fluid (in cases of possible rape) are often found mixed in one stain. When this possibility occurs, further information must be obtained in order to reach any conclusions as to the possible origin of the stain. A blood and saliva specimen should be obtained from the victim and, if made possible by consent or court order, similar specimens should be obtained from the accused. Both individuals should then be tested to ascertain the blood group and whether they exhibit their blood group antigens in their body secretions. "Secretors" exhibit blood group antigens in their body secretions, while "nonsecretors" do not. This individual's ability to secrete or not secrete is referred to as "secretor status." These bits of information might be put together in the following manner:

> Stain on victim's underpants: A antigen present
> Victim's blood grouping and secretor status: secretor, group O
> Accused's blood grouping and secretor status: secretor, group A

It can be reasoned that since the victim is group O, she could not have contributed, via her vaginal secretions, any of the A antigen found on her underpants. The accused, on the other hand, is a group A secretor and definitely could have contributed, via his seminal fluid, the A substance found in the stain. This type of result makes excellent circumstantial evidence.

It Is as Simple as A-B—H

It should be noted here that present theory has blood group antigens A and B arising from a single basic chemical structure which has been designated "H." This H substance is present to some extent in all red blood cells and in the body secretions of secretors. This is an additional factor which can be tested for and is extremely useful in the determination of group O blood. It can also be useful in deciding what blood groups are present in the case of mixed blood stains.

Paternity Testing

Everyone, at the time of his or her conception, obtains certain chemical "codes" or genes from each parent. These genes dictate the characteristics of almost every variable which makes you the individuals you are—eye color, hair color, height, bone structure, a predisposition to certain allergies or diseases, and even if a person will go bald 60 years after birth. Some of these genes do another thing that is of great importance to the serologist. They give rise to a great variety of different blood group factors. These blood group factors, present at birth, are fully developed shortly thereafter and continue unchanged for the rest of a person's life. There are presently more than a dozen different blood group "systems," with each system comprised of two or more related factors, some forty different factors in all. It can be seen that statistically a large number of individual possibilities (some say many millions) can exist if the factors are randomly mixed. It can be likened to an individual having forty different hats with two different numbered markers, say 1 and 2, in each hat. If you then start from the first hat and draw one numbered marker and then continue drawing in turn for all forty hats, you will have the first number combination. Then you start drawing for a second number combination. It can readily be appreciated how many number possibilities there could be and how low is the chance that any two drawings might have exactly the same order of numbers. Members of the same family, of course, have a greater chance to have similar blood factors since the "codes" or genes a child possesses is completely dependent on what genes were received from the parents. A child cannot possess a gene that one or the other of the parents do not possess. This last fact is the basis of all testing in cases of disputed parentage.

Legal disputes often occur when a man disclaims fatherhood of a child and the mother brings suit for some type of support payment or even an alleged father's "name." In these cases, the court might order blood grouping tests to be performed on the mother, child (or children), and the alleged father. These tests determine if the child's (or children's) genes could not have come from either the mother or the alleged father and, hence, must have come from another man— the actual father. In all cases, it must be assumed that the mother is in fact the actual mother of that particular child and that no mix-up of babies occurred shortly after birth. In fact, several important paternity cases have been conducted for just that reason—to return the exchanged babies to their rightful parents. The theory of paternity testing is demonstrated in a simplified case, as follows:

Mother	Blood group A
Child	Blood group AB
Alleged father	Blood group O

Since the child has two codes, one giving rise to his or her blood group factor A and the other to factor B, the child belongs to blood group AB. The mother also has two genes, but these genes can express only a single blood group factor—A (not B). The alleged father's genes express neither the A nor B blood group factors. Hence, he could not have contributed either of these factors, through his genes, to the child in question. The mother could have contributed only the A factor.

Where did the B factor come from? Certainly not from the mother who has only the A factor, nor from the alleged father who has neither factor! It can be concluded that another individual has donated that B factor; the alleged father can be ruled out or excluded as the father of the child in question. The possible combinations are shown in Table 7-1.

Treatment of Seminal Stains

Semen is a body fluid that is frequently encountered in, although not exclusively limited to, crimes of rape. It is a protein-rich

TABLE 7-1: Possible Blood Type Combinations for Mother, Child, and Father

Mother Is	Child Is	Possible for Father
O	O	O, A, B
A	O	A, B
B	O	O, A, B
O	A	A, AB
O	B	B, AB
A	A	O, A, B, AB
B	B	O, A, B, AB
B	A	A, AB
A	B	B, AB
A	AB	B, AB
B	AB	A, AB
AB	A	O, A, B, AB
AB	B	O, A, B, AB
AB	AB	A, B, AB

fluid which, in a nonsterile male, is rich in spermatozoa (the male sex cells).

A preliminary search involves searching the area (clothes, floors, furniture, etc.) with ultraviolet light for the characteristic strong bluish white fluorescence of these stains. This is often useless, however, when the material has been laundered since the laundering agents usually contain "whiteners" which are in themselves highly fluorescent. The stained area may feel "crusty" or appear so when viewed with a stereoscopic microscope. The precautions for packaging and transporting this material to the laboratory are much the same as given for suspected bloodstains.

The observation, using a high-power microscope, of spermatozoa is the best proof of the presence of semen (Fig. 7-6). These may, however, be rendered unidentifiable through mishandling since, especially in the dry state, they are damaged by rubbing, bacteria, and sunlight. In a case of suspected rape, vaginal smears should be taken and examined for spermatozoa. This is the most dependable identification for the presence of semen in the vagina.

A number of chemical tests are also used to examine suspect stains. The acid phosphatase test is the most widely accepted of these tests. Although many body fluids contain the acid phosphatase enzyme, it is present in much higher concentrations in semen. Therefore the demonstration of its presence is strong evidence that the stain is semen.

Research into identifying other unique characteristics of semen is underway. The results to date appear quite promising, particularly using immunological methods.

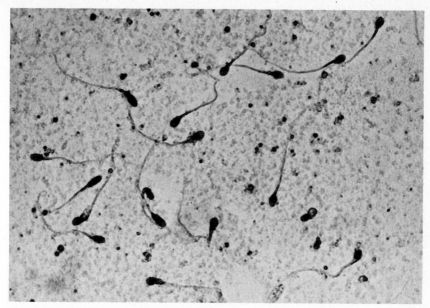

Figure 7-6   Photomicrograph of spermatozoa (Courtesy W. Reid Lindsay, photographer to medical examiner of Westchester County, NY).

Toward the Future

Forensic serology, immunohematology, and immunology are still in their infancy. Someday, however, sophisticated blood grouping techniques will be able to yield conclusive evidence concerning a particular individual's presence at the scene of a crime. Such information will be as indispensible as fingerprints to the criminologists of the future.

Forensic Photography

The camera is essential equipment in a forensic laboratory. It is used in every major aspect of criminalistics. A photograph serves as a permanent record of conditions and circumstances that may change as time passes—wounds, for instance—or altered by someone intentionally or unintentionally moving evidence. In ballistics and fingerprint analysis, photographs have a number of uses. One is side-by-side comparisons of bullets or of fingerprints. Photographs of the scene of a crime are often vital evidence in court. Photomicrographs of such things as blood and semen often play important roles in rape and murder cases.

Imagine the difficulty you would have in describing an automobile to a person who had never seen one. How much simpler it would be to show the person a photograph! It is much the same in a court of law. A photograph—or many photographs—tells a story that cannot be told in words, especially when it represents a scene or object that cannot be brought into court. In addition, special photographs, such as those taken under ultraviolet or infrared light or with a microscope, reveal details that cannot be perceived in any other way.

In this chapter, first you will review how law enforcement agencies make use of photography as part of their standard procedures. Then, you will take a look at the fundamentals of photography itself, with an emphasis on practical tips about taking pictures in situations normally encountered in criminal investigations.

There are a wide variety of cameras available for police work ranging from the press type, 4 by 5 Graphic (see Fig. 8-1) to the miniature spy-type cameras. The Graphic is the traditional police camera. It has a large 4- by 5-in negative suitable for making enlargements, and it is quite versatile. One can make "instant" photographs and negatives using the Polaroid 545 Land Film Holder (see Fig. 8-2). Its main disadvantages are that it is more complicated than many of the small-format cameras, and it is large, heavy, and unwieldy. Many departments are using these smaller, simpler, and more convenient 35mm cameras. They have a much smaller negative, which can be a problem in making enlargements. Even the Instamatic camera is suitable for many purposes. It is a good policy to have one available in each patrol car so that the first officers arriving at the scene can make an immediate photographic record.

No matter what camera is used, a good flash attachment should be available for low-light or night conditions. Flash attachments can be battery-operated using individual flash bulbs or electronic strobes.

The Crime Scene

Photographs of the crime scene are of paramount importance in any major crime, particularly in the case of a homicide. After the location has been secured, the next step is to have it completely photographed (Fig. 8-3). These photographs should represent the scene exactly as it appeared on the arrival of the first officer. They should be taken before anything is moved or even touched. If there is a murder victim, the body should not be moved until after photographs are taken. The body should be photographed from as many angles as possible. Close-ups of wounds should be taken. All other evidence bearing on the case should be included in the photographer's coverage of the scene. There can never be too many photographs of a crime scene.

> **CAUTION:** In crime scene photographs, no identification plates or posters with the name of the police department, date, or location should appear. Photographs with such devices are generally not admissible in court. In homicide cases, photographs should not include police officers or other individuals. In addition, there must be no "cropping" of any negative from which a photograph was produced. Cropping excludes a part of a negative (either sides, top, or bottom) from that which is printed. In court, the photograph must be a true and fair representation of the negative and thus the subject matter.

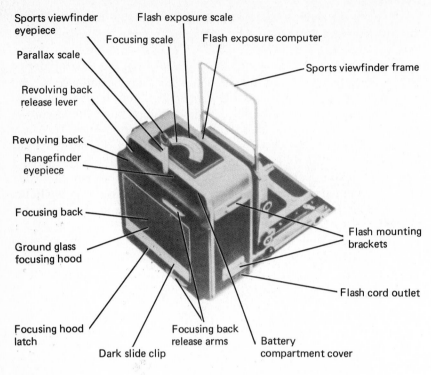

Sports viewfinder eyepiece

Flash exposure scale

Focusing scale

Flash exposure computer

Parallax scale

Sports viewfinder frame

Revolving back release lever

Revolving back

Rangefinder eyepiece

Focusing back

Flash mounting brackets

Ground glass focusing hood

Flash cord outlet

Focusing hood latch

Focusing back release arms

Dark slide clip

Battery compartment cover

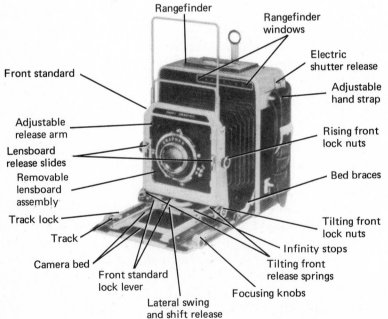

Rangefinder

Rangefinder windows

Front standard

Electric shutter release

Adjustable hand strap

Adjustable release arm

Lensboard release slides

Rising front lock nuts

Removable lensboard assembly

Bed braces

Track lock

Track

Tilting front lock nuts

Camera bed

Infinity stops

Front standard lock lever

Tilting front release springs

Focusing knobs

Lateral swing and shift release

Figure 8-1   Parts of a Graphic camera.

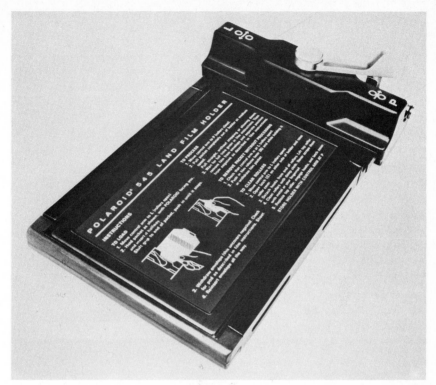

Figure 8-2   Polaroid 545 Land Film Holder for instant photograph and negative (Courtesy Polaroid Corp., Cambridge, MA).

Shooting the Homicide Scene

Most medical examiners or coroners maintain a photographer on their staffs for taking photographs of homicide victims or any questionable death. The medical examiner testifying at a trial about the cause of death will often bring along photographs to show entrance wounds of bullets and other physical marks that help determine the cause of death. Here is a checklist for crime scene photography:

1. Crime scene from all directions.
2. Overall photograph of victim.
3. Close-up photograph of wound or wounds.
4. Overall photograph of evidence in relation to location of victim.
5. Close-up photographs of such evidence as weapons, bloodstains, bullet holes, bullets, cartridges, etc.
6. More refined and detailed photographs of items that can be moved

Figure 8-3 *Top:* simulated crime scene; *bottom:* close-up of simulated crime scene (Courtesy *Law and Order* magazine, New York, NY).

may be taken at the forensic laboratory (weapons containing blood, hairs, fibers, and fingerprints).

7. Color photography is preferred at crime scenes for showing blood, clothing, furnishings, etc.

8. "Instant" cameras, such as those made by Polaroid and Kodak, are useful in determining exposure, angles for shooting, etc. Many police photographers use them for this purpose and then duplicate the shots with their standard Nikon or Graphic, for photographs of better quality (for enlargements, for instance).

Burglaries

The point of entry of a burglary should be photographed—broken glass in a window or door, jimmied lock, or possibly a hole cut through an outside wall or roof of a building. All footprints should be photographed, too. A ruler should be placed alongside the impression so that the photograph will show the footprint's size precisely. Sneakers are common footwear for burglars because of their rubber soles. They are likely to leave impressions on a clean surface when coming from mud or dirt. In one burglary, the outline and pattern of the sole of a sneaker were prominently visible on a dusty screen that had been removed in the break-in.

Photographic Form

Many departments have either a form attached to the back of each photograph or a rubber stamp containing the following information:

Case number
Date
Time taken
Weather
Distance
Subject
Name of photographer
(Type of film, camera, f-stop, and shutter speed may also be
    added.)

A separate form is preferable so that it may be removed for court purposes at any time. A record should be maintained of all photographs taken and made a part of the officer's or laboratory technician's report.

Fingerprints

Photography plays an important role in the preparation of latent fingerprint exhibits when a fingerprint has been identified and a comparison chart is needed for court. If a fingerprint found at a scene is on an immovable object, a photograph will suffice for court purposes. Two court decisions that pertain to this fact are *State v. Connors* [(1915, N.J.) 87 N.J.C. 419] and *Durree v. U.S.* [(1922) 207 Fed. 70].

Ballistics

In ballistics, when a comparison of two bullets is called for, a photograph may be used in court. The photograph enables the expert to show to the jury how the striae or markings on the evidence bullet compare with those on the test bullet. The viewing of a photograph by a juror has a more convincing effect than testimony. Some experts have discontinued the use of photographs in court. Due to the limited depth of field, some of the striae will be out of focus and may cause doubt in the minds' of jurors.

Macrophotography

Macrophotography is used in showing larger-than-life blowups of such things as the markings left by tools, knives, and other implements. Generally, macrophotography commences with magnification of 5X (5 times) the size of the original and progresses to the point where a microscope must be used. Macrophotography is used for photographing an intervening enlargement between a normal lens and a microscopic enlargement.

Photomicrography

Photographs taken through a microscope are called photomicrographs. The lens of the microscope takes the place of the camera lens. Often a 35mm camera body or a camera such as a Linhof Technica, adapted for Polaroid film, will be mounted atop the microscope. Polaroid is playing an increasingly important role in forensic and general police photography. Photomicrographs are taken to prove the presence of semen and blood and to show a specific grouping. Photomicrography is used in many forensic laboratories as an aid in the identification of drugs such as heroin, cocaine, morphine, etc. Generally, most drugs are identified from spectra with one type of instrumentation or another. (See Chap. 15.)

Ultraviolet Light

Photography employing ultraviolet (UV) light is used in the forensic laboratory. A photograph of subject matter under UV light must be taken in a darkened room. Special detection powders that fluoresce under UV light are often used to trap a thief. Such material, when irradiated with invisible UV light, gives off light that is visible. Such powders may be placed on doorknobs that would be touched or dusted on items likely to be stolen. There are also fluorescent crayons that can be used to mark money (bait money) or other items used for trapping a thief. These powders are rarely seen by the naked eye but will fluoresce under UV light. Evidence with fluorescent powder markings must be photographed with black and white film. Generally, it requires a time exposure of 1 second(s) or more to record a subject matter under UV light. A latent fingerprint on a multicolored surface dusted with fluorescent powder will render very good results when photographed under UV light. See Fig. 8-4. Many substances such as papers, tars, glasses, lipstick, oil, grease, and body fluids (urine, semen, and perspiration) fluoresce under UV lighting, making photographing possible for a permanent record.

Infrared (IR) Photography

The chemical compositions of materials vary, and thus it may be possible to distinguish them from one another when they are photographed with infrared light. One subjects the object to infrared light (which is not visible to the naked eye). Photofloods, flashbulbs,

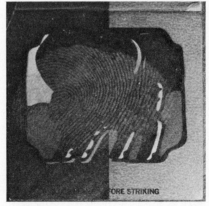

Figure 8-4 *Left:* photograph of matchbook cover not using ultraviolet light; *right:* photograph of matchbook cover under ultraviolet light, showing fingerprint (Courtesy Pennsylvania State Police, Captain John Balshy).

and heat lamps are satisfactory sources of infrared light. A special filter (Wratten 87) must be placed over the camera lens to filter out all light other than IR. Special IR-sensitive film must also be used.

At times, infrared photography will reveal written or printed matter on burned paper. The altering of checks where a different ink having the same color as the original is used to change the amount may be revealed with IR photography (Fig. 8-5).

IR photography will also help detect forgeries in many instances, particularly when one writing or printing is superimposed over former writing. Often the original writing can be made visible where an attempt has been made to obliterate it by blacking it out with some material such as crayon or pen (see Fig. 8-6). It will bring out powder residue on clothing around a bullet hole, which other-

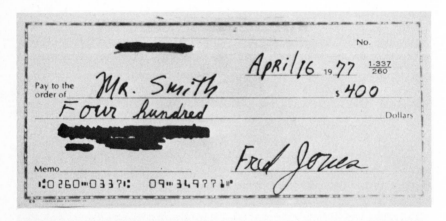

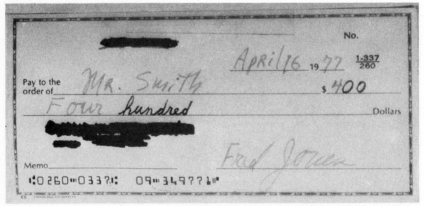

Figure 8-5 *Top:* altered check photographed (Tri-X film) under normal illumination; *bottom:* the same check photographed (infrared-sensitive film) under infrared illumination. Note that the two different inks are readily distinguishable.

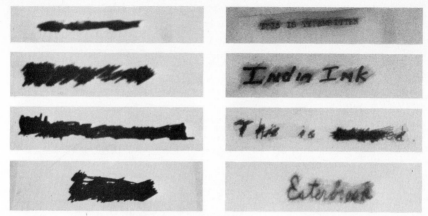

Figure 8-6 Samples of obliterated writing. *Left:* photographed (Tri-X film) with normal illumination; *right:* photographed (infrared-sensitive film) with infrared illumination.

wise would not be seen (see Fig. 8-7). In such instances, a photograph of the powder pattern will help experts make an assumption about the approximate distance from which the gun was fired. IR flashbulbs permit the taking of a photograph in total darkness without detection by the subject.

One of the authors has used a simple variation of infrared photography with great success. This technique involves processing the sample with an ordinary office Thermo-Fax copying machine (Fig. 8-8) (3M Company, 3M Center, St. Paul, MN).[1]

In its normal operation, one places the document to be copied (up to $8^{1}/_{2}$ by 11 in) with a "blank" in the machine. The blank is a material containing a sheet of a substance that blackens when heated. As the blank and the document pass through the instrument, they are exposed to infrared radiation. If the writing on the document absorbs infrared radiation, it becomes warm; since it is in contact with the blank, it blackens, thus transferring the writing to the blank. In other words, the success of the copying process depends on exactly the same phenomena as in the making of an infrared photograph, namely that the details on the object being photographed absorb infrared radiation. The main limitation to the use of the Thermo-Fax machine is that the instrument accepts objects whose size is in the order of $8^{1}/_{2}$ by 11 in and that are roughly no thicker than a few sheets of paper. Figure 8-8 illustrates the use of the Thermo-Fax copier for these purposes.

[1] J. S. Levkov, "A Rapid, Inexpensive Method of Obtaining Infrared Images," *Journal of Forensic Sciences,* Vol. 23, p. 539, July 1978.

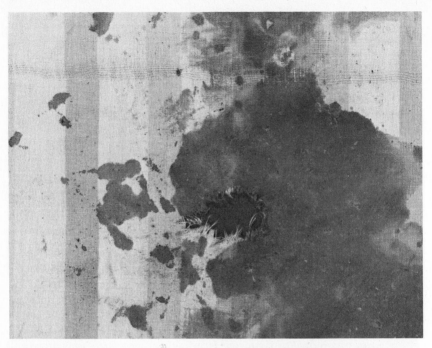

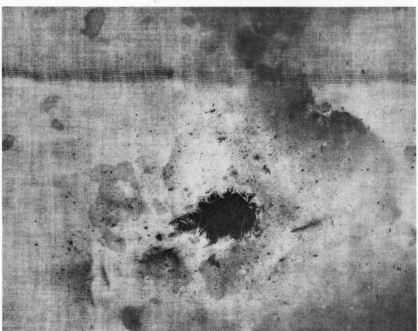

Figure 8-7 *Top:* photograph of clothing showing blood, using panchromatic film, normal illumination; *bottom:* photograph of clothing showing powder markings, using infrared-sensitive film, infrared illumination. Note that the blood is almost invisible, while the powder residue is quite distinct (Courtesy W. Reid Lindsay).

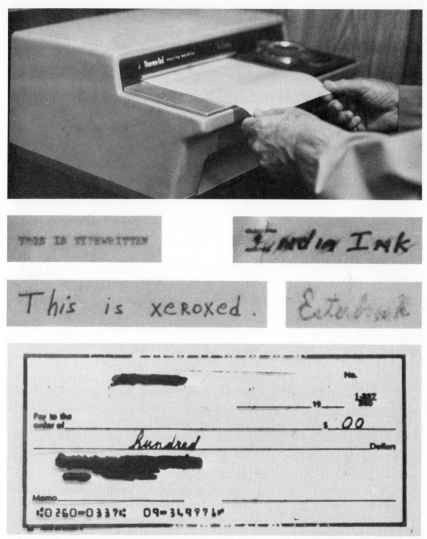

Figure 8-8 *Top:* Thermo-Fax copying machine; *middle:* Thermo-Fax copy of same obliterated writing as shown in Fig. 8-6; *bottom:* Thermo-Fax copy of the same check as shown in Fig. 8-5.

Historical Note

Some years ago the FBI laboratory was asked to examine the identification board of the Deadwood Stage found in Wyoming. IR photography revealed a penciled date of July 23, 1840, making it the oldest stagecoach in existence.

X-Ray Photography

Another type of photography employs X-rays, which make it possible to locate a bullet in any area of a body. X-rays are taken of the teeth of the deceased when there is any question as to identity. These X-rays are compared with those taken by the individual's dentist or with the dental charts on record. X-rays will disclose previous bone fractures that have healed as another means of identifying an individual. The contents of packages or luggage suspected of containing explosive devices can be ascertained with X-ray. The most recent advance in the use of X-rays is the possibility of reproducing for permanent record fingerprints on the skin of a deceased. See Fig. 3-10.

Insurance Photography

Many insurance companies require a photograph of expensive pieces of jewelry for their files when a policy is issued. If the item is stolen, it may be identified from its photography by insurance or police investigators. Police agencies will often send out bulletins showing photographs of expensive jewelry which has been stolen. If the stolen jewelry is found, it can possibly be identified from a photograph. The same procedure is recommended for works of art.

Photography of a special sort may provide a solution to one of the thorniest problems that confront police involved in the recovery of stolen diamonds. That is being able to prove that the recovered stone is the same as the one reported stolen from an individual. Up to the present time, identification depended on a subjective judgment based on the size, clarity, color, and cut of the stone.

The new technique involves use of a machine known as Gemprint. The process involves passing a narrow beam of light from a helium-neon laser through a pinhole in a sheet of Polaroid 55 P/N (positive/negative) film. The beam then strikes the diamond that is to be "fingerprinted." The diamond must be precisely positioned so that the beam strikes its top facet or "table" at a 90-degree angle. The beam will undergo a number of reflections from inside the rear facets of the diamond. The reflected rays will strike the film and expose it, forming tiny black spots on the negative. The positions of these spots are uniquely determined by the multiple angular relationships of the cut diamond and the textural qualities of its individual facets. The result is a fingerprint of the particular stone.

The Gemprint system is currently being evaluated by the New York City Police Department. As it operates now, two positive prints and two negatives are produced. One print goes to the customer and one to the insurance agent. The customer also receives a certificate.

The jeweler keeps one negative, and one is stored in a central computerized file of the gemprints. The latter is a key to the system's successful operation. As soon as a stone is reported stolen, this is noted at the central file. The print can be retrieved from the file when needed.

Fundamentals of Photography

Photography plays such an important role in law enforcement that it is a good idea to have a grasp of the fundamentals, even though you do not intend to specialize as a police photographer. A knowledge of photography will always come in good stead in police work.

To begin at the beginning, the word *camera* comes from the Latin phrase *camera obscura* meaning "dark chamber." A camera is nothing more than a lightproof box containing a lens at one end through which light passes and film that records an image on the opposite end. Of the many different types of cameras in use today, some of which cost thousands of dollars, all function in essentially the same way as transmitters of light to film.

The complexity comes mainly in technological advances in the control of the light entering the camera through the lens. This control is a function of the lens and the shutter in combination. Both the size of the lens opening and the speed of the shutter must be taken into consideration in making proper exposures for the prevailing lighting conditions and the sensitivity of the film being used. The key components of a camera, then, are the lens, the diaphragm (which controls the size of the lens opening), and the shutter (which controls the length of time that light passes through the lens). These three components will be considered separately.

Lens

The lens is generally the most expensive part of a camera. Good lenses are made of finely ground glass, with many separate elements combined. The normal lens for the average 35mm camera is usually 50mm or 55mm in focal length, which is to say that the lens "sees" an area roughly equivalent to that of the focal area of the human eye.

Auxiliary lenses are described as "wide-angle" and "telephoto." Lenses with focal lengths of 35mm, 28mm, or smaller are wide-angle lenses and are used for photographing subjects of wide dimension such as buildings or groups of people. The telephoto lenses range in focal length from 85mm to 150mm or more. As the name implies, they act as a telescope, giving close-up details of faraway subjects.

Diaphragm and f-Stops

The amount of light passing through the lens at a given moment in time is controlled by the size of the opening in the diaphragm. This is called the "f-stop." It is found underneath the lens in markings that indicate the range of f-stops for that particular lens. On the typical single lens reflex 35mm camera, such as the Nikon or the Honeywell Pentax, these markings range from f1.4 (the largest opening for that lens) to f16 (the smallest opening). Some lenses are "wide open" at f1.2, and some may be closed down to f32 or even f64 (a tiny pin hole) (see Fig. 8-9).

Shutter

The shutter speed is regulated in click-stops, ranging (on some cameras) from $1/1000$ to 1 second (Fig. 8-9). A B (for "bulb") exposure means that the shutter will remain open as long as the release lever is held down. T (for "time exposure") means that the shutter opens when the release is pressed once and closes when pressed again.

Fast shutter speeds "stop" action. A fighter taking a swing would be a blur at 60 ($1/60$ second) but would be frozen in sharp detail at 500 or 1000 ($1/500$ or $1/1000$ second).

Of course, there is a functional relationship between the stop and the shutter speed. If, for example, the proper exposure for a scene were 60 at f16, then in order to capture the action at 1000, the diaphragm opening would have to be set much larger—at f4.5. The general rule to follow is that when the shutter speed is increased by one calibration, the f-number must be decreased by one calibration and vice versa. Both exposures admit the same amount of light, but the faster shutter speed freezes the action.

Focusing

Another basic consideration is focusing the lens on the subject as a function of the subject's distance from the camera. Focusing determines the sharpness or clarity of detail in the photograph.

Some cameras have a footage scale which is set by measuring the distance between camera and subject. Modern cameras, how-

Shutter speed set at 1/100 second

f stop set at 16
diaphragm opening

Figure 8-9 Camera lens board with stops and shutter speed.

ever, almost always have built-in devices for focusing—range finders, ground glass, or split image. Simple cameras have "fixed focuses," which means that everything from a few feet from the camera to infinity will be in focus.

Depth of Field

With more complex lenses, *depth of field* must be taken into consideration as well. Depth of field is that part of the picture in which details are in sharpest focus. This area varies with the lens—the larger the lens opening, the smaller the depth of field. A lens opening of $f1.4$, for instance, has a depth of field of only a few inches when the subject is close to the camera. Depth of field can be determined by a scale printed on top of some lenses. One reason for stopping down lens openings to $f11$ or $f16$ is that the depth of field is so much larger than with f-stops of $f2$ or $f1.4$.

Film

Film is available in roll (cassette) or sheet (cut) format. In color or black and white, a wide variety of films are available today which are suitable for many different photographic situations. Color films are usually somewhat slower than black and white films—that is, they may require longer exposures. The most widely used color films have film speeds ranging from 25 to 165. The most common black and white film is rated 400. There are especially sensitive high-speed films (Kodak Recording 2475) suitable for night surveillance photography. Even more sensitive are electronic devices for amplifying low levels of light. These speeds indicate the relative sensitivity to light of the film, rated by the American Standards Association, thus the term *ASA rating* listed on the box in which the film is packaged and on the accompanying data sheet (which always contains excellent information about the proper exposures under varying conditions of light).

> **NOTE:** **The speed of color film has been catching up to that of black and white. High-speed Ektachrome (ASA 160) may be increased to ASA 400 with special processing, and Fuji now produces a color film with a standard ASA rating of 400, without special processing. Both films are considered to render color with fidelity, but many professional photographers believe that the most faithful color reproduction is given by slower films, such as Kodachrome I (ASA 25).**

Automatic Cameras

The trend in recent years in photography has been to increase technical sophistication while at the same time simplifying the camera's operation for the photographer. Most cameras on the market today have automatic exposure controls which guarantee proper exposure. The photographer simply sets the speed of the film in the camera and focuses correctly. Lens opening and shutter speed are electronically set by light-sensitive mechanisms.

Darkroom Techniques

Developing black and white negatives is quite simple and requires no expensive equipment. Negatives must be developed in darkness. Be sure that light does not leak through cracks of the door jamb or around windows.

Three trays made of enamel, glass, plastic, rubber, or stainless steel will serve the purpose. They should be approximately 8 by 10 in with a depth of 2 in. For 35mm film developing, small tanks are available.

Two chemicals are required—developer and fixer—that are available in any photographic shop. It has been found through personal experience that Kodak DK 50 developer will prove most efficient in developing most black and white film, although there are other good developers on the market. The two agents—DK 50 and fixer—are easily prepared by following mixing directions on their respective containers. All that is required is to mix the powders with water at given temperatures. Place the developer in the first tray, water or a stop bath in the second tray, and fixer in the third tray. *Extreme care must be used in handling negatives for they will mar or scratch very easily. Negatives should be handled by their sides or at the extreme edges.* The first step in developing negatives requires about 5 minutes. Depending upon the temperature, it must be performed in total darkness.

The roll or sheet of film should be agitated three or four times in the 5-minute period. Then, the negatives are dipped in the water tray and immediately immersed in the fixer for 5 to 10 minutes; the remaining process may be performed in ordinary light. After the negatives are removed from the fixer, they must be washed under running water for approximately 30 minutes and then hung up to dry. Hypo clearing agent may be used to reduce the washing time.

What Went Wrong

A dark negative or one that is almost completely black is generally caused by excessive time in the developer or overexposure (too slow a shutter speed or too large an f-stop).

A negative that is very faint or one in which the image can hardly be seen (referred to as "thin") is caused by too little developing time or underexposure (too fast a shutter speed or too small an f-stop).

NOTE: (1) Negatives have a shiny side and a dull side. The dull side of a negative is the emulsion side. Photographic

papers also have two sides with *the shiny side of the paper being the emulsion side.* A basic rule is that the emulsion side of the negative must face the emulsion side of the paper in printing or enlarging. (2) Kodak will provide any law enforcement agency with an affidavit when processing color film and photographs. This helps to maintain the chain of evidence from the time the film is taken, through its processing, until its return to the agency.

Making Prints

The object in making a print is to pass light through the negative onto photographic paper, which in turn records the image. Photographic paper cannot be exposed to light (except safelight, which is amber), or else it will "fog" and become useless.

Enlargers project the negative onto light-sensitive paper, the exposure is made, and then the paper is developed by the same method as that described below for making a contact print. A contact printer is needed for making prints that are the same size as the negative.

The dull side (or emulsion side) of the negative must face the emulsion (shiny side of the paper). The negative rests on the glass of the contact printer with the paper placed over the negative. The printer handle is depressed, and the negative is exposed to the paper for approximately 7 seconds. The length of exposure varies from one negative to another. This is a trial-and-error procedure. Count seconds to yourself: "1001, 1002," and so on. Of course, the second hand of your watch or a timer will be more efficient.

At the end of the exposure, the handle of the printer must be released immediately, and the paper is placed in a previously prepared tray of Dektol. [There are many good developers on the market for making prints from negatives. One, often used by the authors, is Dektol. This is available in quart size and must be prepared according to the instructions on the container. Dektol is placed in the first tray, water or a stop bath in the second, and fixer (the same as is used in developing negatives) is placed in the third tray.]

The exposed paper should be turned over a couple of times with the image visible in the solution. When the image appears of satisfactory contrast, the paper is removed, dipped in water, and immediately placed in the fixer for 10 minutes. There can be no hesitation between the steps once the paper is removed from the Dektol. At the end of 10 minutes, the print must be washed in running water for 30 minutes and dried. Again Hypo clearing agent may be used to reduce the washing time.

Photographic papers come in various types, and one that renders a good rendition of contrast and tone is AZO F-3. This paper can generally be used to make a contact print from the average negative.

Kodak makes a resin-coated (RC) paper that requires little washing and dries in a very few minutes. RC paper does not require an electric dryer, as does AZO F-3 or any of the other conventional papers. AZO photographic paper may be used in contact prints and Kodabromide or polycontrast paper for making enlargements.

Kodak manufactures what is known as a Kodak Ektamatic Processor that will develop, fix, and dry a contact print or enlargement in less than 15 seconds, thus eliminating the manual process of developing, rinsing, fixing, washing, and drying.

"Instant" Photography

Polaroid's MP-3 Multi-Purpose land camera is shown in Fig. 8-10. It is an ideal camera for photographing latent fingerprints or other evidence, i.e. guns, knives, or other weapons. Care must be exercised in photographing fingerprints in grease, oil, wet paint, putty, or some other soft substance; the lights must not be too close to the subject matter because the heat may distort the print.

The MP-3 has an arrangement of four lights which can be easily

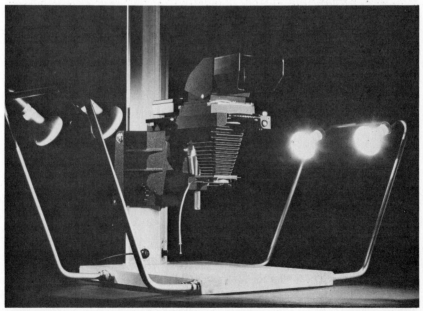

Figure 8-10　Polaroid MP-3 Multi-Purpose camera. There is now an MP-4, which is an update of the MP-3 (Courtesy Polaroid Corp., Cambridge, MA).

altered thus saving considerable time in photographing difficult objects. One can use Polaroid film (including P/N film which produces both a photograph and a negative) or the conventional 4- by 5-in cut film or a film pack adapter with the MP-3. Various lenses are available for performing macrophotography up to a magnification of 14X. It can be easily converted to an enlarger.

Figure 8-11 shows Polaroid's CU5 camera. This camera is portable and may be used at the crime scene to photograph fingerprints or other small evidence. It comes with a battery pack for powering its light source, or it may be used with 110-volt current. A photograph can be taken of a subject on a one-to-one basis, which means recording the image on film to its exact size. The camera may be used with the 545 holder.

Figure 8-11   Polaroid CU-5 camera (Courtesy Polaroid Corp., Cambridge, MA).

Impressions as Evidence

Many different kinds of physical impressions at the scene of a crime may provide valuable evidence leading to the apprehension and conviction of the criminal. Of these, the most common are footprints and tire tracks. Both are usually found in loose earth, sand, mud, or snow. Marks left by a tool used in the commission of a crime also constitute valuable clues.

Impressions are important because, like fingerprints, they reveal individual characteristics. No footprint, tire track, or tool mark is exactly like another, even though the article making the impression is mass-produced in a standard design. Scratches, cuts, abrasions, and imperfections of all kinds form distinctive patterns that on occasion can be preserved and used as evidence.

For this reason, the search for such physical impressions takes a top priority when investigators arrive at a crime scene. It goes without saying that the area must be carefully secured to ensure that spectators do not trample footprints and tire tracks or otherwise disturb the potential evidence.

Footprints and Tire Tracks

In order to identify an impression with a specific shoe or tire, it is necessary to find matching characteristics. The following is a list of some of the characteristics based upon which an identification may be made:

1. Design
2. Shape
3. Worn areas (sole or heel of shoe, tire tread)
4. Size of tire tread
5. Worn name of manufacturer on rubber heel
6. Width of heel, widest part of sole, length of impression
7. Distance between repeating patterns in tire tread
8. Imperfections in tire tread (small bits of rubber missing from cuts or gouges)

> **NOTE:** A tire impression may represent only a small portion of the 7 or 8 ft of tire tread (varies with the size of the tire). At times, it is possible to determine the manufacturer from the tread design. However, identification of a specific tire requires finding identical characteristics in the impression as well as on the tire itself. In dealing with shoe, sneaker, or other footwear impressions, an investigator is confronted with similar problems. With footwear impressions the investigator is more likely to be dealing with most of a shoe or sneaker. The complete tread impression of one or more tires can sometimes be obtained when the car has made a turn on a soft surface. The FBI maintains a reference library of tire treads.

With footprints, one can determine size, width, and often the manufacturer (from heel marks on shoes and the patterns of ridges on the soles of sneakers). Millions of rubber heels and sneakers of the same design are made each year, and the investigator's job is to make a comparison with the footwear of one individual. Again, the object is to find a worn area or some imperfection visible in the impression and also on the suspect's footwear. The identifying feature could be a small piece of the design missing in the pattern of a sneaker sole or an imperfection in a rubber heal. The imperfection or wear would be visible in the sole of the footwear. The fact that the impression is similar in size to that of the suspect's shoe is insufficient in itself. What is required is some identifiable feature or characteristic that can be found in the impression and also in the footwear. (Fig. 9-1.)

First Step: Photography

Before any attempt is made to make a cast of a shoe or tire impression, a photograph must be taken. The proper procedure is to place a ruler alongside the impression so that the dimensions can be easily determined on the finished print. There will be little difficulty in photographing impressions in the sunlight, but if they are found in the shade or a dark area, side lighting may be necessary to make the impression more visible. Tests have shown that contrast can be improved by spraying the impression with a very fine mist of matte white paint for dark surfaces or matte black paint for light surfaces (e.g. snow).[1] An identifying gummed label may be placed on the ruler showing the date, case number, location of impression, and initials of the photographer. The person who found the impression should make a record of that fact, listing all pertinent data.

The ideal impression is that found in loose dirt, such as a flower bed that has been recently cultivated. Equally good is an impression in mud that dried after the impression was made. Examine the impression carefully and remove any loose debris.

Making Casts

The next step is to construct a cardboard or wooden frame around the impression. The purpose is to contain the soft cast mix. The four sides of a shoe box, cut to a height of 2 in [50.8 mm], make an ideal framing device.

The most common and economical substance used in casting is plaster of Paris. It is available at most hardware, building supply, or art supply stores. Generally 7 parts plaster to 4 parts water or roughly 2 parts plaster to 1 part water will suffice. Approximately 1.5 lb [0.68 kilograms (kg)] of plaster will suffice for one foot impression. Usually, 1 pint [0.47 liter (l)] of water will be enough for mixing plaster for one footprint. A somewhat larger amount will be necessary for a tire impression, which varies in size. The plaster may be mixed in a metal or plastic pail or pan or any other object that is watertight. The plaster is sprinkled into the water until it will not hold any more and mixed to a uniform texture or consistency similar to that of heavy cream, pudding, or pancake batter.

[1] K. Carlsson and A. C. Maehly, "New Methods for Securing Impressions of Shoes and Tyres on Different Surfaces," *International Criminal Police Review* (Paris) **299**: 158–167, 1976.

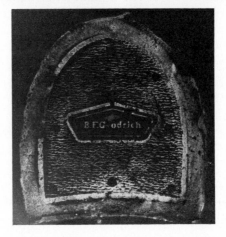

Figure 9-1 *Left:* Actual heel; *right:* actual heel with white powder; *bottom:* simulated rubber lift of white heel print. Note missing *o* in *Goodrich* and other identifying elements.

Before the plaster cast is made, it is good practice to spray the impression with a fine mist of shellac or hair spray. Two or three coats of spray will bind all loose material. Never hold the spray too close to the impression, for that may distort it. When the spray has dried, the impression may be sprinkled with talcum powder or sprayed with a light oil. The purpose of the spray and powder is to facilitate the removal of the cast from the impression. It is almost impossible to make two casts of the same impression.

The mixture of plaster of Paris should not be poured directly on the impression. It should be gently ladled on with a spoon or spatula or poured into the impression using the spatula held a couple of inches above it to break the fall; otherwise, pouring would probably injure the surface. The thickness of the first pouring should be limited to roughly ½ in [12.7 mm]. The casting should be reinforced with wooden tongue depressers, twigs, or wire mesh. Reinforcement material must be carefully placed on the impression.

A second layer of the mix is poured over the reinforced cast to a height of about 1 in [25.4 mm]. The initials of the investigator and the date should be set in the cast. Generally, the cast will be dry in 20 minutes, and then carefully removed. A small amount of salt added to the original mix will hasten the drying time of the cast as soon as it hardens sufficiently. When it is perfectly dried, the cast may be cleansed under slowly running water to remove foreign debris. Soaking a cast in sodium bicarbonate will increase its hardness.

To make a cast of a footprint or tire impression in snow requires great care. As the plaster sets, heat which can melt the snow is given off. The obstacles will vary according to the temperature and whether the snow is moist or hard and dry. In making a cast in snow, it is recommended that a thin coat of talcum powder be sprinkled over the impression followed by shellac or hair spray. This process is repeated two or three times. Then the casting is performed as previously explained. In this case, however, one should not pour until the plaster has partially set. This can be determined by dropping test amounts into the snow. When a drop does not cause the snow to melt, the plaster is ready. (*Note:* Do not use salt to hasten the drying time of the plaster; it will melt the snow.)

Another means of preparing an impression in snow is by spraying with cellulose acetate dissolved in acetone. After the mist has settled on the surface of the snow, the acetone evaporates. All that remains is a transparent film of cellulose acetate. This serves as a foundation upon which the plaster of Paris may be placed. Melted sulfur has been used as a substitute for plaster of Paris with some degree of success.[2]

A fourth, very promising method uses paraffin as follows[3]:

1. Loose snow threatening to fall into the impression from its surroundings is removed or patted down.

2. Paraffin spray (e.g. Xmas decoration "snow-spray") is applied over the whole impression from a distance of about 4 in. and from various angles. During the spraying operation the aerosol can is slowly losing its

[2] *Criminal Investigation and Physical Evidence Handbook*, Wisconsin Dept. of Justice, 1973. Order from State of Wisconsin Dept. of Administration, Document Sales, 202 S. Thornton Ave., Madison, WI 53702.
[3] Carlsson and Maehly, p. 166.

pressure and is cooling down as a result of evaporation. It is therefore advisable to have two or three spare cans at hand, preferably in a moderately warm place (pockets, car). Spraying is done three times, allowing a 3-minute interval for drying each time (if the whole operation is carried out in one go, cracks can appear in the sprayed-on layer). The paraffin layers should have a total thickness of about 1 mm.

3. After an additional drying period of 10-15 minutes, melted paraffin (heated just above its melting point) is slowly and carefully poured into the sprayed paraffin layer. The paraffin used in our experiments had a m.p. of about 52°C and a light grey color when melted.

4. In order to avoid damage to the cast during transportation, it is advisable to reinforce it by placing wooden sticks over the sprayed and dried layers of paraffin and pouring the melted paraffin over these. Care must be taken so that no paraffin runs under the print.

5. The finished cast is cooled with snow and lifted when thoroughly cold.

Instead of reinforcing the cast as described above, the cast can be placed into a wooden box, a shoe carton or the like and secured by pouring additional paraffin around it."

Materials for Making Casts

It is a good idea to keep available the materials for making a plaster cast:

Plaster of Paris (finely divided artist grade for best results)
Water container
Mixing pail
Wooden spoons
Talcum powder
Shellac for spraying
Hair spray
Ruler
Shoe box or wooden slats for framing
Reinforcing material (tongue depressors, metal or plastic screening)

Plaster of Paris is the traditional and the cheapest medium for making these casts. In the last few years materials have become available that promise to be easier to work with, to give cleaner casts, and to reproduce fine detail. One of these is silicone rubber (General Electric Co., Silicone Products Dept., Waterford, New York 12188). These are liquids and will set only after they are mixed with a suitable catalyst. The main drawback is their greatly increased cost.

Adapt to Circumstances

Making plaster casts of impressions is always a delicate business because of the nature of the materials and the possibility that significant markings may be distorted. The authors remember a homicide case in which tire marks appeared as crucial evidence. Suddenly, it began to rain, threatening to obliterate the tire marks. An alert police officer quickly threw his raincoat over them. Then, the investigators mounted a tent over the impression. Photographs were taken and a cast was made. This is a good example of the obstacles confronting investigators and of how a little ingenuity can help in police work.

Tool Marks as Evidence

Tools leave distinctive marks because they are generally made of metals harder than the surfaces with which they come in contact. Tool marks may be divided into two types: friction marks and compression marks. The striking of a hammer against a surface leaves a compression mark, and a knife drawn over a surface leaves friction marks. As a tire impression may place a suspect's car at the crime scene or footprints point to his or her presence there, so also may a tool mark link the tool's possessor with a criminal act.

Most tools in common use leave identifying marks. Here is a list of those most often encountered by police:

Hammers	Wrenches (all types)
Screw drivers	Jimmy
Pry bar	Socket tools
Pliers	Cold chisels
Wire cutter	Stapling machines
Bolt cutter	Steel wedges
Knife	Crow bar
Ax or hatchet	Tire iron

Any time a tool is used to force open a window or door or pry open a cash box, safe, or metal cabinet, a close examination will usually reveal the mark or configuration of that tool. When a metal tool is used forcibly against another metal surface, striations are likely to be found.

Examination of any tool under 5X magnification will reveal markings caused during manufacture, irregularities, and grooves caused by wear or use on its surface. However, although a file or saw will have distinctive markings, it is almost an impossibility to find their counterparts on the surfaces with which they come in contact.

The point of entry or scene of the break-in in a burglary is an excellent area to search for tool marks. A careful examination should be conducted of the window sill, door jamb, or any other point of forced entry. Particular attention should be given to painted surfaces. Close inspection will reveal markings in the paint or complete absence of the paint by scraping or rubbing. Should the tools be recovered, they should be examined for matching bits of paint. Whenever safes, cash boxes, or metal locked cabinets have been forced open, be on the lookout for broken bits of tools. This is ideal evidence because if the tool is located, the broken pieces can clearly indicate its use in the crime. When this occurs, a macrophotograph (see Fig. 9-2) should be taken to illustrate how the broken part of the tool fits into the missing area of the tool.

Some burglars leave their tools at the scene of each burglary, particularly where safes are involved. They do this so that, if arrested, they cannot be charged with possession of burglary tools in general or, more to the point, the tools used in the particular crime in question.

Tool Mark Procedures

The first step upon finding a tool mark is to take a photograph with a ruler or measuring tape adjacent to the mark. Print the identifying data—date, case number, and initials of photographer—on a gummed label and stick it to the ruler. This procedure will begin the chain of evidence as far as the tool mark is concerned. It is recommended that a fingerprint camera or any camera capable of taking a one-to-one photograph be used. In other words, the photograph of the impression should be the same size as the impression being recorded. If such a camera is not available, one merely has to make a photograph with a ruler included, so that it may be used to produce the exact dimensions in enlarging the negative. One should take a second photograph showing the impression in relation to its surround-

Figure 9-2 Tool parts found at crime scene fitted onto tools found in suspect's car (Courtesy San Diego, California, Police Department and Eastman Kodak, Rochester, NY).

ings. When the surface containing the tool mark may be easily moved, take the object to your laboratory for photographing. The Polaroid MP-3 Multi-Purpose camera will render excellent minute detail in a matter of minutes along with a negative for producing high-quality enlargements.

In instances where the tool mark is found on an immovable object or surface, a cast of the impression may be made. A variety of casting materials are available from commercial suppliers—cellulose acetate butyrate, liquid silicone rubber, and such common substances as clay or putty. These materials will render a much more detailed impression of a tool mark than that obtained from plaster of Paris, because they have a finer texture.

A technician may make more than one casting of a tool mark. This technique produces a negative cast which is a replica of the tool that made the mark. From this cast a positive cast must be made with a substance that can be separated from the first cast. This second, or positive, casting will produce a reproduction of the original tool mark impression.

At times, it is possible to place the tool next to the impression so that a photograph may be taken showing the similar configuration of both. If the substance containing the mark is soft, a similar impression may be made in it by the suspected tool, and a comparison can then be made of both surfaces. The comparison may be performed by placing the two photographs side by side and showing the similar identifying characteristics.

If striations are found on a metal surface, do not attempt to use a suspected tool to make a similar mark on another metal surface, because it may alter or destroy the ridges on the tool that made the markings. Use clay, putty, or some other soft substance. Some experts make test marks in lead, an exceptionally soft metal.

The services of a microscopist are necessary where metal surfaces are concerned. Firearms examiners, accustomed to working with striations and markings on bullets and cartridges, are highly qualified to make identifications of tool marks on metals. If a soft metal such as copper is involved, little change will occur on a wire cutter when a sample cut is made for comparison purposes (Fig. 9-4). The comparison microscope used in firearms identification is excellent for viewing a metal mark from a crime scene and a test mark made in lead. A split-image photograph of each, showing the matching characteristics, can be made. (Figs. 9-3 and 9-4.)

Other Impressions

Certain kinds of impressions do not lend themselves to casting, but they are valuable as evidence and should be preserved. Often, for instance, a burglar will stand on a chair to gain access to a high cabinet. If her or his shoes were wet, soiled, or muddy, there will be an imprint on the chair. Similarly, when a safe is open, the insulation and cement scatter on the floor, and the burglar leaves prints in the residue.

Such impressions should be photographed and "lifted" with rubber lifters. The method is similar to lifting fingerprints, and various types of lifters are available. Of course, if the impressions are on glass, paper, tile, or any other portable material, they should be brought intact to the crime laboratory.

Capsule Cases

During a recent burglary of a home in Westchester County, an aluminum screen was removed from a patio to

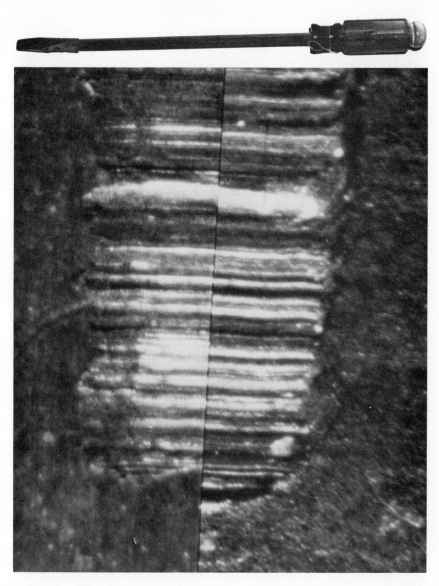

Figure 9-3 *Top:* doorplate with tool markings and screwdriver; *bottom:* (left), mark from screwdriver used to force open door and (right), test mark (Courtesy Marshall Robinson, Forensic Laboratory, Connecticut State Police).

Figure 9-4 *Left:* edge of copper slug; *right:* mark from machine from which slug was produced (Courtesy James McDonald, New Haven, Connecticut, Police Department).

gain access to the house. An almost complete design of the rubber sole pattern of a sneaker was observed on the screen. Were it not for the accumulation of dust on the screen, the impression would never have been recorded. The same sneaker pattern was observed on the painted surface of the patio.

In an unusual assault and rape case, the attacker left a prominent bite mark on a girl's thigh. A quick-thinking investigator made a cast of the bite impression. In this instance, the rapist had a slight imperfection in his bite that was visible in the impression. Shortly afterward a suspect was arrested, and a court order was obtained to get a bite impression of his teeth. The cast from the girl's leg and that from the suspect's bite were identical and helped bring about his conviction.

In another rape and murder case in a quiet area, someone recalled hearing a scraping noise and a car speeding off. A search of the scene disclosed a rock with scrapings on its surface. When the suspect was arrested, an examination of his car disclosed a dent in his oil pan. The impression in the oil pan was found to coincide with the surface of the rock where the scrapings were observed on its surface. This fact placed the car at the scene and helped bring about the conviction of the murderer.

Criminals often wear gloves to avoid leaving fingerprints, but gloves themselves may leave impressions. The FBI reported a case in which a glove impression was found in soft dirt at a burglary scene. A plaster cast was made. Distinctive marks in the glove cast were observed and matched to a pair of gloves of a suspect. On the basis of the cast a conviction was obtained.

In a hit-and-run case, the victim clutched the car's side mirror, and it was found in his hands. Striations on the base of the mirror and on a suspected vehicle were found to be identical. Faced with this damning evidence, the suspect confessed.

The partial outline of a shoe and a small portion of a sole on a rug were enough to make another suspect confess to a crime. Evidently the shoes had picked up dirt or other foreign matter, which caused the impression on the rug. The impressions were sharp enough to be photographed. Confronted with this evidence, the suspect confessed.

Summary

It is not always easy to get impressions that can lead to arrests and convictions, but they rate a top priority in the search for evidence in any crime scene. Footprints, tire marks, and tool marks figure prominently in the solution of many crimes, and care should always be taken that all such evidence is noted, recorded, and preserved.

In gathering impressions as evidence, remember these essential investigatory procedures:

1. Always photograph the impression, using a ruler to clarify scale.
2. Send portable impressions to the crime laboratory when possible.
3. Take a cast, with plaster of Paris or other casting material.
4. Label all casts properly.
5. Be on the alert for marks that may lead to an identification of the tool used in the crime.

chapter

Drugs and Poisons

Aspirin, heroin, Valium, LSD, coffee, morphine, cigarettes, Librium, marijuana, Scotch whisky, curare, airplane glue . . . What do these things have in common? They are drugs. They alter the user's biochemistry, with resultant modification of cell structure and of behavior.

Of course, this is but a partial listing. The pharmacopoeia of drugs ranges from mild pain relievers and cough suppressants to dangerous mind- and mood-altering substances illegal almost everywhere in the world. To be sure, most drugs have therapeutic value when used properly. The problem arises when they are abused— when they are taken at such high levels of concentration or with such frequency that they injure the user's health. Physical and psychological dependence, in varying degrees, often accompanies their use. Many drug abusers are forced to commit illegal acts, from prostitution to theft, in order to support a drug habit. Thus, the spread of the drug culture in recent years becomes the proper concern of society and its lawmakers.

There have been laws against certain drugs, such as heroin, morphine, and cocaine, throughout most of the twentieth century (but not during the nineteenth century, when anyone could buy any drug in any drugstore for a few pennies). The advent of new drugs and the great increase in the number of drug users prompted the United States government to make renewed efforts to control their sale and use.

The task is overwhelming. A DEA (Drug Enforcement Administration) study in 1974 reported the following statistics:

1. Approximately 500,000 registered private enterprises supply drugs to those in need of medication.
2. Approximately 20,000 different brand names for controlled drugs are involved.
3. This includes about 185,000 lb [83,990 kg] of opium derivatives, 45,000 lb [20,430 kg] of synthetic narcotics, 4172 lb [1894 kg] amphetamines, more than 1 million lb [454,000 kg] of barbituates, 2 billion dosage units of various tranquilizers, 60 million dosage units of stimulants, and more than 25 million 4-oz bottles of codeine cough syrup.

No wonder a computerized system has been developed to monitor these substances!

It is also not surprising that pharmacies are a focal point for obtaining these drugs illegally. In 1973, 5640 pharmacies in the United States were broken into and robbed. More than 32 million dosage units were stolen, with an estimated street value of $23.6 million. In the first half of 1975, Philadelphia experienced a 57 percent increase in such crime. Forged prescriptions and lax or even illegal issuance of prescriptions on the part of some physicians have been on the increase. Many remedies for the situations have been tried. The most successful are better security (monitored alarm systems) and a hot line (pharmacists have voluntarily agreed to alert one another to forged prescriptions).

The Controlled Substances Act of 1970 was passed to try to stem widespread drug abuse. This act establishes the different categories of illegal drugs; rules and regulations for importing, distributing, and exporting them; and penalties for their unlawful possession.

The intent of this act is to minimize the amount of drugs of abuse which are available to potential drug abusers. A substance may be placed on the list following the investigation of the drug by the DEA. This investigation can be initiated in a number of ways—petition by the Department of Health, Education, and Welfare or by any interested party (e.g. manufacturer, public interest group, local government, etc.). The purpose of the investigation is to determine whether the drug satisfies the criteria listed under the appropriate schedule.

A key criterion for controlling a substance, and the one which will be used most often, is the substance's potential for abuse. If the Attorney General determines that the data gathered and the evaluations and recommendations of the Secretary of Health, Education, and Welfare constitute substantial evidence of potential for abuse, he or she may initiate control proceedings.

The reasons for placing a substance in each schedule along with the penalties for trafficking (first offense) are listed below.

Schedule 1

1. The drug or other substance has a high potential for abuse.
2. The drug or other substance has no currently accepted medical use in treatment in the United States.
3. There is a lack of accepted safety for use of the drug or other substance under medical supervision.

Penalties: 15 years/$25,000 (narcotic)

Schedule 2

1. The drug or other substance has a high potential for abuse.
2. The drug or other substance has a currently accepted medical use in treatment in the United States or a currently accepted medical use with severe restrictions.
3. Abuse of the drug or other substances may lead to severe psychological or physical dependence.

Penalties: 15 years/$25,000 (narcotic)
             5 years/$15,000 (nonnarcotic)

Schedule 3

1. The drug or other substance has a potential for abuse less than the drugs or other substances in schedules 1 and 2.
2. The drug or other substance has a currently accepted medical use in treatment in the United States.
3. Abuse of the drug or other substance may lead to moderate or low physical dependence or high psychological dependence.

Penalties: 5 years/$15,000 (narcotic)
             5 years/$15,000 (nonnarcotic)

Schedule 4

1. The drug or other substance has a low potential for abuse relative to the drugs or other substances in schedule 3.
2. The drug or other substance has a currently accepted medical use in treatment in the United States.
3. Abuse of the drug or other substance may lead to limited physical dependence or psychological dependence relative to the drugs or other substances in schedule 3.

Penalties: 3 years/$10,000 (narcotic)
             3 years/$10,000 (nonnarcotic)

Schedule 5

1. The drug or other substance has a low potential for abuse relative to the drugs or other substances in schedule 4.
2. The drug or other substance has a currently accepted medical use in treatment in the United States.
3. Abuse of the drug or other substance may lead to limited physical dependence or psychological dependence relative to the drugs or other substances in schedule 4.

Penalties: 1 year/$5000 (narcotic)
             1 year/$5000 (nonnarcotic)

In making these findings, DEA and HEW are directed to consider eight specific factors:

1. Its actual or relative potential for abuse
2. Scientific evidence of its pharmacological effect, if known
3. The state of current scientific knowledge regarding the drug or other substance
4. Its history and current pattern of abuse
5. The scope, duration, and significance of abuse
6. What, if any, risk there is to the public health
7. Its psychic or physiological dependence liability
8. Whether the substance is an immediate precursor of a substance already controlled under this title

Two agencies share responsibility for enforcing the controls of the act—the Food and Drug Administration (FDA) in the Department of Health, Education, and Welfare and the Drug Enforcement Administration (DEA) in the Department of Justice.

The nine control mechanisms imposed on the manufacturing, obtaining, and selling of substances listed under the act are as follows: registration of handlers; recordkeeping requirements; quotas on manufacturing; restrictions on distribution; restriction on dispensing; limitations on imports and exports; conditions for storage of drugs; reports of transactions to the government; and criminal penalties for illicit trafficking. The first two controls are equally applicable to substances listed in every schedule; the others vary, depending upon the schedule involved.

The enforcement of drug laws requires great expenditures of ef-

TABLE 10-1: Price of Heroin from Farmer to Street

Market	U.S. $ per kilogram	U.S. $ per kilogram of raw opium, equivalent
United States		
Price to Farmer for Opium (in Turkey)	60	—
Wholesale Price for Heroin, Marseille	7000	700
Border Price for Heroin, New York	12,000	1200
Wholesale Price for Heroin, New York	40,000	4000
Retail Price for Heroin, New York	400,000	40,000

Source: DEA, U.S. Department of Justice, *Fact Sheets*, U.S. Government Printing Office, 1973, 0-507-933.

fort, time, and money. At present, the proportion of drug analyses in the average crime laboratory is so large that other (and perhaps more important) investigations are unable to compete successfully for the time of the overburdened criminalists.

Consider the following statistics: a recent study reported that for crime laboratories in ten jurisdictions, 54 percent of the cases involved drugs. In three cities—Berkeley, Buffalo, and Portland—the average submission rates for drugs were 92, 72, and 67 percent.[1]

From 1968 to 1969 the number of examinations in the categories of burglary and robbery decreased in New York City while the narcotic analyses increased over 60 percent.[2] New York City alone has about 1500 law enforcement agents involved in drug investigations.

The estimates of drug users vary. For heroin alone, the National Institute on Drug Abuse estimates between 400,000 and 500,000. Every year 5000 people die of overdoses. Some 90,000 addicts are being treated in methadone maintenance clinics and another 60,000 in other rehabilitation programs. The crimes committed by heroin addicts cost the United States more than $6 billion a year.

Why is it so difficult to stop the use of some of these drugs, most of which are imports? Huge profits are certainly one reason. Table 10-1 illustrates this for heroin (these are estimates made in 1973.)[3] Perhaps more informative are the street drug price and purity indices issued quarterly by the DEA. (These figures vary from one part of the country to another.) For July, August, and September

[1] W. R. Benson, J. E. Stacy, Jr., and M. L. Worley, *Systems Analysis of Criminalistics Operations*, LEAA Grant NI-044, Midwest Research Institute, Kansas City, Mo., 1970.

[2] R. H. Ward, "The Investigative Function: Criminal Investigation in the U.S." Unpublished D. Crim. dissertation, School of Criminology, University of California, Berkeley, 1971.

[3] Drug Enforcement Administration, U.S. Dept. of Justice, *Fact Sheets*, U.S. Government Printing Office, 1973, 0-507-933.

1975, heroin averaged about $1.15 per milligram (mg) and was about 6 percent pure. (The average addict needs about 50 mg per day.) Its price was up from the previous quarter, indicating a decrease in supply. Cocaine averaged about $0.50 per milligram (average purity about 13 percent) and had decreased in price, indicating a good supply. Thus 1 oz would cost about $14,000. The 1977 selling price has dropped considerably. Now 1 oz costs about $2000 (or $0.07 per milligram). A single dose costs about $10.

What are these drugs of abuse? The most widely used fall into several broad categories.

Narcotic Analgesics

According to medicine, narcotic analgesics include any drug that produces sleep or stupor and relieves pain. According to law, a narcotic analgesic is any drug so labeled in federal or international law. Examples are opium and opiates (opium derivatives such as codeine, morphine, heroin), synthetics such as meperidine (Demerol) and methadone (Dolophine). The naturally occurring opiates are derived from the poppy plant grown in various parts of the world (Fig. 10-1).

As a result of the analgesic action on the central nervous system (CNS), lethargy, drowsiness, and reduced sex and hunger drives result. When they are taken in more than therapeutic amounts, symptoms such as constriction of the pupils, lowered blood pressure, constipation, nausea, vomiting, and itchiness of the nose may be observed. An overdose leads to death through respiratory failure. Tolerance develops with repeated use, and addicts can take many times the lethal dosage without experiencing adverse or pleasurable effects. Before this immunity develops, intense pleasure often accompanies the use of some of these drugs. Afterward, the drug is taken mainly to prevent withdrawal symptoms.

Narcotics are used medicinally to relieve pain, diarrhea, and coughs. Aside from the danger of an overdose (which is most likely in the case of new users), death may occur as a result of the addict's neglect of nutrition or hygiene (using dirty needles and other conditions likely to lead to infection).

The addict may unwittingly purchase a bag of heroin mixed with ground glass or high levels of cyanide. The Food and Drug Administration does not protect the addict. He or she is at the mercy of the supplier. In Washington, D.C., in 1976 four addicts died and twenty-five others became ill when they purchased and used "Mexi-

Figure 10-1 Opium poppy (Courtesy Paul Fuqua).

can mud" heroin having a content of 12 percent heroin. The Mexican heroin they normally purchased and were accustomed to using was 2 to 3 percent pure.

It has been estimated[4] that a heroin addict spent over $17,000 to purchase enough heroin to support his or her habit in 1973. To approximate the value of the goods stolen to obtain this amount of money, the figure must be multiplied by a factor of 3 to 5—the "fence" factor—or $51,000 to $85,000.

The withdrawal symptoms are extremely unpleasant—gooseflesh, running nose, watery eyes, chills, instability, loss of appetite, nausea and vomiting, dilated pupils, yawning, involuntary muscle spasms, and insomnia.

As a result of its usual method of introduction into the body,

[4] Bureau of Narcotics and Dangerous Drugs, U.S. Department of Justice, *Director's Report on Federal Performance Measurements*, U.S. Government Printing Office, Washington, D.C., 1972.

there are a number of telltale physical signs of heroin addiction. The maximum effect is derived by injecting directly into the blood. Probably 85 to 90 percent of users choose to inject the drug. Heroin powder is placed in a spoon with some water. It is heated until dissolved; then it is drawn into a syringe (or often an eyedropper with a hypodermic needle fastened at the end) through a small piece of cotton as a filter. It is injected into a vein in the arm or leg. Sores or "track marks" may appear at the point of injection (Fig. 10-2). The walls of

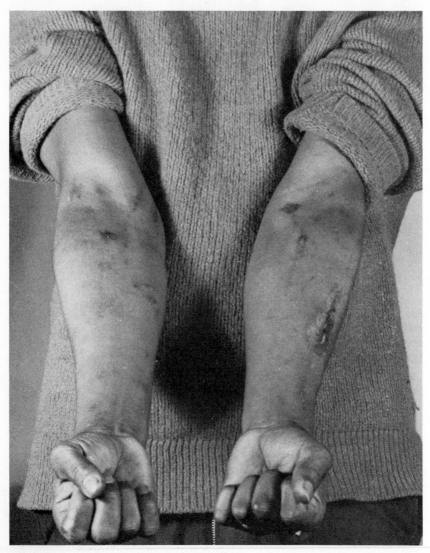

Figure 10-2 Track marks on arms of addict.

the veins collapse after repeated injections, and new sites are sought——between the fingers and toes, for instance.

About 15 percent of users sniff heroin. This is generally true only of beginners or rather wealthy users, since one gets only 30 to 50 percent of the drug's effect in this way. Prolonged use in this manner results in the destruction of the membrane between the nostrils. There are a number of chemical tests which may be applied to samples of the drug or urine samples. See Tables 10-2 and 10-3.

TABLE 10-2: Composition of Some Chemical Mixtures Used in Drug Identification

Test Name	Ingredients	Amounts
Koppanyi	cobalt acetate	0.1 g
	methyl alcohol (absolute)	100 ml
	glacial acetic acid	0.2 ml
Van Erk	P-dimethylaminobenzaldehyde	12.5 g
	concentrated hydrochloric acid	6.5 ml
	water	3.5 ml
Marquis	formaldehyde (40%)	5 ml
	concentrated sulfuric acid	50 ml
Duquenois	vanallin	2.0 g
	acetaldehyde	1 ml
	95% ethyl alcohol to make	100 ml
Cobalt thiocyanate	cobalt thiocyanate	2.0 g
	water to make	100 ml
Mayer	mercuric chloride	1.3 g
	potassium iodide	5.0 g
	water to make	100 ml
Mandelin	ammonium vandate	1.0 g
	concentrated sulfuric acid	100 ml
Stannous chloride	stannous chloride	5 g
	concentrated hydrochloric acid	10 ml
	water to make	100 ml

Depressants—Ethyl Alcohol and Barbiturates

Examples are ethyl alcohol (the active ingredient in all alcoholic beverages—beer, whiskeys, etc.); phenobarbital (Nembutal, "yellows"); secobarbital (Seconal, "red devils"); Amobarbital (Amytal, "blue heavens"); and Tuinal (amobarbital plus secobarbital, "rainbows"). Alcohol is produced by fermentation and distillation of certain food materials. Barbiturates are made synthetically.

This class of drugs is also a CNS depressant, producing drowsiness, general anesthesia, coma, respiratory depression, and death. A mild dose of alcohol—3 oz [88.7 milliliters (ml)] of 90 proof whiskey

TABLE 10-3: Color Reactions of Various Drugs

Narcotic	Test Name	Reaction
Opium	Mayer	white precipitate
	Marquis	violet coloration
Morphine	Mayer	white precipitate
	Marquis	purple coloration
Codeine	Mayer	white precipitate
	Marquis	violet coloration
Dilaudid	Mayer	white precipitate
	Marquis	red to violet
Heroin	Mayer	white precipitate
	Marquis	red-violet coloration
Demerol	Mayer	white precipitate
	Marquis	yellow to light green
Methadone	Mayer	white precipitate
	Mandelin	yellow to blue-green
	cobalt thiocyanate	blue precipitate
Amphetamine	Marquis	orange to brown
	Mandelin	olive green
Barbiturate	Koppanyi	blue to violet
Cocaine	Mayer	white precipitate
	cobalt thiocyanate	A blue precipitate which remains blue on the addition of stannous chloride, indicating that cocaine *could be* present. If blue precipitate disappears on addition of stannous chloride, cocaine is not present.
Quinine	Mayer	white precipitate
Cannabis	Duquenois test	purple coloration

(the actual percentage of alcohol is half of the proof rating, thus this is 45 percent alcohol by volume)—will produce a 50.0 mg percent blood level in about 30 minutes. This produces a sense of well-being and no significant impairment of driving skills. (It should be noted that there is a wide variation from individual to individual in reactions to all drugs.) Yet 6 oz [1.67 deciliters (dl)] produces a sixfold increase in driving accidents (the blood level is then 100 mg percent, which is the legal definition of intoxication in many states), and 9 oz [2.66 dl] produces a 150 mg percent blood level, which is considered legally intoxicated in Oregon. Gross intoxication, 18 oz [1.6 liters (l)], can cause death.

Alcohol is probably the most abused drug in American society. It is found in about 50 percent of all suicide cases and 50 percent of all homicides. Psychological and physical dependency often occurs. In addition, alcohol causes irreversible damage to the brain, liver, pancreas, kidney, and other body tissue.

The reactions to barbiturates are very similar to those for alcohol. They do have medicinal use (whether this is true for alcohol is open to dispute), mainly for inducing sleep. Physical dependence may occur when taken above therapeutic levels for one or more months. For all these depressants (including chloral hydrate and glutethimide) there are dangers to the individual and to society—drunk driving, antisocial behavior, homicidal tendencies, potentiation (the effect of using two drugs is greater than that of either one used alone. Alcohol and a barbiturate may be fatal when taken in combination, but nonlethal when taken separately). In the United States, barbiturates are the leading prescription drug used in suicide. Approximately 75 percent of all suicides in which drugs are used involve barbiturates.

Withdrawal symptoms are similar for alcohol and barbiturates— tremors, nausea, anxiety, perspiration, cramps, vomiting, hallucinations, convulsions, exhaustion, circulatory failure, and death. Barbiturate withdrawal is considered more dangerous than heroin withdrawal. It takes about 7 days to withdraw a patient from a barbiturate habit as compared to 1½ to 3 days for heroin addiction.

Alcohol can be detected by the odor of the breath and, more quantitatively, by use of various techniques for directly or indirectly measuring the blood alcohol level (with a breathalyzer). It is the blood alcohol level that is important because it is directly related to the amount of alcohol in the brain. The breathalyzer determines alcohol level in the lungs. The alcohol level in the blood is 2100 times greater than that of the lungs. Barbiturates can be recognized by the presence of pills of various colors. They are sometimes taken by injection. If so, the user's body will show needle marks. There are also a number of chemical tests which can be applied to blood or urine samples.

Similar in action to the barbiturates are certain hypnotics such as glutethimide (Doridan) and chloral hydrate.

Milder in action than all these and less likely to produce psychological dependence are tranquilizers like meprobamate (Miltown, Equanil), chlordiazepoxide hydrochloride (Librium), and diazepam (Valium). These are relaxants to skeletal muscles. Physical dependence has been demonstrated for some and is probably true for all these, but to a lesser degree than with alcohol and barbiturates. It is believed that many develop a psychological dependence on tranquilizers.

Other types of depressants are the volatile solvents. Examples include benzene, gasoline, toluene, glue, paint thinner, lighter fluid, acetone, and ethyl acetate. These are sniffed or inhaled and produce effects similar to those of alcohol, as a result of CNS depression. They are most often used by youngsters who may enclose their heads and the solvent, e.g. airplane glue, in a paper bag to concentrate the vapors. There is a tendency to psychological dependence but none physiologically.

Sustained use may lead to coma, unconsciousness, and death. Lower doses cause symptoms similar to an alcohol high with the same tendency for accidents. Because many of these chemicals are absorbed by fatty tissue, e.g. nerves, permanent damage to the brain, heart, kidneys, and liver may occur.

Stimulants

Examples of stimulants include methamphetamine (Methedrine, "speed"), amphetamine (Dexedrine, Benzedrine), cocaine, caffeine (found in coffee, tea, and cola drinks). These drugs act by stimulating the CNS, causing symptoms of excessive adrenalin production, e.g. alertness, rapid speech, wakefulness, attentiveness, reduced appetite, hyperactivity, dilation of pupils, higher blood pressure and increased sweating, fast pulse, and involuntary rapid eyeball movement. Higher doses may produce irritability, anxiety, and psychotic reactions. A likelihood for psychological dependence exists, but withdrawal symptoms are usually mild. A user often exhibits deep depression, severe cramping of the abdominal muscles, and symptoms of an asthma attack. Amphetamines are used therapeutically to reduce appetite (diet pills) and to overcome fatigue. Recently the combination of amphetamine and morphine has been found twice as effective as morphine alone in relieving pain.[5]

When taken intravenously, these stimulants lead to orgiastic experiences known as flashes or rushes. A user develops a tolerance to amphetamines and requires larger and larger doses. A user may take the drug for days at a time, injecting every 2 hours, thus maintaining a hyperactive state without sleep, eventually becoming confused and exhibiting irrational behavior. After perhaps 5 days the user stops, becomes semicomatose for perhaps 15 hours, wakes up in a lethargic state, and needs to resume the use of the drug. These runs often produce (or accentuate already present) aggressive, paranoid, psychotic, and violent behavior.

Users may be detected by the presence of pills of varying colors, excessive smoking, as well as the application of chemical tests to the pills or to urine samples (see Tables 10-2 and 10-3).

Cocaine is obtained from the leaves of the erythroxlyn coca

---

[5] W. H. Forrest, Jr. et al., "Dextroamphetamine with Morphine for the Treatment of Postoperative Pain," *New England Journal of Medicine*, vol. 296, no. 13, p. 712, March 31, 1977.

plant which grows most abundantly in the Andes mountains. It has much the same effect as the amphetamines. In pure form, it is a white crystalline powder. It is said to be the strongest stimulant known, and it is either sniffed or injected. An overdose of injected cocaine can stop respiration instantly. Its normal effects last over a short period, and tolerance does not seem to develop. Repeated sniffing causes the nose lining to bleed and rot. Cocaine has become a fashionable drug of the well-to-do in the past few years. (See Tables 10-2 and 10-3 for some chemical tests for these drugs.)

Hallucinogens

Marijuana is by far the most widely used of all illegal drugs. It takes three forms: marijuana (bhang), hashish (charos), and tetrahydrocannabinols (THC, the chemically active ingredient). It is a mixture of leaves, stems, and flowers from the plant *cannabis sativa*. Potency varies widely with the location and conditions where it was grown. Hashish contains more of the active ingredient (THC) from the resins given off by the plant (perhaps six to ten times more THC).

The plant is extremely hardy and is frequently cultivated by individuals for their own use. The female plant is far more potent than the male. The stalk is hollow, leafy, and four-cornered. It is about 4 in [10.2 cm] thick and 20 ft [6.1 m] high in a full-grown plant. The leaves resemble those of a palm tree. They have an odd number of leaflets, five to eleven, on a single stem. They are serrated, 2 to 6 in [5.1 to 15.2 cm] long, with the outer two leaflets being the shortest. The top side of the leaf is dark green, and the underside is a lighter green. Microscopic hairs grow on the underside which are used for identification in laboratory tests. Ridges run diagonally from the center to the edges (Fig. 10-3). The most potent parts of the plant are the leaves, then the flowers and the small stems.

The effects of marijuana vary with the amount taken (usually smoked) and the previous experience and expectations of the user. The marijuana user seems more in control over the effects than alcohol or other hallucinogen users. These vary from the sense of well-being and pleasurable feelings of a mild alcohol high through hallucinations. At low doses there does not seem to be an effect on coordination. There is some potential for psychological dependence, but no physical dependence. There have been a number of studies to determine if any adverse physiological effects result from use of the drug, but none have been conclusive or widely accepted. It has been shown to remain in the body some 7 to 8 days. Probably no cases

Figure 10-3 *Left:* marijuana growing wild; *right:* close-up of marijuana leaf (Courtesy Westchester County, NY, sheriff's office).

exist where death has occurred as a result of an overdose of marijuana. Its use can be recognized from the characteristic odor of the smoke (burning rope), special (pot) pipes, and cigarette paper. There are also a number of chemical tests. (See Tables 10-2 and 10-3.)

Other Hallucinogens

Examples of other hallucinogens include *d*-lysergic acid diethylamide tartrate-25 (LSD), psilocybin, dimethyltryptamine (DMT), diethyltryptamine (DET), mescaline (peyote), dimethoxymethylamphetamine (STP, or DOM). These hallucinogens have much stronger effects than marijuana. Some are obtained from natural sources; others are produced synthetically. They act directly on the brain, producing profound, as yet not understood, alterations in nerve activity. The senses are greatly amplified. The "tripper" is bombarded with sensation, "feels" color, or "sees" sound. The individual may feel removed from his or her body. There are great swings in emotion. Whether an individual experiences a good trip (users claim to gain a fundamental understanding of themselves) or a bad one (resulting in a psychotic experience) depends very much on the environment and the suggestions of other individuals who are present. Pupils dilate markedly; hot and cold flashes, increased flow of saliva, nausea, lack of appetite, and increased pulse and blood pressure have all been observed.

The pure LSD is a colorless, odorless, tasteless powder. It is taken in tablet, powder, or liquid form. Probably the most powerful known hallucinogen, a dose of 50 to 200 micrograms (μg) (the size of a pinhole) is sufficient for a "trip" of 8 to 16 hours. To achieve similar effects, 10 times the amount of psilocybin, 2000 times the amount of DMT, and 4000 times the amount of mescaline would be required. One ounce of LSD is enough for 280,000 such doses and has been estimated to have a value of $1,430,000. There is no physical dependence but some tendency for psychological dependence, with no withdrawal symptoms. Tolerance builds up rapidly so that these drugs cannot be taken daily without greatly increased doses. This tolerance disappears a few days after cessation of drug use.

The main proved dangers are psychological—prolonged psychotic episodes, impairment of motivation, flashbacks (i.e. recurring hallucinogenic experiences without taking the drug again). There is evidence of chromosomal damage and birth defects.

Role of the Law Enforcement Officer

The investigation of drug abuse and the trafficking in controlled substances involve all the techniques previously described for the investigation of a crime, and then some. Because of the huge amounts of money involved, drug traffickers are often willing to bribe and even murder to protect their interests. Both the perpetrator (pusher, junkie, etc.) and the victim (addict or user) will usually conspire to deceive the police since they are accessories in the crime. This makes it difficult to obtain evidence. Usually, infiltration by undercover agents and/or the use of informants is employed. An attempt is made to observe as well as to film or electronically record the drug transaction.

Elaborate methods of concealment have been devised to hide and transport these drugs (Fig. 10-4 and 10-5). This requires the investigator to be ever alert and as clever and imaginative as the adversary. Dogs trained to detect specific substances such as marijuana are widely employed. Some case histories will illustrate these points. In a case recently reported in the *Journal of the American Medical Association*,[6] a man, age 19, arrived in a stupor at a hospital in Framingham, Massachusetts. Among other problems he had a grand mal seizure shortly after he arrived. The surprising cause of his assorted symptoms was the fact that two days before, while in Columbia, South America, he had swallowed 180 rubber bags of cocaine, and some of

[6] *Journal of the American Medical Association*, vol. 237, 1977.

Figure 10-4 Trick seat.

it had entered his system. Nearly all the bags were eventually recovered.

Washington, D.C.—DEA agents and Arlington County police cooperated on a buy that netted a kilogram of cocaine and the arrest of four South American smugglers. The action began with an informant's phone call advising police that he had possible access to a large amount of cocaine. The drug, smuggled into the United States taped to the bodies of women couriers, was offered by a Peruvian identified as "Coco." The police requested DEA's help and together they set up two surveillance teams. After the informant had actually seen the cocaine in a suburban Washington motel room, he returned with a DEA undercover agent. The surveillance teams moved in once the substance was positively identified as cocaine. The kilogram cache was retrieved from its

Figure 10-5 Dummy bottom of a trunk (Courtesy Westchester County, NY, sheriff's office).

hiding place under a bed, and four Peruvian nationals were arrested.[7]

Greensboro, N.C.—As a result of a DEA compliance investigation, prompted by reports of large orders of amphetamines from pharmaceutical houses, a physician was convicted in a federal court on five felony counts. The investigation revealed that he himself had been a user of narcotics and had once entered the Public Health Hospital in Lexington. He received a three-year suspended sentence and five years probation. The court also ordered his federal narcotics license revoked for five years.[8]

[7] *Drug Enforcement*, Spring 1974, DEA, U.S. Justice Department, U.S. Government Printing Office.

[8] *Drug Enforcement*, Summer 1974, DEA, U.S. Justice Department, U.S. Government Printing Office, 1974, 0-734-331/3.

Hong Kong—Prices on the illicit market recently rose sharply after the Hong Kong Narcotics Bureau seized two heroin laboratories in a single night. In an apartment near Kowloon, 54 pounds of morphine base, 32 pounds of No. 3 heroin, and large amounts of precursor chemicals and equipment were seized. A heroin chemist and his wife were arrested. The second police effort resulted in the arrest of 14 traffickers and seizure of 146 pounds of heroin. The Bureau was using its newest recruit, a black Labrador retriever, in the case. In his first field trial the dog detected 44 pounds of morphine base concealed behind the wall of a hut.[9]

Drugs have been found in many odd locations: sewn inside shirt collars, taped under soles of feet, in the hollowed heel of a shoe, in body cavities, hat bands, belts, and ties. Automobiles provide numerous hiding places—under the horn, under upholstery, in tires, air vents, and door panels. It probably would be easier to list the parts, if any, that have not been used (Figs. 10-4 and 10-5). Buildings —homes, offices, etc., offer innumerable possibilities; in a waterproof bag suspended in the water tank of a toilet; in the zippered cushions of couches or chairs, in heating and air-conditioning ducts; in various secret compartments; hollowed out bars of soaps; in all sorts of cosmetics (lipstick containers, submerged in cold cream); under floorboards or rugs—the list is incomplete but should alert the investigator to the need for the utmost care and thoroughness in conducting such a search.

NOTE: One should conduct the search legally, with a warrant or valid consent, or with reasonable cause in the case of a search made incidental to an arrest. Many cases have been thrown out of court for such infractions. Any evidence that is seized should be properly labeled and placed in evidence bags for analysis at the laboratory.

NOTE: *It is important not to taste or smell substances that are thought to be drugs.* Many of them are potent in extremely small doses, and a bit on the tongue is sufficient for them to have a serious effect. Be careful not to scratch yourself with confiscated syringes—infectious hepatitis is common among addicts.

It is often difficult to recognize if an individual is misusing a drug.

[9] Ibid.

Many of the symptoms are common to those of a cold or allergy, e.g. sniffles, running eyes; or a person may be carrying a hypodermic needle because he or she is diabetic, etc. There are some signs that may indicate drug abuse:

1. Changes in work or school attendance.
2. Change from normal abilities at work, etc.
3. Lack of concern for physical appearance.
4. Wearing sunglasses constantly at inappropriate times to conceal dilated or constricted pupils and also to make up for the eye's inability to adjust to sunlight. Marijuana, for example, causes bloodshot eyes.
5. Going out of way to cover arms in order to hide needle marks.
6. Associating with known drug users.
7. Stealing items whose sale is a source of ready cash.

Table 10-4 on pp. 190–192 summarizes the pertinent facts concerning these drugs. Of particular importance to police personnel are the possible identifying symptoms. Also important are the slang and street terms used to name them. Many of these are listed in Table 10-5 on p. 193.

Poisons: Forensic Toxicology

Drugs, which cause so many deaths by their misuse and abuse, are related to the role of the specialist in poisons—the toxicologist. Toxicology is the science of poisons. Of course, many more substances than the drugs included in the first part of this chapter are poisonous. Many common house plants can be lethal—the poinsettia, mistletoe, and rhubarb (leaves and roots). Hemlock and the aminata mushroom, though not exactly household plants, are well-known poisons readily found in many parts of the world. When such plants cause trouble as poisons, it almost always is an accident. Many household cleaning agents (lye, Drano, etc.) are also the causes of accidental poisonings.

In a toxicological analysis, the investigator tries to establish the presence or absence of a particular drug. At least, that is the most favorable situation—when the investigator has some idea of what to look for.

Less favorable is when the toxicologist is asked to determine whether there is any drug or poison in the body. This is a complex question. It is impossible to approach anything like an analysis for

TABLE 10-4: Controlled Substances: Uses and Effects*

Drugs	Schedule†	Often Prescribed Brand Names or Chemical Name	Medical Uses	Dependence Potential: Physical	Psychological	Tolerance	Duration of Effects (in hours)	Usual Methods of Administration	Symptoms/Overdose/Withdrawal
Narcotics									*Possible Identifying Symptoms*
Opium	2	Dover's Powder, Paregoric	Analgesic, anti-diarrheal	High	High	Yes	3 to 6	Oral, smoked	Needle marks, "works," slow pulse and respiration, euphoria, drowsiness, constricted pupils, nausea, loss of appetite (These generally apply to heroin, morphine, and opium; much higher doses of the others may produce some of the same effects.)
Morphine	2	Morphine Sulfate	Analgesic	High	High	Yes	3 to 6	Injected, smoked, oral	
Codeine	2, 3, 5	Codeine, Methyl-morphine	Analgesic, antitussive	Moderate	Moderate	Yes	3 to 6	Oral, injected	*Effects of Overdose*
Heroin	1	Diacetyl-morphine	None	High	High	Yes	3 to 6	Injected, sniffed	Slow and shallow breathing, clammy skin, convulsions, coma, possible death
Meperidine (Pethidine)	2	Demerol, Pethadol	Analgesic	High	High	Yes	3 to 6	Oral, injected	*Withdrawal Syndrome*
Methadone	2	Dolophine, Methadone, Methadose	Analgesic, heroin substitute	High	High	Yes	12 to 24	Oral, injected	Watery eyes, runny nose, yawning, loss of appetite, irritability, tremors, panic, chills and sweating, cramps, nausea
Other narcotics	1, 2, 3, 5	Dilaudid, Leritine, Numorphan, Percodan	Analgesic, anti-diarrheal, antitussive	High	High	Yes	3 to 6	Oral, injected	
Depressants									*Possible Identifying Symptoms*
Chloral Hydrate	4	Noctec, Somnos	Hypnotic	Moderate	Moderate	Probable	5 to 8	Oral	Pills and capsules of various colors, slurred speech, disorientation, drunken behavior without odor of alcohol; small doses serve to relax and make good-humored; symptoms increase with dosage
Barbiturates	2, 3, 4	Amytal, Butisol, Nembutal, Phenobarbital, Seconal, Tuinal	Anesthetic, anti-convulsant, sedation, sleep	High	High	Yes	1 to 16	Oral, injected	*Effects of Overdose*
Glutethimide	3	Doriden	Sedation, sleep	High	High	Yes	4 to 8	Oral	Shallow respiration, cold and clammy skin, dilated pupils, weak and rapid pulse, coma, possible death, very dangerous when taken with alcohol
									Withdrawal Syndrome
									Anxiety, insomnia, tremors, delirium, convulsions, possible death

	Trade or Other Names	Medical Uses	Physical Dependence	Psychological Dependence	Tolerance	Duration (hours)	Usual Method
Methaqualone	2	Optimil, Parest, Quaalude, Somnafac, Sopor	Sedation, sleep	High	High	Yes	4 to 8	Oral
Tranquilizers	4	Equanil, Librium, Miltown, Serax, Tranxene, Valium	Antianxiety, muscle relaxant, sedation	Moderate	Moderate	Yes	4 to 8	Oral
Other Depressants	3, 4	Clonopin, Dalmane, Dormate, Noludar, Placydil, Valmid	Antianxiety, sedation, sleep	Possible	Possible	Yes	4 to 8	Oral

Stimulants

		Trade or Other Names	Medical Uses	Physical Dependence	Psychological Dependence	Tolerance	Duration (hours)	Usual Method
Cocaine‡	2	Cocaine, Methylester of Benzoylecgonine	Local anesthetic	Possible	High	Yes	2	Injected, sniffed
Amphetamines	2, 3	Benzedrine, Biphetamine, Desoxyn, Dexedrine	Hyperkinesis, narcolepsy, weight control	Possible	High	Yes	2 to 4	Oral, injected
Phenmetrazine	2	Preludin	Weight control	Possible	High	Yes	2 to 4	Oral
Methylphenidate	2	Ritalin	Hyperkinesis	Possible	High	Yes	2 to 4	Oral
Other Stimulants	3, 4	Bacarate, Cylert, Didrex, Ionamin, Plegine, Pondimin, Pre-Sate, Sanorex, Voranil	Weight control	Possible	Possible	Yes	2 to 4	Oral

Possible Identifying Symptoms
Pills of various colors, multicolored capsules, increased alertness, excitation, euphoria, dilated pupils, increased pulse rate and blood pressure, insomnia, loss of appetite, erratic and aggressive behavior

Effects of Overdose
Agitation, increase in body temperature, hallucinations, convulsions, possible death

Withdrawal Syndrome
Apathy, long periods of sleep, irritability, depression, disorientation

Hallucinogens

		Trade or Other Names	Medical Uses	Physical Dependence	Psychological Dependence	Tolerance	Duration (hours)	Usual Method
LSD	1	Lysergic acid diethylamide	None	None	Degree unknown	Yes	Variable	Oral
Mescaline	1	3, 4, 5-Trimethoxyphenethylamine	None	None	Degree unknown	Yes	Variable	Oral, injected
Psilocybin-Psilocyn	1	None	None	None	Degree unknown	Yes	Variable	Oral
MDA	1	Methylenedioxyamphetamine	None	None	Degree unknown	Yes	Variable	Oral, injected, sniffed

Possible Identifying Symptoms
Depression, exhilaration, illusions and hallucinations (with exception of MDA); poor perception of time and distance, gastric distress (Mescaline)

Effects of Overdose
Longer, more intense "trip" episodes, psychosis, possible death

Withdrawal Syndrome
Withdrawal syndrome not reported

(Continued)

TABLE 10-4: Controlled Substances: Uses and Effects* (Continued)

Drugs	Schedule†	Often Prescribed Brand Names or Chemical Name	Medical Uses	Dependence Potential Physical	Dependence Potential Psychological	Tolerance	Duration of Effects (in hours)	Usual Methods of Administration	Symptoms/Overdose/Withdrawal
Hallucinogens, cont.									
PCP§	3	Sernylan, Phencyclidine	Veterinary anesthetic	None	Degree unknown	Yes	Variable	Oral, injected, smoked	*Possible Identifying Symptoms* Pungent odor, euphoria, relaxed inhibitions, increased appetite, disoriented behavior, talkative, may sit and stare
Dimethyltryptamine (DMT)	1	Dimethyl-tryptamine	None	None	Degree unknown	Yes	Variable	Oral, injected	*Effects of Overdose* Fatigue, paranoia, possible psychosis
Cannabis Marijuana Hashish Hashish Oil	1	Cannabis sativa, Tetrahydro-cannabinol	None	Degree unknown	Moderate	Yes	2 to 4	Oral, smoked	*Withdrawal Syndrome* Insomnia, hyperactivity, and decreased appetite reported in a limited number of individuals

* This table is adapted from *Drugs of Abuse*, 3rd edition, U.S. Department of Justice, Drug Enforcement Administration.
† Scheduling classifications vary for individual drugs since controlled substances are often marketed in combination with other medicinal ingredients.
‡ Designated a narcotic under the Controlled Substances Act.
§ Designated a depressant under the Controlled Substances Act.

TABLE 10-5: Street and Slang Terms for Drugs

Amphetamines	Bombidos, Beans, Bennies, Black Beauties, Blackbirds, Black Mollies, Bumblebees, Cartwheels, Chalk, Chicken Powder, Copilots, Crank, Crossroads, Crystal, Dexies, Double Cross, Eye Openers, Hearts, Jelly Beans, Lightning, Meth, Minibennies, Nuggets, Oranges, Pep Pills, Speed, Roses, Thrusters, Truck Drivers, Turnabouts, Uppers, Ups, Wake-ups, Footballs, Peaches, Greenies
Barbiturates	Barbs, Block Busters, Bluebirds, Blue Heavens, Blue Devils, Blues, Christmas Trees, Downers, Green Dragons, Marshmallow Reds, Mexican Reds, Nebbies, Nimbies, Peanuts, Pink Ladies, Pinks, Rainbows, Red and Blues, Redbirds, Red Devils, Reds, Sleeping Pills, Stumblers, Yellow Jackets, Yellows, Phennies, Double Trouble, Goofballs, Seggy
Cocaine	Bernice, Bernies, Big C, Blow, C, Coke, Dream, Flake, Girl, Gold Dust, Heaven Dust, Nose Candy, Paradise, Rock, Snow, White, Stardust, The Leaf
Glutethimide	C.D., Cibas
Hashish	Black Russian, Hash, Kif, Quarter Moon, Soles
Heroin	Big H, Boy, Brown, Brown Sugar, Caballo, Chinese Red, Chiva, Crap, Doojee, H, Harry, Horse, Junk, Mexican Mud, Powder, Scag, Smack, Stuff, Thing, Scat, Snow, Joy
LSD	Acid, Beast, Big D, Blue Cheer, Blue Heaven, Blue Mist, Brown Dots, California Sunshine, Chocolate Chips, Coffee, Contact Lens, Cupcakes, Haze, Mellow Yellows, Microdots, Orange Mushrooms, Orange Wedges, Owsley, Paper Acid, Royal Blue, Strawberry Fields, Sugar, Sunshine, The Hawk, Wedges, White Lightning, Window Pane, Yellows
Marijuana	Acapulco Gold, Broccoli, Bush, Dry High, Gage, Ganga, Grass, Griffo, Hay, Hemp, Herb, J, Jay, Jane, Mary Jane, Mota, Mutah, Panama Red, Pod, Pot, Reefer, Sativa, Smoke, Stock, Tea, Weed
MDA	Love Drug
Mescaline	Beans, Buttons, Cactus, Mesc, Mescal, Mescal Buttons, Moon, Peyote
Methamphetamines	Crystal, Meth, Speed
Methaqualone	Quas, Quads, Soapers, Sopes
Morphine	Cube, First Line, Hocus, Miss Emma, Morf, Morpho, Morphy, Mud, White Stuff, M., Dreamer
Phencyclidine	Angel Dust, DOA (Dead On Arrival), Hog, Killer Weed (when combined with marijuana or other plant material), PCP, Peace Pill
Psilocybin/Psilocyn	Magic Mushroom, Mushroom
Dimethyltryptamine	DMT
Diethyltryptamine	DET
Codeine	Schoolboy

all possible drugs in a reasonable time, or perhaps in any time. As was seen in the chapter on the crime laboratory, some drugs, notably LSD, act at such low concentrations that they may be difficult to detect with today's techniques. (A typical dose is perhaps 100 mg, which is then diluted into the blood, liver, urine, etc.) Detection may require the most sophisticated and expensive instrumentation that is usually only available in major crime laboratories.

Even if it could be identified, there will be a question about whether the drug contributed to the death. Did the barbiturate cause the victim to drive carelessly or was the victim so depressed that he committed suicide by driving off the highway into a brick wall?

Or, was the level of drug in the body high enough to cause death? This is a thorny question. Individuals vary widely with respect to their tolerance depending on their size, body metabolism, and previous experience with the drug. Some years ago, several men died from drinking wood alcohol. The man who supplied the alcohol survived the drinking spree and was subsequently arrested. He was charged with homicide, but after trial he was found not guilty. He proved that the wood alcohol was not toxic to himself.

A most interesting case was brought to light when a woman on the verge of death had her stomach pumped. In her stomach was found a large quantity of arsenic. Her husband was questioned about the matter, and he revealed that he had used arsenic spray on vegetables to control bugs and insects. Even though he had eaten the same food as his wife, it did not affect him. Evidently his body passed the arsenic in excretion or waste whereas hers did not.

The lethal dosages of some of these drugs are listed in Table 10-6. These are known as the LD 50 values, that is, the amount (expressed as milligram of chemical per kilogram of body weight) that will kill 50 percent of all test animals in a single oral dose. For example, if a 150-lb [68-kg] individual ingested $68 \times 70 = 4760$ mg (about $1/6$ oz) of nicotine, there would be a 50 percent chance of death occurring.

Of course, there is a danger in extrapolating such evidence from animals to humans. Humans may be more or less sensitive than the particular animal used to establish these figures.

How Poisons Enter the Body

The method of introduction of a poison has a lot to do with its effect. Some poisons—hydrogen cyanide gas, as well as a number of solvents—are effectively absorbed through the skin. Usually, however, the skin, unless broken, is an effective barrier. Poisoning through the skin is most frequently encountered in industrial situations. Inhalation is a much more effective and common method for toxins to enter the body, because the substance (which is usually a vapor, asbestos particles being one exception) can be absorbed rapidly through the tiny air sacs in the lung. They have a surface area of a little less than 0.02 acre, or 753 ft² [69.9 m²], across which this absorption takes place. Gases and vapors—carbon monoxide, hydrogen cyanide, and gasoline—are absorbed directly into the blood-

TABLE 10-6: Comparison of Toxicity of Various Substances*

Chemical	Use	LD 50†
Arsenic (as arsenic trioxide)	Laboratory and industrial chemical	45
Aspirin	Pain relief	558
Caffeine	Coffee, tea, cola	192
Chloral hydrate	Drug	285
Curare	Drug	1.2 (intravenous)
DDT	Insecticide	113
Dimethytryptamine (DMT)	—	43 (intravenous)
Heroin hydrochloride	—	38 (intravenous)
Librium	Drug	56
Mescaline	—	880
Morphine	Drug	745
Nicotine	Smoking	70
Phenobarbital	Drug	66
Sodium chloride	Ordinary table salt	3000
Sodium cyanide	Laboratory and industrial chemical	6.4
Strychnine	Medicinal drug	16

* H. E. Christensen, T. T. Luginbyhl, and B. S. Carroll (eds.), *Toxic Substances List,* 1974 ed., U.S. Department of Health, Education, and Welfare, Public Health Service, Center for Disease Control, National Institute for Occupational Safety and Health, Rockville, Md. 20852.

† These are oral doses (except where stated otherwise) expressed as milligrams of chemical per kilogram of body weight (mg/kg). All studies were done on some animal population.

stream, where they can be carried most rapidly to the rest of the body. The most common form of poisoning occurs via oral ingestion. This does have its drawbacks (from the viewpoint of the perpetrator) since the poison will be at least partially neutralized by the liver as it passes out of the stomach. The liver is like a chemical factory. One of its most important tasks is the metabolizing of toxins, and it is one of the first organs analyzed in a case of suspected poisoning since many of the toxins concentrate there.

Homicide by Poison

A case of homicide by poisoning may very well go undetected. Unless there are some grounds for suspicion (which is often left up to the medically untrained investigating officer to decide), the medical examiner's office is not called in and any physician who has seen the deceased in the recent past may sign the death certificate. Many poisons may not show obvious symptoms.

When an officer responds to a call for help, he or she must remember that all may not be what it appears to be. The suicide may be actually murder by a toxic substance (see Table 10-7). Any bottles containing pills or suspected of having contained pills should be examined for fingerprints and the remaining pills or residue exam

TABLE 10-7: Poisons and Associated Physical Manifestations*

Type of poison	Symptom or evidence
Caustic poison (Lye)	Characteristic burns around lips and mouth of victim
Carbon monoxide	Red or pink patches on chest and thighs
Sulfuric acid	Black vomit
Hydrochloric acid	Greenish brown vomit
Nitric acid	Yellow vomit
Silver salts	White vomit turning black in daylight
Copper sulfate	Blue-green vomit
Phosphorous	Coffee-brown vomit, onion or garlic odor
Cyanide	Burned almond odor in air
Ammonia, vinegar, Lysol, etc.	Characteristic odors
Arsenic, mercury, lead salts	Pronounced diarrhea
Methyl (wood) alcohol	Nausea and vomiting, unconsciousness,
Isopropyl (rubbing) alcohol	possibly blindness

* R. H. Fox and C. L. Cunningham, *Crime Scene Search and Physical Evidence Handbook*, LEAA U.S. Government Printing Office, stock no. 027-000-00221-8.

by a toxicology laboratory. In a suspected suicide case, fingerprints of the deceased should be on a pill bottle. If an officer's observations point to a suspected toxic substance as the cause of death, the job of the toxicologist can be greatly simplified. If no specific substance is suspected, testing can be a long, drawn-out affair.

Any suicide note must be handled with care so as not to destroy any fingerprints it may contain. The note should be placed in an evidence bag for safekeeping and future examination. The actions of the first officer on the scene will have a bearing on all future investigations. He or she must therefore use good judgment.

In the late 1960s, newspaper headlines carried the story of Dr. Coppolino, who was found to have killed his wife using succinylcholine chloride by injection.[10] It was only after the victim was legally buried that some suspicion was aroused. The body was exhumed, and since records indicated that the doctor had ordered such a drug from a drug supply house, a needle mark was sought and found. Special tests to show the presence of this toxin had to be developed. In spite of the fact that these tests were never used before in this way, their results were sustained in court.

Report from One County

In Westchester County, New York, there are approximately 6000 deaths a year. About 40 turn out to be homicides. Approximately 20 percent of the 6000 wind up in the medical examiner's office, and autopsies are done in about 650 cases. Approximately 100 of

[10] *Coppolino v. State* 223 So. 2d 68 (Fla. App. 1968).

these will have full drug screening tests done, and perhaps 25 will be determined to have death caused by drugs. Analysis may be aided by the fact that most drugs, poisons, and their breakdown products stay in the body for days or weeks and perhaps longer. A drug screen involves analyzing tissues and fluids from the body. The various classes of drugs are separated from one another by some type of extraction process. This depends on their differing solubilities, which are a reflection of their differing chemical makeups. The blood, urine, bile, liver, brain, lung, and kidneys are subjected to this analysis.

The identification of a drug is the job of the forensic chemist, or toxicologist. This is crucial. Depending on the state involved, the penalty for drug trafficking may depend not only on what is present but on how much. Both must be determined in the laboratory and be presented convincingly and with certainty to a jury if necessary. When presented with an unknown drug, the chemist faces a formidable task. The strategy, if no other information is presented, is to perform some screening tests to try to narrow down the possibilities to some manageable number. Any information that can be supplied by the investigating officer such as noticeable odor, pill boxes or bottles that might have been present, how the suspect was behaving (e.g. drowsy or excited), results of preliminary tests (there are commercially available kits for performing initial screening tests in the field) can save many hours of work (Fig. 10-6).

Initially some chemical color tests might be performed. These consist of adding specific chemical reagents to small samples of the suspect drug. Depending on the resultant color, an estimate can be made as to what may or may not be present. For example, the Marquis reagent [5 milliliters (ml) of 40% formaldehyde and 50 ml of concentrated sulfuric acid] turns violet with most opium derivatives but orange to brown with amphetamines. A partial listing of these reagents is shown in Table 10-2. Table 10-3 lists some of the characteristic colors observed. Additional screening may be provided by performing microcrystalline tests. Reagents are added which, in this case, cause characteristic crystals to form; these can be viewed with the aid of the microscope.

Positive identification can be achieved after the drug is separated from any impurities that are present through the use of gas chromatography (Chap. 15). They may then be identified using infrared and/or mass spectrometry (Chap. 15).

Nondrug Poisons

Some of the more commonly encountered nondrug toxins follows:

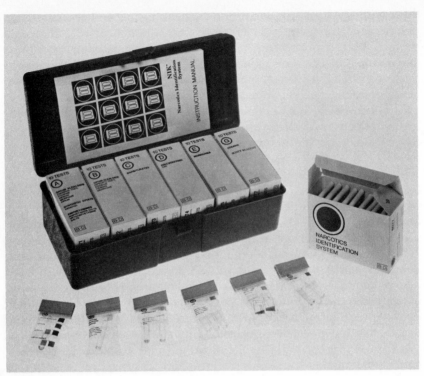

Figure 10-6   Narcotics field-test kit (Courtesy Beckton, Dickinson and Co., Arlington, TX).

CARBON MONOXIDE (CO)   This gas is formed by the incomplete combustion of carbon (as in a burning building or a car engine). It is a colorless, odorless gas, which can explode when mixed with air. Its poisonous action is a result of the combining of the carbon monoxide molecule with the hemoglobin of the blood. This displaces the oxygen which is normally bound to the hemoglobin (and is carried by it to all parts of the body), causing death from a lack of oxygen. The skin turns a purplish to cherry red, as a result of the carbon monoxide–hemoglobin combination. This color is used to indicate death from possible carbon monoxide poisoning. Table 10-8 lists the effects of various concentrations of carbon monoxide on the body. Table 10-9 lists CO levels produced by various sources. A measurement of the CO level in the blood can be used to distinguish between murder and accidental death where the victim is found at the scene of a fire. If the victim was killed prior to the fire, low blood levels of CO will be found, and vice versa.

HYDROGEN CYANIDE (PRUSSIC ACID, HCN)   Hydrogen cyanide is a colorless gas with the odor of bitter almonds. It is highly

TABLE 10-8: Concentration of CO and Effect at 8-Hour Exposure

CO concentration in air		Carboxyhemoglobin, Percent Concentration in Blood	Physiological Effect
Percent	Parts per Million (ppm)		
0.005	50	8.5	Impaired vision and coordination
0.01	100	14.0	Headache, fatigue
0.02	200	25.0	Drowsiness
0.05	500	45	Loss of consciousness
1.00	1000	65	Death

toxic and acts by combining with an enzyme preventing sugar metabolism. This can be formed by the burning of certain synthetic materials such as orlon, thus presenting a danger in case of fire where furnishings may be made of such synthetics. The skin assumes a brick red or purplish color that is called cyanosis, and a burned almond odor may be observed. Ingestion of solid sodium or potassium cyanide has the same effect.

HEAVY METAL POISONS Lead (Pb), mercury (Hg), arsenic (As), copper (Cu), and many others are heavy metal poisons. Almost all metals and their compounds are poisonous. Generally, the more soluble the substance, the more toxic it is. Many of these are cumulative; they build up in the body. *Lead* affects CNS and bone marrow and causes feeblemindedness, convulsions, and kidney damage. It is found in plumbing, paint, pottery glaze, and the antiknock agent in gasoline. There have been cases where people died from drinking or eating from pottery covered with lead-containing glazes. It is a common problem in ghettos where children may eat lead-containing paint. *Arsenic* interferes with important enzymes, accumulates in the hair and nails, and can be detected there. Table 10-7 lists some of these poisons along with symptoms that may indicate their presence to the investigating officer.

There is an additional class of toxins that is occasionally involved in both intentional and accidental poisonings.

NEUROTOXINS These poisons act specifically on the nervous system (see Fig. 10-7). The nerves are long, threadlike tissues that

TABLE 10-9*: CO Content of Various Sources

Mine explosion, 1 day after explosion in coal mine	1.0%
Gas range burning natural gas	0.2%
Room heater burning natural gas	0.5%
Automobile exhaust	7.0%
City fire (black smoke from burning building)	0.1%

* M. B. Jacobs, *Analytical Chemistry of Industrial Poisons, Hazards, and Solvents,* Interscience Publishers, Inc., New York, 1941.

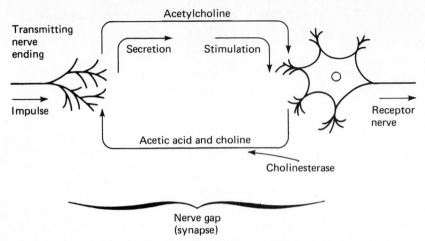

Figure 10-7   Diagram of the path of nerve transmission.

meet end to end at junctions called synapses. The "messages" are
carried along the nerves by electrical impulses. When they reach a
synapse, a chemical (acetylcholine) is released which rapidly diffuses
to the adjacent nerve ending, triggering the electrical impulse which
is carried along the next nerve; this might then cause, for example, a
muscle to contract. This chemical must now be removed to prevent
repeated nerve firing. An enzyme (cholinesterase) does this. Some of
the most powerful poisons act by interfering with this process.

Anticholinesterase agents prevent the enzyme from removing
acetylcholine, causing uncontrolled muscle contraction. Examples
are strychnine, war gases, and phosphate insecticides.

Receptor-site blocking agents prevent acetylcholine from transmitting the impulse, which results in relaxation of the muscles and
paralysis. Examples are atropine, nicotine, curare, and succinylcholine chloride.

Botulin toxin prevents acetylcholine from being released. It is
probably the most deadly toxin known.

Document Examination

Society runs on paper. From birth to death, every individual accumulates important pieces of paper—a birth certificate, driver's license, marriage license, deeds, checks, mortages (even paper money itself is a kind of document). Think a minute, and you will realize that society as it is today could not function without the vast network of paper that reaches into nearly every aspect of life. Bad checks (forgeries, those issued with insufficient funds, or written with no account or account closed) add greatly to the workload of the document examiner.

Forgery, counterfeiting, and the alteration of documents constitute a major area of crime, simply because there are so many opportunities—and so many temptations. Document analysis seeks to uncover such crimes. It is the province of highly trained specialists skilled in examination of handwriting, printing, paper, and ink—the four basic variables by which the authenticity of documents are usually determined.

This chapter summarizes the important techniques of document analysis as they relate to the study of criminalistics. Particular emphasis is placed upon the examination of handwriting, because the forging of checks and credit cards is a major criminal activity encountered by law enforcement officials everywhere. (See Fig. 11-1) Also considered will be how document examiners evaluate paper ink, and printing in determining a document's authenticity.

Figure 11-1 Comparison of two handwriting samples using CP-6 (Courtesy Unitron Instruments, Woodbury, NY).

Document Analysis—One of the Oldest of the Forensic Sciences

Document analysis figures in the earliest cases of civil and criminal law. Forgeries began to be a legal problem as soon as there were legal documents to be forged, that is, from the beginning of the art of writing itself. Roman law permitted the comparison of a person's normal handwriting with the handwriting on a particular document in question as evidence in court. A Roman handwriting "expert" could testify in court that he had studied samples of the person's handwriting and could swear that a certain specimen was or was not executed by the same person.

In English law, however, such expert testimony regarding a "comparison of hands" was not admissible for hundreds of years. The English believed that the only hard evidence concerning handwriting was that of a witness swearing that he or she had actually seen the person writing the document in question.

This restriction began to soften in the nineteenth century when scientific methods began to be applied to document analysis, especially handwriting. But the courts remained doubtful about expert testimony; sometimes they were willing to accept it in civil cases, but never in criminal cases.

In the United States, a step toward a resolution of the problem was made in 1902 in *University of Illinois v. Spalding* (71 N.H. 163, 51 Atl. 731). The court issued this ruling:

History

> This true rule is, that when a writing in issue is claimed on the one hand and denied upon the other to be the writing of a particular person, any other writing of that person may be admitted in evidence for the mere purpose of comparison with the writing in dispute, whether the latter is susceptible of or supported by direct proof or not; but before any such writing shall be admissible for such purpose, its genuineness must be found as a preliminary fact by the presiding judge, upon clear and undoubted evidence. This involves, indeed, a marked departure from the common law. It does away with the common-law limitation of comparison to standards otherwise in the case . . . . In some states . . . legislation has been deemed essential to bring about such changes; but in others . . . the same result has been accomplished by judicial action.

In 1913, Congress enacted a statute that further encouraged the comparison of handwriting in United States courts and judicial proceedings. It said, in part: "In any proceeding before a court or judicial officer of the United States where the genuineness of the handwriting of any person may be involved, any admitted or proved handwriting of such person shall be competent evidence as a basis for comparison by witnesses, or by the jury, court, or officer conducting such proceeding, to prove or disprove such genuineness."

A little more than ten years later, in 1924, expert testimony pertaining to document examination was explicitly favored by the court in the case of *State v. Gummer* (51 N.D. 445, 200 N.W. 20). "The study of handwriting has become a scientific matter and with modern theories as to individual characteristics as expressed in handwriting and the scientific means for measurement and demonstration that have been devised, the status of handwriting evidence has wholly changed. That being the case, the rules of evidence with respect to handwriting have had to be enlarged accordingly. It is another case of the growth and progress of the law to meet modern requirements."

Since the courts opened the way for professionalism and the development of scientific techniques in document analysis, there have been a number of outstanding cases in which expert testimony has been decisive. An English newspaper, for example, was about to buy the alleged diary of Mussolini for half a million dollars when analysis of the paper on which the diary was written revealed that it was manufactured after Mussolini's death. In a famous kidnapping case, the handwriting on the ransom note was compared with two million public records, and the kidnapper was identified. The ransom notes of Bruno Hauptmann were also instrumental in bringing about his conviction in the Lindberg kidnapping case, when handwriting experts testified that he alone could have written them. (*Note:* The defense brought in its own experts in an attempt to refute the testimony of the prosecution's experts.)

Handwriting Analysis and Comparison

A person's handwriting is dependent upon a combination of coordinated actions involving the brain, the eyes, the arm, fingers, muscles, and nerves. It is affected by a person's mental attitude, emotions, and physical condition at the time it is written. Further, handwriting is affected by the position of the writer—whether one is seated, standing, or writing on one's lap—the speed of writing, etc. Taking all this into consideration, it is obvious why the remark is made that a person never signs his or her name twice in the exact same manner. Any time two signatures are found precisely alike, one has been traced or reproduced by some method.

Handwriting comparison is based upon similarities or differences between the material in question and that of the sample. These similarities and differences may be the ways in which a letter is started or ended, idiosyncracies in capital or small letters and ways in which an individual shapes the letters, how they are placed in relationship to a lined paper, and many other writing characteristics. Microscopes and other magnifying aids are widely used (Fig. 11-2).

How to Obtain Writing Specimens

A sample of a person's handwriting or the way in which he or she ordinarily writes is called a "standard." The importance of standards cannot be overstressed, for herein lies the backbone of the case

Figure 11-2　Examining document under low-power stereoscopic microscope.

and a successful conclusion is almost wholly dependent upon them. Some rules for obtaining standards follow:

1. Always try to have the individual use the same type of writing implement as was used in the questioned document.
2. Never show the individual the questioned document. If necessary, dictate the text to the person.
3. Obtain as many samples or specimens of the subject's normal writing as possible. This will enable one to observe normal variances in handwriting.
4. Attempt to learn of any handwritten application for credit where true samples will be obtained.
5. If handprinting is involved, attempt to obtain printed samples.
6. Offer no suggestions as to spacing, punctuation, spelling, or capitalization.

7. Once a page has been completed, have it removed or give it to another individual so as not to allow the suspect to see his or her style of writing.

8. Ask that suspect sign his or her name or at least initial each page.

9. Witness all specimens by writing your signature or initials on each page.

10. Try to obtain samples of both the right and left hands.

11. Repeat words to see if the subject is consistent in the formation of letters.

12. If the subject's signature is obtained on a license, try to get a verification by someone who knows the signature.

13. Try to be evasive if you are asked how to spell a certain word.

14. Obtain samples at various speeds, both rapid and slow.

If there is no known sample of a person's handwriting, the signature alone will be of assistance. There are many documents that will contain a person's signature, such as all types of licenses (driver's, automobile registration, marriage), bills of sale, invoices, a will, mortgages, application for utilities (telephone, gas, electric), and affidavits and petitions. A good sample is a handwritten letter or application for credit, because the applicant will fill out the entire form. *An investigator can never have too many samples.* As a rule, the comparison is actually done by individual letters, not words.

Handwriting Characteristics

A handwriting expert will examine script for many more characteristics, but Fig. 11-3 gives an indication of some of the techniques for comparison. One must always remember that when people have become crippled, mentally ill, physically ill, or injured, their writing will show some change in its normal style. Such circumstances must be taken into consideration in an examination of a document or signature.

Typewriter Identification

Identification of typewritten material is another area in which the document examiner will be called upon for an expert opinion. As with handwriting, differences and similarities in letter formation, spacing, and alignment play a major role in effecting an identifica-

1. Slant of writing.

book   book   book

2. Manner of formation of capital letters.

a   a   a

3. Upward strokes in the first letter of a word.

door   door

4. The size and shape of the loop in the letters **l, t, f, d, p, g, h,** and **q.** Notice the similarity in the "loop" portion of the **h** letters and also the similarity in the lower portion. Note also that either from the way the pen was held or from a fault within it, one side of the loop part of the letter **h** is not a solid line.

hope   hear

5. Hesitancy in the writing of certain letters where there is a stoppage of the writing implement on the downward stroke.

thrust   starting   bring   shifting

6. Manner of crossing **t**'s.

start   start   start

7. Angle and height of crossing **t**'s.

start   start

8. Separation of letters in a word; ordinarily, it is more pronounced in words containing **t**'s and **i**'s, where it is necessary to cross a **t** or dot an **i**. Note the similarities in the **th** in the following three words: **that, the,** and **therefore.** Notice how the **t** is disjointed from the remainder of the word and how the crossing of the **t** extends through the top of the letter **h.** Also note that the letter **h** contains no upward loop.

that   the   therefore

Figure 11-3 Handwriting characteristics.

9. Variation in ratio between top portion of a letter and that written below the line, as in **f**, **g**, **y**, **z**, and **p**.

10. Closed or open space between upward stroke and circular loop in **d**, **p**, **q**, and **g**.

11. "Hooks" in capital letters that may be found at the start or end of the letter.

12. Open or closed letters, as in **a** or **o**.

13. Words ending in **t**, whether the letter is crossed or terminated with a short, upward stroke.

14. Relationship of dot of the **i** to remainder of letter.

15. Words ending in **s**, where there is a finishing stroke or an abrupt termination. Notice the similarity in the ending **s** in each word.

16. Size or relationship of small letters to capital letters.

17. Ending stroke when words end in **y** or **g**.

tion. In Fig. 11-4 note how the letter **e** is set slightly higher than the letters **m** and **n**. In the same figure, the lower portion of the letter **j** is worn, giving it a distinctive figure.

With any typewriter there could be one or more letters out of

men .j .j

Figure 11-4   Typewriter identification.

alignment, or a letter might have a worn area that would be apparent. Again, it is a matter of identifying a sample (typewritten material from a known typewriter) with the typewritten material in question. The typewritten material in question could be in the form of an extortion letter, kidnapping ransom request, or other typewritten matter of evidentiary matter. The important thing is to recognize the possibility of finding an oddity or idiosyncracy in a typewritten document.

A Note on Fingerprints

Latent fingerprints may be made visible on papers provided the individual has not used gloves or taken other precautions to prevent their being deposited. Iodine fuming, ninhydrin, silver nitrate, the Magna-Brush, or conventional powders may be used to raise them. It is recommended that the techniques be used in this order. If a technique is not successful, it will not interfere with the application of the next one. (Success here depends on the prints being relatively fresh—a matter of hours.) X-ray photography has also been used successfully (see Chap. 3). Once the latent fingerprints appear, they should be photographed, thus establishing a permanent record of the results of the testing.

Principal Methods of Forgery

The study of handwriting and typewriting usually involves forgery of one kind or another. In cases that come to the average law enforcement officials, the most frequent crime is that of forgery of checks or credit cards (the criminal finds or steals the credit card and attempts to use it, faking the signature of the card owner). Generally speaking, there are four kinds of forgery:

1. *Freehand.* The individual tries to imitate a signature or style of writing.

2. *Traced.* A piece of thin paper is placed over a signature in an attempt to follow the lines of the original script.
3. *Transfer of signature.* An attempt is made to remove a signature from one document and place it on another.
4. Reproduction of signature by offset printing, photography, or copying machine.

Technology is constantly making possible new ways of recording, storing, and transmitting information. As these are introduced into wide usage, for example, as in the use of credit cards to transfer money, criminals will think of ways of altering them for their own profit or gain. Computers are now widely used to record deposits and withdrawals to bank accounts and security holdings as well as to make transfers of these from one account to another. Information of a personal nature, e.g. health records, credit ratings, criminal records, etc., is also commonly stored in a computer's memory.

It is not surprising that a new crop of white-collar criminals have sprung up to exploit the computer for their own advantage. What might be surprising is the magnitude of the crimes. Statistics in this area are not easy to come by. Often, these crimes go undetected because there is usually no written record or ledger of figures that is routinely audited. Auditing a computer is much more difficult than auditing a set of ledgers. Furthermore, people tend to blindly accept what the computer printout says. Often it is pure luck that the crime is discovered. (In one case the computer system in a bank failed and the accounts had to be checked manually, leading to the discovery of the fraud.)

Perhaps most important is the fact that the parties involved are often reluctant to prosecute because of the publicity involved. Imagine how embarrassing it would be for a bank to have it known that millions were swindled from its accounts. What would the customers' reaction be?

To repeat, the fact that these thefts occur is not surprising. What may shock the reader is the magnitude of the amounts involved. Some examples will make this clear.

A 1973 study of sixty-four noncomputer-related white-collar crimes committed in 1970 showed an average of $100,000 per crime. Twelve computer-related embezzlements averaged $1 million per incident. It has been estimated that there were more than $200 million involved in computer-related crimes in 1974. There was a case where the manager of the computer facilities for a stockbroker embezzled over $80,000 by having checks made out to fictitious people. In another case an individual illegally sold the names and addresses of a firm's employees to a life insurance company for use as a mailing list.

One clever individual managed to have the roundoff—the fraction of a dollar past the hundredths (or cents) place that is normally kept by the bank—credited to his account. This occurs, for example, in computing interest: $593 at 4.25 percent interest yields an interest of $25.2025. The individual holding the account gets $25.20 and is happy. The thief gets $0.0025 in his account. If 100,000 such transactions occur in a single day (not unreasonable in a large bank), the thief has made $250 and is also happy (he or she will be happier after 100 days).

The blockbuster of these swindles, the largest on record, known as the Equity Funding Scandal, occurred in California. It involved about twenty-two people, working together over a period of about ten years, making up fake insurance policies. They were indicted in 1973 on 105 counts. They swindled more than $2 billion.

The foregoing examples illustrate a type of crime not traditionally handled by a document examiner but which nevertheless does involve the alteration of "documents" produced by twentieth-century technology.

Rules for Handling Document Evidence

Because the qualified examiner will apply a sophisticated arsenal of chemical and physical techniques to determine the authenticity of the document, it is very important that the law enforcement officer take utmost care in its handling. Here are five suggestions for the proper method of handling all documents that may appear as evidence in court:

1. Place the document in a transparent plastic envelope. Do not unfold the document; leave it in its original condition.
2. Handle as little as possible and only by tweezers. (This is necessary to protect latent fingerprints for examination.)
3. If possible, have a photograph taken of the original document. Use a white ruler with black markings, along with the initials of the individual who found the evidence, date, and place of finding of evidence. This information must not be placed on document but on an identification slip.
4. Never use a wet-process copier when reproducing a document. If there is a malfunction of the equipment, it may destroy, wrinkle, or stain the original document.

5. Remember that the document examiner will always want to work with the original document, for photographs or photostats will not ordinarily reveal tracing or other alterations.

Questions Confronting the Document Examiner

In order to be familiar with how the examiner approaches each paper given for analysis, it is well for the student to keep in mind the kind of questions that the examiner may be called upon to answer in the course of investigating a document:

1. What is the age of the ink?
2. Were two documents written with the same ink?
3. Was all the writing on a document written with the same ink?
4. Was the signature written on the document on the original date, or was it placed there subsequently?
5. Are folds in the document recent, or do they date back to the origin of the document?
6. What is the approximate age of the document?
7. Is a watermark identifiable or present; if so, does the date of the document coincide with the date of manufacture of the paper?
8. Did the suicide victim write the suicide note?
9. Is the signature or writing on the document genuine or a forgery?
10. Were any erasures made on the original document?
11. Was any writing removed by bleaching with chemicals?
12. Is printing or stamping on the document genuine? (Many documents have seals and rubber stamps to authenticate them.)
13. When a document has been torn apart, did the pieces come from the original document?
14. What was the writing on a burned paper document?

The examiner will also look for erasures or alteration of figures; (that is, a check for $1 changed to $100); changing the number one to a nine, four, seven, or six; nine to a ninety; four to a forty. Other points to look for in a questioned document include:

1. Words or phrases squeezed in an area

2. Different colors of ink
3. Spelling errors
4. Uncommon phrases
5. Inconsistency or variation in size of letters, numbers, or words
6. Noticeable discrepancies in signatures

Role of Photography in Document Analysis

Seldom do document examiners testify or present evidence in court without supporting photographic exhibits. By using enlargements they can explain similarities between exhibits while pointing to specifics. They can make copies in whatever sizes desired. They can utilize individual letters from a handwriting specimen to form a word for comparison purposes with the questioned document. This was done in the Lindbergh kidnapping case where photographs of handwriting samples were pieced together to reproduce some of the extortion notes.

Photographic enlargements may reveal erasures or other altered writings. Erasure marks may be brought out by holding the document in front of a bright light. Polarized light may cause the remaining graphite from a pencil erasure to appear black, thus exposing the erasure. Photographing the document using infrared-sensitive film (see Chap. 8) may reveal that an erasure has occurred. This technique has been used successfully to show "overwriting" that has occurred. (Overwriting is the attempt to obliterate writing by writing over it with some dark material.) This is shown in Figs. 8-6, 11-5, and 11-6. The success of the technique depends on the upper ink being transparent to infrared while the lower must be relatively opaque. It is difficult to predict which inks will or will not be opaque.

If it is suspected that writing has been erased, an infrared picture should be taken. Some of the original writing material may be left behind; it will be an infrared absorber and will therefore appear as a dark area on the print. The technique has been used to bring out faded or aged writing and even to read material on letters in sealed envelopes.

Photography with ultraviolet light has been successful where an ink eradicator was employed, or where invisible writing was used, to reveal the alteration or make the writing visible. This technique may also be successful in cases where tickets, money, or other material have been counterfeited or where art works have been al-

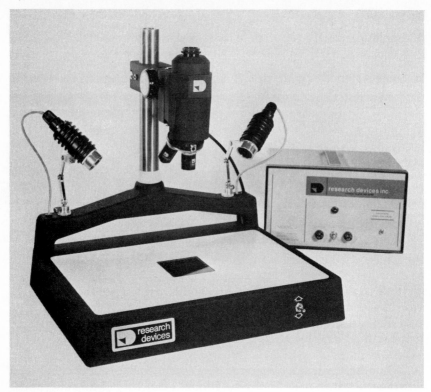

Figure 11-5 Infrared microscope (Courtesy Research Devices, Inc., Berkeley Heights, NJ).

tered. In each case one looks for a difference in fluorescence between the rest of the material and the questionable area.

Charred Documents

Charred documents may prove of value, if they are properly handled. They can be examined by infrared photography, for example, and the writing will sometimes become legible. It is most important, however, that extreme care be taken with them.

The Federal Bureau of Investigation's laboratory in Washington, D.C., will examine charred pieces of documents if they are transmitted properly. One suggestion is to place a layer of cotton in the bottom of a rigid corrugated box. Next, a layer of tissue paper should be placed on the cotton. A second layer of tissue paper should be placed over evidence (charred paper) and another layer of cotton used to fill the box. The top layer of cotton is to prevent movement

Figure 11-6 *Left:* photograph of seemingly genuine lottery ticket; *right:* infrared photograph of same lottery ticket (Courtesy Research Devices, Inc., Berkeley Heights, NJ).

and destruction of the charred paper. The carton should be marked fragile. The utmost care must be taken in packaging, as the entire examination will be contingent upon the condition of the evidence when received by the laboratory.

Charred paper may be treated for several days in a wet moisture chamber. This process should return moisture to the paper, giving it body for handling. Once the fragments have a body and have lost their brittleness, they may be placed between two pieces of glass for examination and photographing. If the paper has been subjected to complete combustion, it will be impossible to develop any writing from the minute ash fragments. Another method is to spray the charred fragments with a lacquer diluted with thinner by means of a fine atomizer similar to the type used by women for perfume. Some recommend placing the charred paper in contact with the emulsion side of film for several days. The fogging of the negative may reveal the printed or written matter, when developed in the normal manner.

In general, in dealing with material as damaged as charred or water-soaked paper, it is advisable to handle it as little as possible and to call in the services of an experienced document examiner to process it.

The Royal Canadian Mounted Police use a technique which involves heating the document in an oven fitted with a quartz window. In some cases the writing becomes visible and can be photographed. (See Fig. 11-7.)

Research done in their laboratories has produced some useful results, particularly with relatively flat documents that can be sep-

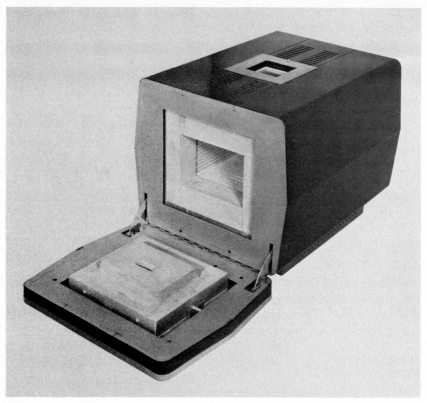

Figure 11-7 5100 series muffle furnace (Courtesy Lindberg Division of Sola-Basic Industries, Watertown, WI).

arated into separate sheets without the use of special solutions.[1] The effects of burning are summarized below.

The Effects of Burning

Stage 1 At 200°F (approximately) the paper turns *brown*. This colour darkens as the temperature rises but the writing remains legible.

Stage 2 At 550°F (approximately) the paper turns *black* and the writing is generally invisible. In some cases it may be read by oblique illumination, at an almost horizontal inclination, but generally the lack of translu-

[1] Albert Bartha and Eric Schroeder, *Charred Documents—Their Preservation and Decipherment*, Document Section, Centre of Forensic Sciences, 25 Grosvenor Street, Toronto, Ontario, Canada.

cence and contrast renders any attempts at decipherment unfruitful. The shrinkage is noticeable.

Loss of Fluorescence: At this stage papers which fluoresced under Ultra-Violet radiation began to lose this property.

Stage 3 At approximately 650°F the paper is reduced to a dark *grey ash,* which gradually lightens. It shrinks and curls even more and any careless touch or the slightest movement of the air will cause it to break up into a mass of dust.

Legibility: Shortly after this stage, the writing becomes legible again. It appears white in colour, the paper being now a blackish-grey ash, much reduced in size.

Stage 4 At 750°F (approximately) the grey ash turns slowly into a *cream-white ash,* with a further reduction in size to about a quarter of the original. Though its thickness was not measured the paper also appeared to be considerably thinner.

Legibility: The writing is clearly legible at this stage. Its white colour has now changed to dark brown, reddish-brown or black, depending on the composition of the ink. Since the background has changed to cream-white the clarity and crispness of the writing is enhanced. It may be photographed with emulsions used routinely in document work, and enlarged to the original size of the document.

Further burning up to 1200°F causes the paper to crumble and renders restoration of the writing impossible.

When the papers are burnt in an open flame, all these stages follow hard on each other. Each portion of the paper will burn at its own rate, depending on the supply of oxygen available at that point.

Results with specific writing materials will vary from this depending on their particular composition.

The Examination of Ink

Ink is difficult to analyze. Of two ink samples, the examiner can ascertain with much greater certainty that they are not alike than that they are. This unsatisfactory situation arises from the nature of the materials in inks and the way they are manufactured. The principle modern inks are:

1. Ball-point ink—originally olein base with oil and soluble dye but now usually polyethylene glycol formulations containing certain soluble synthetic dyes and/or insoluble pigments. Dyes constitute about 45 percent of the ink. The rest is mainly solvent plus additives that give the ink its characteristic properties.
2. Iron inks—contain iron salts plus some dye material and gallic and tannic acids.
3. Dyestuff ink—many blue and all colored inks, usually marked nonpermanent. They contain synthetic (analine) dyes (about 1 percent), gum arabic, polyethylene, glycols, hydrochloric or sulfuric acid.
4. Carbon black ink (India ink)—the coloring material here is an aqueous dispersion of carbon in gum arabic.

These inks may be examined by a number of chemical and physical tests such as (1) observation with magnifying glass or microscope, (2) separation of components by means of thin-layer chromatography (Fig. 11-8) or electrophoresis, (3) ultraviolet and/or infrared photography, and (4) analysis of reflectance spectrum. In particular, see the case of the Vinland map in Chap. 15.

Ball-Points

Ball-point pen writing presents a particularly difficult problem. This type of writing instrument tends to introduce many irregular-

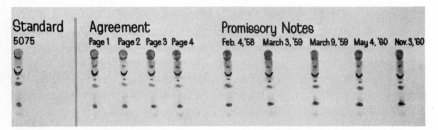

Figure 11-8 Detail of a chart of thin-layer chromatograms presented in court as evidence in a perjury trial [*U.S. v. Sloan,* Memphis, TN (1970)]. These were made using the ink in a four-page agreement dated 1958 and in a series of promissory notes dated as in the figure, all introduced by Sloan in his defense. Because the chromatograms were similar, it was concluded that the identical ink was used in all the writings. Matching of these with a chromatogram in the library of the Bureau of Alcohol, Tobacco, and Firearms showed that all had been written *after 1960,* since that was the date this ink formulation was first produced. A conviction resulted.

ities in the writing, making detection of the writer's own nuances much more difficult than with fountain pen writing. Dating of the ink and writing is also more difficult. (It should be remembered that ball-point pens were first marketed in 1945.) There may be millions of pens manufactured with the same formula of ink. No success seems to have been attained in dating the age of ball-point inks except by comparison with thin-layer chromatograms in the reference library (over 3000 inks) of the Bureau of Alcohol, Tobacco, and Firearms. It has been suggested that manufacturers tag their inks with an easily identifiable dye which would be changed annually, thus enabling writings to be dated.

Iron Inks

As a result of the nature of their chemical components, the iron-type inks do undergo progressive color changes which can be used as a crude indication of their age. However, their aging depends quite critically on the environment in which they were stored (humidity, exposure to light, heat, whether the ink in the bottle was already aged, etc.).

Neither the carbon or analine inks change with age and therefore are difficult to date.

The Examination of Paper

Paper made its first appearance in Europe during the eleventh century. The first paper mill appeared in England around 1490. The watermarks in paper are said to have originated in Italy near the end of the thirteenth century. A watermark is a latent mark or design, embedded in the paper during the processing. It is the way the manufacturer identifies the product. Many times it is visible by merely placing a sheet of paper up to a light source. Unfortunately, not all papers contain watermarks. Its importance can be easily understood by the following incident.

In an income tax evasion case involving hundreds of thousands of dollars, a businessman produced worksheets allegedly used to prepare his 1962 income tax return. The FBI document analysis section revealed a watermark that was not used until 1971 by the manufacturer of the paper. This proved that the taxpayer had never made out work papers to prepare his return during 1962.

Paper may also be checked for purposes of comparison and

identification with respect to chemical composition, size, weight, and composition of fillers and sizing used.

Paper is composed of various substances, for example, cellulose obtained from vegetable fibers and at one time from old cloth or rags. Some expensive papers are made from linen and cotton, while others are made from vegetable filbers, a filler, and a sizing such as starch, casein, and presently fluorocarbon. Very special paper is used in the making of United States currency, which is why counterfeit money is rarely undetected.

Some of the more obvious characteristics that may be observed by one examining counterfeit paper money are listed for your benefit.

1. The identical set of serial numbers appearing on different bills
2. Color of the green ink
3. Failure of paper to contain tiny red and dark blue threads
4. The feel of paper money (there is a distinctive feel of authentic paper money that is difficult to imitate)
5. Quality of engraving of face and lines around the edges of paper money

Generally speaking, the recognition of counterfeit money is not a police function. However, the possibility exists of an investigator finding it during a legal search of premises or possibly a vehicle in the course of an investigation. The crimes of possession of counterfeit money and the making of such are a violation of the federal statutes and come under the jurisdiction of the United States Secret Service. (See Fig. 11-9.) Counterfeiting is known to flourish when the

Figure 11-9 Counterfeiting paraphernalia seized by the Westchester County Sheriff's Office: plates, engraving tool, bogus bills.

economy is at a low and was prevalent during the Depression of the 1930s.

This chapter should make clear the large scope of cases in which the services of a document examiner may be required. As with a fingerprint or ballistics expert, the training is unique and specialized. It requires a knowledge of many aspects of technology whose number grows as new methods of writing and reproduction are developed.

Arson

According to the National Fire Protection Association, 12,000 people die annually in the United States as a result of approximately 3 million fires. About 57 percent of the deaths occur in residential fires. Property loss is estimated at $4 billion annually. Statistics for 1975 disclose that fires due to arson accounted for about $634 million. If half the fires listed as due to an undetermined cause were included, the total cost for the year would be more than $1.2 billion.

Arson, the deliberate burning of property for malicious or fraudulent purposes, confronts the police investigator with circumstances quite different from those of other crimes. Arson is a crime that often is not even suspected until long after it has been committed. The arsonist has plenty of time to flee the scene and prepare an alibi. Arson is a crime in which much of and sometimes all the best evidence is likely to go up in the blaze, leaving the investigator with little to work with. Arson is a crime in which the criminal may have no record of past crimes. In fact, he or she may be a "respectable" businessperson who, suffering business reverses, burns down a house or factory to defraud an insurance company or destroy records that an audit might find damaging.

This chapter outlines the police investigator's role in cases of suspected arson. Usually, the investigator is not alone in arson cases. He or she works with the fire department, the fire marshall, the crime laboratory, and fire underwriter investigators from insurance companies, who bring special experience and expertise to the job of determining what and who started a fire (especially when there are large insurance claims involved).

The Investigation

Is This Fire of Suspicious Origin?

First on the scene, firefighters are almost always the ones who point to the possibility of arson. Routinely, they report their suspicions to the police. In the first stages of the investigation, they work closely with police investigators in gathering the evidence needed to prove that a given fire was criminally started.

There are countless clues that might arouse a suspicion of arson. Among the most frequently encountered are:

No readily observed cause (most accidental fires present a clear-cut origin)
Telltale odors of flammable fluids (such as gasoline)
Sprinkler system or extinguishers rendered inoperable
More than one place of origin
Empty cans or jugs with the odor of gasoline
Water shut off
Fire hoses cut
Electrical fuses missing
Evidence of forced entry
Remnants of trailers (strips of cloth or paper used to spread fire)
Holes cut in walls or ceiling
Suspicious attitude of building's owner or occupants
Absence of valuable materials that would normally be in the building (a warehouse, for instance, with little stock; a store without merchandise; a house without much furniture)
Account books near origin of fire (with the obvious purpose of destroying them)
Coverings over windows and doors
A broken bottle, possible remains of a Molotov cocktail, that incendiary bomb made by filling a bottle with gasoline and using a cloth or string as a wick (The wick is lighted, and the bottle thrown. When the bottle breaks on impact, the gasoline explodes, spreading flames in all directions.)

Color of Flame

Eyewitnesses to a fire can often provide clues to the possibility of arson. Short of a witness seeing the arsonist in the act of setting the fire or leaving the building, an eyewitness description of the blaze may prove extremely helpful. Much can be determined, for instance, by the color of the flames. Here's a tabulation from the Chicago Fire Department:

Combustible	Color of Smoke	Color of Flame
Wood	Gray to brown	Yellow to red
Paper	Gray to brown	Yellow to red
Cloth	Gray to brown	Yellow to red
Gasoline	Black	Yellow to white
Naphtha	Brown to black	Straw to white
Benzine	White to gray	Yellow to white
Lubricating oil	Black	Yellow to white
Lacquer thinner	Brownish black	Yellow to red
Turpentine	Black to brown	Yellow to white
Acetone	Black	Blue
Cooking oil	Brown	Yellow
Kerosene	Black	Yellow

The color of smoke becomes darker with the presence of more hydrocarbons (gasoline, oil, etc). The color also varies from red to yellow to white (colorless) with an increase in temperature.

What Kind of Fire?

Firefighters classify all fires by the nature of the combustible material. There are five categories:

Class A Fires. Wood, rags, paper—the most common materials are the base of the most common fires.

Class B Fires. Liquid hydrocarbons in many forms—primarily petroleum products—make up the combustible material in this category.

Class C Fires. Electric equipment, conduits, transformers, appliances, and motors are the source of these fires.

Class D Fires. Magnesium, potassium, zinc, and other combustible metals, which are usually found in large industrial plants, made up this category.

Class E Fires. These involve radioactive materials.

Accidental Fires

Many—in fact, most—fires are not of an incendiary nature. They happen by accident. Here is a list of the most common causes of accidental fires:

Faulty wiring
Overloaded electrical outlet with numerous extensions
Children playing with matches
Children turning on gas stoves
Gas or electric stove left burning for long time
Cleaning fluid ignited by carelessness
Smoking in bed

For the Record

The police investigator should always obtain copies of the fire department's record of the fire. Should the case eventually come to court, these will be needed to establish the fact that a fire did occur. These are the pertinent facts:

Date of fire
Time of fire department notification
Name of person who notified
Address of property burned
Type of structure (dwelling, factory, warehouse, etc.)
Owner of building
Insurance company
Assessment of damage

The Fire's Origin

Much of the investigation will concentrate on answering the question, Where and how did the fire start? This question should be answered as soon as possible.

There is no direct or simple way to determine a fire's origin. Generally, fire spreads in an upward direction, so it is wise to start the search on the lowest level at which there is evidence of a fire. Often, the place where the fire started reveals itself in the depth of the charring of thick wooden beams. Sometimes, the smell of gasoline or kerosene lingers in the air, which is a good indication of arson and of the place of its origin.

Of course, inflammable liquids are volatile and are often completely consumed in the blaze. However, it is always possible for such liquids to soak into a surface and still be detectable after the blaze has been extinguished. Water from fire hoses tends to preserve volatile liquids, slowing down the time of evaporation so that there may be evidence of their use long after a fire has been put out.

Testing for Flammables

Any evidence suspected of being saturated with flammable liquids should be placed in an airtight container, such as a mason jar. The jar should be marked for identification with the initials of the person placing the evidence therein. Also, the date, time, location of burned premises, specific place where evidence was found, and the case number should be noted. *Remember:* Always get a receipt from the crime laboratory when turning over such material.

Gas Chromatograph

Since most crimes of arson employ gasoline, kerosene, or paint thinner (also found are rubbing alcohol, charcoal lighter fluids, naphtha, etc.), the gas chromatograph is the instrument most widely used on arson evidence in the crime laboratory. The gas chromatograph separates the hydrocarbon components of a wide range of petroleum products into distinctive patterns, characteristic of each.

In the laboratory, the evidence is placed in a sealed glass bottle. When heated, volatile residues in the evidence are driven off and trapped. The vapor is removed and placed into the gas chromatograph, where the separation takes place. The patterns reflected by the chromatograph are then compared with the known patterns of a whole series of petroleum products, and a sure identification is made (Fig. 12-1). The gas chromatograph is extremely sensitive and can detect infinitesimal residues of hydrocarbons. Thus, it is useful in determining arson cases in which investigation of the origin of the fire may have been delayed. As we have seen, the problem in testing for hydrocarbons is that they are volatile and evaporate quickly. It has been possible to detect accelerants that soaked into material such as wood even weeks after the fire. (A hint to the investigator: The chances for a successful laboratory analysis of such material are greatly enhanced if porous materials such as wood, drapery, and carpeting, rather than nonporous material like glass or ceramics, are submitted.)

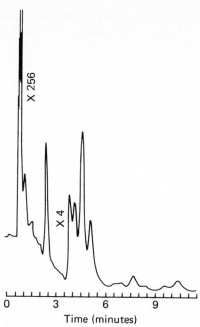

Figure 12-1 Gas chromatograph of distillation vapors from soil recovered at fire site; shows presence of gasoline. The time at which various peaks are recorded, as well as their relative heights, is used to identify the substance (Courtesy Varian Associates, Palo Alto, CA).

Other Tests

Infrared spectrophotometers are also used in the crime laboratory for identifying unknown liquids used as accelerants in cases of arson. Sometimes, however, quick tests can be easily done by investigators with only a limited knowledge of laboratory techniques.

TEST 1 Any object suspected of containing a flammable substance may be heated in water to a temperature of 70°C. When the container is opened, it is often possible to determine the type of flammable material by its odor.

TEST 2 A suspected substance may be broken into pieces and put into a distillation flask with a little water. The flask is then heated so that the material inside is distilled. The fractions passing off may be roughly identified by odor—gasoline being among the more volatile will come first, then kerosene a few fractions further on.

Photography

The scene of the incendiary fire should be completely photographed, with an overall shot of the building and the surrounding area. If possible, try to show the building's location by including a street sign or a neighboring building in the picture. If your department has a police photographer, he or she will be most helpful. Should no photographer be available, an inexpensive camera, such as an Instamatic, will serve the purpose. *Remember:* Fire generally results in charred wood, black ashes, and dark debris, all of which require a fairly good light. Use a flash for catching important details, especially in close-ups. Color photographs are especially useful not only in showing the results of a fire but in recording the actual color of the flames.

Each area of the building or fire should be photographed, with close-ups of all possible evidence and the suspected point of origin. Do not crop borders of the negative. Reproduce the entire negative. This is the court-accepted procedure for presentation of photographs. It is also suggested that no identifying plates showing department, date, location, or the like be used in the photograph. All negatives must be kept in a secure place until the time of the trial. They should be accessible to authorized personnel only. Under today's disclosure rules, a defense attorney is entitled to view all photographs. There have been cases where photographs of the spectators have led to the identification of the arsonist who appeared in several of the pictures.

Photographs will be a supplement to your notes and, after a period of a year or two, will refresh your memory of the circumstances of the fire.

The Detailed Search

Concerted effort should be made to search for evidence at the fire's point of origin. This can at times be determined by a high concentration of burning ashes and debris in one area. If such is not possible, the questioning of witnesses may reveal the fire's origin. After this point has been looked into and after the photography has been done, a thorough investigation of the arson scene is necessary.

One good place to start is a search for tool marks, indicating that a door or window was forced open to gain entry. If the building is completely consumed, the metal area around the lock and the door jamb should be examined for markings. As with any type of evidence, a photograph should be taken showing the location.

Trash areas should always be examined for containers of flammable fluids. The container should be handled carefully and dusted for latent fingerprints. The can should be immediately sealed to prevent evaporation of any remaining liquid, as well as for security reasons (such fumes are easily ignited).

Special attention should be given to light fixtures which have a broken bulb but with the remains of the screw base visible in the socket. An electric bulb left burning will produce a temperature varying from 200 to 500°F [93.8 to 260°C] depending upon the wattage. The bulb may be covered with cloth or paper, which will ignite with sufficient heat. Generally, trailers are used to direct the fire to a specific area. This type of ignition gives the arsonist sufficient time to be out of the area when the fire begins to rage.

A sure indication of arson is when investigators discover streamers joining one area to another in an attempt to envelope an entire building. In some cases accelerants (excelsior, flammable plastics, rags, or papers saturated with volatile liquids) are found between building studs, between ceiling beams, or in holes in walls or ceiling. A photograph of such circumstances will readily point to the arson attempt (Fig. 12-2).

Figure 12-2   Paper and wood were set afire after being soaked in an accelerant. The point of fire is about 8 inches from the ground (Courtesy Putnam Valley, New York, Fire Department, Mike Lane).

Motive for Arson

Arson is often called the white-collar crime. It is frequently committed by people who have no criminal record, by so-called respectable businesspeople, by loners who are withdrawn but usually pleasant and unaggressive in their social behavior, by adolescent dreamers who start a fire and then act out their hero fantasies by discovering it and ringing the fire alarm.

In the investigation of most crimes, motive is not usually an important consideration. When a burglary takes place, for instance, the motive is clear enough. Throughout this book, in looking at the criminalistic side of law enforcement, the motive of the suspect receives little attention. But arson is a different matter—not so much when the case comes to court as in pinpointing suspects. In arson, the search for a motive is an essential part of the investigation. Why would people burn down their own property—or that of others? This question is foremost on the mind of the arson investigator.

There is some truth to the often-repeated observation that the incidence of arson is an accurate barometer of the national economy. In bad times, when businesses are in danger of failing, arson cases rise in number in a readily observable pattern. In times of prosperity, arson drops off. This phenomenon was first observed in the Great Depression of the 1930s, when among certain marginal businesses arson became almost epidemic. Nowadays investigators routinely check financial status and insurance claims of businesses involved in fires of any kind; often their findings are the first leads to arson.

A well-known, and perhaps not untypical, case is that of the manufacturer who claimed the loss of thousands of dollars worth of coats and suits in a factory fire. Investigators determined that the buttons used in his products were fireproof. And yet they found *not one button* among the factory's charred ruins. Obviously, the manufacturer was guilty of fraud—and probably of arson, too (though of course that would have to be proved by hard evidence).

Here is a list—partial, to be sure—of the possible motives for arson. They should be kept constantly in mind as the investigation proceeds:

To defraud an insurance company.
To remove business competition.
To get revenge (on the part of a disgruntled employee, a rejected lover, the loser in a dispute or fight).
To get a thrill (arson is often an act of pure vandalism, usually done by teenagers high on drugs or alcohol).

To destroy business records (before auditors discover damaging discrepancies for tax evasion of financial manipulation).

To satisfy a psychotic need. Pyromaniacs cannot suppress impulses to start a blaze and see the flames, smoke, and excitement they created by their own actions.

In other words, the motives of arson range the gamut of human weaknesses, from cold greed to fevered madness. It should be noted, too, that arson can be part of a well-considered *modus operandi* of organized crime. Arson gangs operate in some areas—for fees paid by clients for whom a big fire would relieve financial difficulties by insurance fraud, the destruction of damaging accounting records, or the elimination of a competitor. Arson gangs also engage in "protection" rackets in which a fire is the ultimate penalty for nonpayment.

Deception Detectors

Devices to detect deception are a well-established part of criminal investigation and law enforcement. They are also widely used in many nonforensic areas—in routine preemployment examinations and private investigations by industries, for instance.

The best known and most widely used detection device is the polygraph, popularly known as the lie detector. Two other detection devices in use today are the Mark II Voice Analyzer and the Dektor Psychological Stress Evaluator. In this chapter, we will discuss these three devices.

The polygraph warrants more detailed study, because it has been in use longer than the others and because it is currently the detection device of choice in most law enforcement agencies. The results of a polygraph may be admissible in court in cases where the defendant, prosecuting official, and defense attorney all agree to its use (stipulation). In the absence of such unanimous agreement, polygraph evidence is generally not admissible. However, the results of polygraph examinations may have value in investigations regardless of their role in court. Often, the polygraph helps an innocent suspect corroborate his or her testimony, for instance. Not infrequently a guilty suspect confesses when confronted with a polygraph examination because of the psychological pressures arising from the suspect's realization that his or her lies will be revealed.

How the Polygraph Works

Contrary to popular opinion, the lie detector is not a simple box that rings a bell when a person lies and flashes green when she or he tells the truth. It is not that simple or clear-cut. The polygraph is an instrument that records changes in respiration, blood pressure, pulse, and the skin's sensitivity to electricity. When a person lies, fear of detection may affect his or her nervous system, giving rise to uncontrollable physiological reactions which the polygraph indicates by lines on a moving paper chart. The chart is then examined and interpreted by a trained examiner. (See Fig. 13-2.)

The Role of the Examiner

It is obvious that a polygraph examination is only as good as the examiner. The role of the examiner is crucial. He or she prepares the questions, administers the test, and analyzes the printed results. It requires a thoroughly trained professional. It cannot be left to someone who has merely learned the techniques of applying the polygraph sensors and running the machine. The instrument merely records physiological responses. It is the examiner who decides whether these indicate that the subject was or was not lying.

The Examiner's Qualifications

The standards of education and experience for professional polygraph examiners have been set forth by authorities in the field. All persons wishing to qualify as polygraph examiners should:

1. Possess a college degree.
2. Spend at least a 6-month internship under an experienced and competent examiner with a high volume of case work.
3. Have at least 5 years' experience as a specialist in polygraph examinations.
4. Be able to serve as a competent witness in court in all matters related to polygraph records and produce such records for cross-examination purposes.
5. Have a stable personality, the ability to deal with persons in sensitive situations, and a basic understanding of human nature.

The Polygraph in Police Work

The polygraph is not meant to replace good police investigation. Finding a witness who saw the crime committed and gathering hard evidence are the basis of sound investigative practice. Often, when all other means have failed, the polygraph examiner is expected to perform the miracle of solving the case by testing a suspect. This rarely happens. A complete investigation must be conducted before the polygraph examination is administered.

Investigating officers must give the polygraph examiner a complete history of the case, including every minute detail. This does not mean merely suspicions but detailed, verified facts.

For example, if the case is a murder, the examiner must know what weapon was used, the location of wounds, where the body was found, if money or jewelry was taken from the victim, and the exact or approximate time of death.

If the crime was a robbery, the examiner must know the exact amount of money taken, denomination of bills, location of money, and any other missing articles. He or she must be informed of any strange or obscene act at the crime scene and must be told of any fact that will connect the suspect with the crime. The examiner should be given a copy of any laboratory tests of blood, ballistics, hair, fingerprints, etc. The foregoing examples are by no means complete and are merely representative of the type of information that the polygraph examiner must be given. If a suspect has an alibi, it should be verified before he or she is subjected to a polygraph test. If more than one investigator worked on the case, the examiner should be given each individual's report and be given an opportunity to discuss the case with each investigator.

Conducting the Polygraph Examination

Whenever there is the possibility of using a polygraph during an investigation, it is absolutely essential that all pertinent facts regarding the crime or incident be omitted during questioning by investigators. In other words, the suspect should not be told what the police know regarding the crime. Discussion or questioning of a suspect regarding a specific fact would preclude it from being used as a vital question during a polygraph test. Generally, better results are obtained when the individual has been subjected to a limited amount of questioning before a polygraph test.

Those Not Qualified for Polygraph

Polygraph examiners have determined that many individuals should not be examined because of certain mental or physical conditions. It is strongly recommended that the following not be subjected to testing:

The demented or abnormal
The emotionally upset
A person with a heart condition (should not subjected to undue stress because of possibility of heart attack)
An individual who has been incarcerated a long time (tends to be hardened and unresponsive when tested)
A person who is hungry or thirsty

Figure 13-1 Polygraph examination session (Courtesy Lafayette Instrument Co., Indianapolis, IN).

A person under medication or drugs (narcotics)

A child under the age of reason

An overtired individual

An intoxicated person

A person with a cold, sneezing, coughing, or stuffy nose

A psychopathic liar

An individual with emphysema (irregular respiration would be more pronounced under tension)

Test Environment

A polygraph examination should be conducted in a quiet room, having neither telephone or intercom. It is suggested that the room be windowless with no clock, pictures, paintings, or ornaments that could cause distraction. The room should be thermostatically controlled for comfort. It should be free from outside noises—typewriters, telephones, street sounds. Some recommend a hidden microphone so that the interview or questioning may be listened to by others or recorded. (*Note:* Such devices for eavesdropping are subject to state laws. Use of them may make polygraph results or any evidence obtained as a result of eavesdropping inadmissible in court.) A one-way mirror may be placed in the room so that a third person can observe the interview and refute statements of abuse of the suspect or possibly sexual advances. A one-way mirror will also permit students to witness testing.

Pretest Interview

A pretest interview should take place before the actual polygraph test is given. It is at this interview that an examiner is able to make many important observations regarding the subject. Particular attention should be given to any outward signs reflecting emotions, such as coughing, sniffing, swallowing, wetting lips, twitching, movement of body, readjustment in a chair, movement of feet, etc. The examiner should make notes of any such reactions. Generally, if a subject displays these reactions during the actual examination and not at the interview, it is an attempt to distort the readings. On the other hand, if the subject reacts in the same manner during the pretest interview, it could be his or her normal manner.

Subjects should be told of their rights and given the now familiar Miranda warning. The purpose of the examination should be carefully explained. The examiner should assure the individual that the polygraph will affirm the truth of an innocent individual and at the same time detect deception. Also, it is a good policy to assure subjects that they will be questioned solely regarding the incident or crime in question and nothing else. There should be no attempt to determine an individual's deception or truthfulness at this interview. Generally, an innocent individual will display anxiety to get the testing completed.

It is a common policy to ask if the subject has ever taken a polygraph examination. This alerts the examiner and enables him or her to contact the former examiner and learn the subject's reactions to testing, if that seems desirable.

A great deal of attention should be focused on the subject's comfort. Ask the subject if the room temperature is satisfactory and whether he or she is thirsty or wants to use the toilet facilities.

To put the subject at ease, she or he should be assured that the voltage of the instrument is very low and absolutely harmless. It is natural for a person to be concerned about being connected to an electrical device.

The interview should not be a prolonged affair. There should be a limited amount of questioning. Many times at this stage of the pretest interview, the subject will admit guilt or at least give honest answers.

Administering the Test

Once the pretest interview is complete, the subject should be seated in the chair adjacent to the polygraph. The pressure cuff should be affixed to the arm or wrist and the special type of rubber tube should be placed around the chest or waist. A pair of sensors are attached to the finger or hand to record the GSR, galvanic skin reflex. (See figs. 13-1 and 13-3.) Sample tracings should be made before and after testing to obtain and observe the subject's norm. The Miranda warning may be repeated at this time. Also needed is a consent form signed by the subject giving permission for the test. *An individual should never be forced to take a polygraph test.* The subject should be told what questions are going to be asked. However, during the interview itself, the order of questions may be changed. Some questions will be asked more than once. The examiner should inform the subject that the test will be repeated—possibly as many as four times.

The examiner should use a moderate tone during the questioning. The questions should be brief. Should a long question be necessary, its meaning must be clearly understood. All questions must be specific and unambiguous. Simple words should be used that are familiar to subject. Generally ten to twelve questions constitute the average test, with an approximate 15-second interval between questions. Extreme care must be used in formulating questions. It often happens that the subject is involved in the crime but not in the way the examiner thinks. The number of the question must be placed on the moving response chart when it is asked along with a *plus* or *minus* sign to indicate an answer of yes or no. The plus or minus sign must be recorded the instant the actual answer is given. There should be no surprise questions.

Remember: Any questions may be repeated three or four times so that consistent reactions may be observed.

"Peak of Tension" Question

Some examiners use a "peak of tension" question which may be a particular fact about the crime—specific amount of money, exact

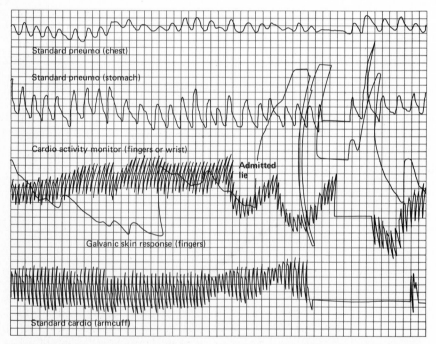

Figure 13-2 Polygraph tape. The lines record the responses from the various parts of the body where the polygraph belts have been attached to the subject. Standard pneumos (top two lines) record the responses from the chest and stomach area. Cardio activity monitor is attached to either the fingers or the wrist. Galvanic skin response (GSR) is from the fingers. Standard cardio shows the response recorded from the armcuff (Courtesy Stoelting Co., Chicago, IL).

time, type of weapon used, type of item stolen, or some detail that will be known to only the suspect. When this method of questioning is used, the subject is told the questions and their order. This is to cause apprehension on his or her part in anticipation of the one specific peak-of-tension question whereby his or her reaction will be reflected on the chart. For example, in a case where the murder weapon is known only to the investigators and presumably to the perpetrator to be a knife, five out of a total of ten to twelve questions might be:

1. Was the murder weapon a gun?
2. Was the murder weapon a hammer?
3. Was the murder weapon a hatchet?
4. Was the murder weapon a knife?
5. Was the murder weapon a car?

Card Test

There are polygraph examiners who recommend the use of what is called a "card test." Several cards are used, each containing a different number. The subject is told to pick one without showing the card to the examiner and then to replace it with the others. The subject is told to answer no when shown each card at an interval of approximately 15 seconds. In other words, the subject is being forced to give a deceptive answer. The test should be administered twice for verification or consistency of the deceptive answer to the chosen card. By this method the examiner is able to determine if subject can be tested and also what reaction is recorded at the time of deception. As with all testing, the number of the question is recorded (which in this case is the actual number on the card), and at the instant of reply a negative sign is placed on the moving chart. The purpose of this test is to establish a norm for the examiner to use.

Irrelevant-Relevant–Type Questions

A third method that can be used in questioning utilizes irrelevant questions. An irrelevant question is one not connected to the crime or incident and one which the subject will answer truthfully. For example, in the case of a murder committed with a knife, the questions might be (Note: 1, 2, 3 are irrelevant, 4 is relevant):

1. Are we in New York City now?
2. Is it daytime?

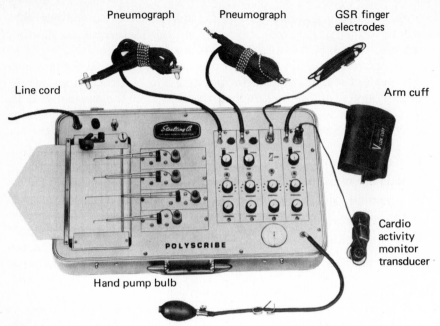

Pneumograph   Pneumograph   GSR finger electrodes

Line cord

Arm cuff

Cardio activity monitor transducer

POLYSCRIBE

Hand pump bulb

Figure 13-3   Portable polygraph, model 22770 Polyscribe (Courtesy Stoelting Co., Chicago, IL).

3. Are you a male?

4. Did you kill John Smith with a knife?

This type of examination is not considered very effective and is generally used only as a last resort. The types of questions themselves are likely to evoke an abnormal response just by their inflammatory nature, regardless of the guilt or innocence of the suspect.

Other Considerations

Testing must be halted whenever coughing, sighing, or yawning is observed. Resume testing only after they have ceased. A notation should be made on the chart whenever a person holds his or her breath and generally causes a distortion to the readings.

It is a good policy to keep the investigator available during the testing, should a point arise that is unfamiliar to the examiner. At no time during the testing should the examiner engage in conversation about the incident. Once the testing has been completed and deception is indicated, a complete interrogation may take place.

Some departments have the tested individual sign the chart at the end of the examination.

Development of Detection Devices

The idea that a way could be found to determine whether a person was lying has been around a long time. As early as 1895, Cesare Lombroso, known as the father of criminology, conducted tests to determine deception. He used a hydrosphygmograph, a small water tank that responded to changes in blood pressure and pulse in a subject tested by it. The changes were recorded on a smoked drum. In 1914, V. Benussi researched changes in respiration resulting from a subject's reaction to lying. Seven years later, John Larsen, working in the police department of Berkeley, California, devised an instrument that simultaneously recorded blood pressure, pulse, and respiration. By 1926, Leonarde Keeler added the galvanometer to record the galvanic skin reflex. It is Keeler's four-pronged polygraph that is in use today. (There have been some refinements, but basically the polygraph that Keeler designed is still used.)

In recent years, detection devices based on different principles have been developed. They were attempts to answer the need for less complicated and more efficient instruments.

Voice Analyzers

In 1966, two veteran polygraph examiners, John Reid and Fred Inbau, wrote *Truth and Deception* (*The Polygraph Technique*), a book in which they emphasize the desirability of better detection devices than the polygraph. They wrote:

> The authors have long held the opinion that the ultimate goal in detection of deception or monitoring would be that of a physiologic data acquisition without sensors being placed on the subject.

The idea of obtaining physiological data without sensors attached to the subject came into being with the introduction of voice analyzers. Two new devices utilizing the voice have been introduced in the field of criminal justice in the last few years, the Mark II Voice Analyzer and the Dektor Psychological Stress Evaluator (PSE).

The authors of *Criminalistics for the Law Enforcement Officer* witnessed a demonstration of the Mark II by its inventor, Mark Fuller, who claims that the Mark II is as accurate as a polygraph and that it renders more consistent results. This invention does not require any attachments (sensors) to the person being tested and records subaudible tremors in speech on a digital (numbered) tape (see Fig. 13-4).

In other words, it is capable of recording sounds on a digital tape that the human ear cannot hear. It processes speech electronically and provides immediate results for single- or multiple-word answers to questions. The device requires a limited amount of simple training to operate. It is capable of processing a recorded voice, one heard over a telephone, or spoken words. Tests have been performed in which deception could be accurately detected with three questions that take less than 10 seconds to ask, process, and evaluate. The instrument analyzes certain qualities of the voice which are claimed to change with and therefore to be indicative of stress. The speed with which deception can be detected places it in an advantageous position compared to the polygraph.

The other device, Dektor Psychological Stress Evaluator (PSE) (Fig. 13-5), is similar to the Mark II in that it does not require any body sensors be attached to the individual. The PSE records and analyzes stress-related components of the human voice. The device may

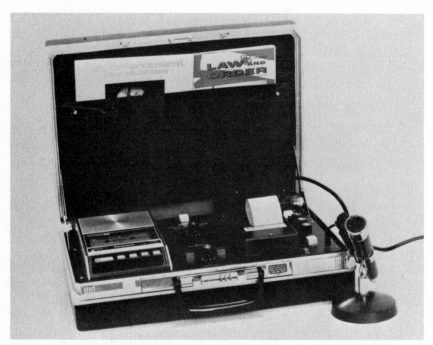

Figure 13-4   Mark II Voice Analyzer (Courtesy HLB Security Electronics, Ltd., New York, NY).

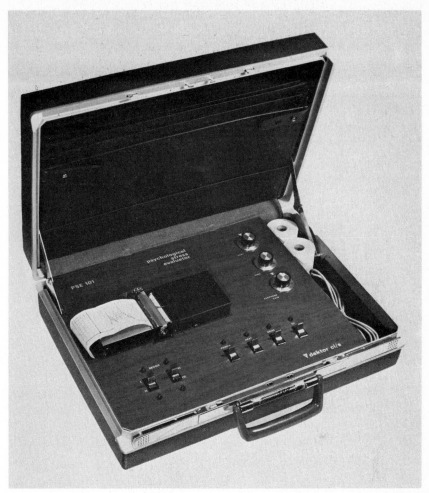

Figure 13-5   Psychological Stress Evaluator (Courtesy Dektor Counterintelligence, Springfield, VA).

be used with or without the knowledge of the individual. Short responses to questions, such as yes or no, may be analyzed. Further, it records vibrations of the voice mechanism not audible to the human ear by using a heated, inkless stylus on heat-sensitive paper. (See Fig. 13-6 for a sample tape printout of the PSE.) Like the Mark II, it is completely contained in an attaché case. The elimination of sensory attachments to an individual appears to reduce physiological stress and affords more perceptible readings.

In evaluating the detection devices discussed in this chapter, it should be kept in mind that they all are based on measurement of

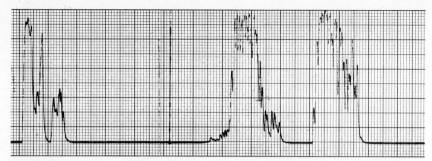

Figure 13-6 Psychological Stress Evaluator (PSE) tape printout. The middle peak indicates the greatest amount of stress. (Courtesy Dektor Counterintelligence, Springfield, VA).

certain physiological changes. That they can do this is not really in question. It is the interpretation of these changes as proving a lie or truth that is in question. As an example, one may ask an innocent individual if he or she killed someone with a knife. Suppose, unknown to the examiner, the suspect was involved in a fight or accident with a knife some years in the past and suffered a severe injury. The subject may now have an emotional reaction to any question involving or mentioning knives in any context. He or she may then show stress on the examination and thus an erroneous conclusion may be reached by the examiner. As a result of such considerations, it is doubtful that the polygraph will ever be admissible in court (without stipulation by all parties). It can provide useful information or indications about how an investigation should proceed.

chapter

Voiceprint Identification

The human voice is almost as individually distinctive as the fingerprint. This is the basis for the branch of criminalistics known as voiceprint identification.

Before the development of the voiceprint, voice identification in courts of law depended completely upon subjective judgment. A witness might testify that he was familiar with the accused's voice, had heard him speak face to face on a number of occasions, and that his was the same as the voice on the wiretap saying, "OK Charlie, that's five across the board on Snowbiscuit in the fourth at Pimlico." Such evidence was—and is—acceptable in court, but its reliability is often in doubt. There is always the real possibility that voices over the phone and on tape might be deceptive and fool even the most honest and expert witness.

Voiceprinting is an attempt to use sophisticated technology to overcome the problem of subjectivity in voice identification. A voiceprint is a record of human speech made on a sound spectrograph. The print itself is called a "spectrogram," and it consists of a complex of wavy lines representing changing levels of pitch and frequency in the recorded voice. According to Lawrence G. Kersta, one of the leading contributors to its development, the voiceprint has been used in more than 750 cases for municipal, county, state, and government agencies.

Its admissibility as evidence in court first occurred in *People v. Straehle* (criminal No. 9323164, Supreme Court, Westchester County

Court, 1966), a case involving the prosecution of a police officer for perjury. The trial resulted in a hung jury. As in all cases where scientific instruments or techniques are introduced into court, they must satisfy the requirements of the Frye decision (page 2). From December 1970 to August 1974, it had been admitted in court in twenty-one states, the District of Columbia, and Ontario, Canada.

One of the reasons that questions still arise about the reliability of voiceprints is that it is a relative newcomer to the law enforcement scene. Its development began during World War II when there was a need to identify the voices of radio operators in military units, so that each of the unit's movements could be followed simply by identifying the voice of its operator.

The early work on the sound spectrograph was done by Green, Kersta, Kopp, and Potter at the Bell Telephone Laboratories in Murray Hill, New Jersey. Kersta later developed a spectrograph specifically for voiceprints, which is now commercially available, manufactured, and sold by a number of companies. Figure 14-1 shows a commercial model. The analysis is based on Kersta's fundamental hypothesis that there exist unique and reproducible characteristics which can be associated with an individual's speech pattern, and that these characteristics may be translated and recorded in a form suitable for identification and comparison purposes.

This hypothesis arises from the mechanics of the speech process in the human body. Kersta observed that an individual's voice is determined by the size of the vocal cavities, or resonators, and the interaction among these cavities. Figure 14-2 shows these oral cavi-

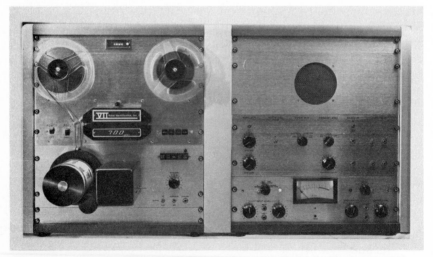

Figure 14-1   Voice analyzer (Courtesy Voice Identification Inc., Somerville, NJ).

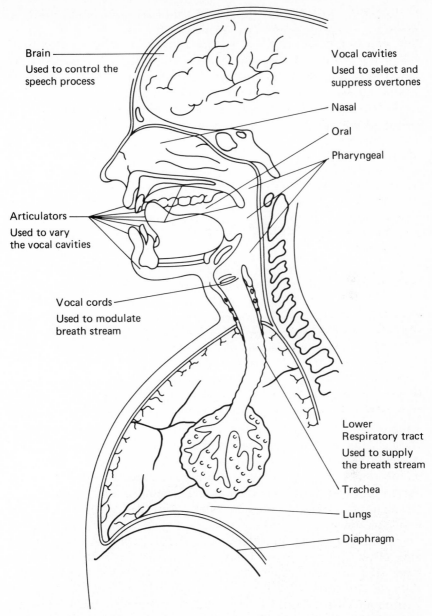

Brain
Used to control the
speech process

Vocal cavities
Used to select and
suppress overtones

Nasal

Oral

Pharyngeal

Articulators
Used to vary
the vocal cavities

Vocal cords
Used to modulate
breath stream

Lower
Respiratory tract
Used to supply
the breath stream

Trachea

Lungs

Diaphragm

Figure 14-2   Schematic of the vocal mechanism (Courtesy Base-Ten Systems, out of business).

ties—throat, nasal passage, and the two oral cavities formed in the mouth by the tongue. The other important factor determining the uniqueness of individual speech—as shown in the spectrogram—is the way the "articulators" (lips, teeth, tongue, soft palate, and jaw muscle) are manipulated to produce speech.

Kersta has written: ". . . The chance that two individuals would have the same dynamic use patterns for their articulators would be remote. The claim for voice pattern uniqueness, then, rests on the improbability that two speakers would have the same vocal cavity dimension and articulator use patterns identical enough to confound voiceprint identification methods."

What Is Speech?

Speech begins at birth with crying and, a little later, babbling. After several months, babies mimic sounds of "Da Da" and "Ma Ma" and other one-syllable words and sounds. To help the baby learn to talk, parents make exaggerated facial movements to encourage the baby to mimic them and produce the accompanying sound.

In all humans, speech occurs when the lungs force air up through the windpipe to the larynx or speech box.

When you speak, your vocal chords are stretched and relaxed by muscles that are attached to them in your throat. The vocal chords vibrate in the same way as violin or guitar strings when these are actuated by a violin bow or guitar pick. The average female has shorter vocal chords than the male, resulting in a higher pitch voice. Speech is a coordinated effort of the lungs, larynx, vocal chords, tongue, lips, mouth, facial muscles, all of which are activated by the brain. You are familiar with how your voice changes when you have a head cold or stuffy nose, thus proving that the nasal passages have an effect upon the voice.

Sounds may be interpreted in a general way as energy in the form of waves or pulses which causes the eardrum to vibrate. These vibrations are sent to the brain, which identifies the words or sounds. The sound spectrograph records on paper what the brain records and identifies in its memory. The brain contains a unique quality whereby you can identify members of your family, friends, business associates, and many others when you hear their voices over the telephone. Some blind people have the ability to ascertain the distance to a speaker or the size of a room because of their keen hearing. Sound has certain characteristics such as intensity or loudness and pitch (high or low tones or frequency).

How the Spectrograph Works

The sound spectrograph produces a visual display of both the frequency of the sound and the intensity with which it is uttered as a function of the time at which it occurred. As it now works, the spectrograph records a voice on high-quality magnetic tape. The instrument will then analyze 2.5 seconds of the tape by scanning it electronically. It takes approximately 80 seconds for 2.5 seconds of a recorded voice to be printed in a spectrogram. The output of the scan is then recorded in one of two types of voiceprints by means of an electric stylus writing on paper attached to a rotating drum. The two types are bar and contour voiceprint.

Bar Voiceprint

The bar voiceprint (Fig. 14-3) is used for the subjective determination of speaker identity. It is the type used in the courtroom. The horizontal axis records the time (2.5-second duration). The frequency of the sound spoken at a particular time appears on the vertical axis. The density of the recording indicates the intensity (loudness of speech). Two individuals enunciating the same word will produce different voiceprints. For example, the spectrogram of the word *voice* as spoken by one person (Fig. 14-5a, first two rectangular areas) is easily distinguished from the spectrogram of the same word spoken by a second person (Fig. 14-5c or d, first two rectangular areas).

Contour Voiceprint

The contour voiceprint (Fig. 14-4) is used in the automated classification of speakers (as in security identification situations). Again, the horizontal axis is time, and the vertical is frequency. Now, however, points of equal loudness are connected by contour lines (much as in a topographical map of a mountain).

For a successful identification one needs a sufficient number of sounds for comparison in the standard and in the suspected recording. Generally, it is recommended that the following ten common words be used for comparison purposes: *the, to, and, we, you, on, is, I, it,* and *a*. Short or one-syllable words are easier to identify.

The more extensive the suspect recording (perhaps from a recorded telephone call), the greater the chance of success. Basically, one makes a visual comparison between the two spectrograms, looking for regions of similarity. An aural comparison is also often made. Kersta tested his instrument extensively, reporting great success.

Figure 14-3   Bar voiceprint (Voiceprint Laboratories).

Kersta wrote:

The first police application, which occurred in Connecticut, interestingly proved a suspect innocent. A man,
therefore, is free today because his voiceprints showed
that he was not the depraved caller who made violent
death threats to a family living there. During an emotional scene at police headquarters, the principal victim
proclaimed insistently that it was the suspect who made
threatening telephone calls. He, just as vigorously, pro-
tested it was not he. As the debut of voiceprints in a
police case, tape recordings were made of the death
threat calls and the suspect's voice. The proof of his as-
sertions by using voiceprint identification gave him his
freedom and subsequently established the guilt of two
suspects picked up later who eventually pleaded guilty.
The nature of the disguises these men used during the

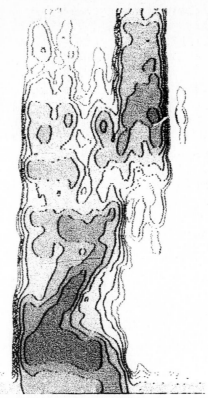

Figure 14-4   Contour voiceprint (Voiceprint Laboratories).

frenzied telephone calls tricked the ears of the victim,
who was not even aware that two men were involved.[1]

Criteria for Taking Voiceprints

Dr. Oscar Tosi, head of the Department of Audiology and
Speech Sciences at Michigan State University, has done extensive research in voiceprint identification.[2] He has established criteria for
the taking of voiceprints that are intended to promulgate uniform
standards of accuracy and reliability.

[1] L. G. Kersta, "Voiceprint Identification," brochure published by Base-Ten Systems, Inc.
[2] O. Tosi et al., "Experiment of Voice Identification," *J. Acoust. Soc. Am.*, **51:** 2030–
2043, 1972.

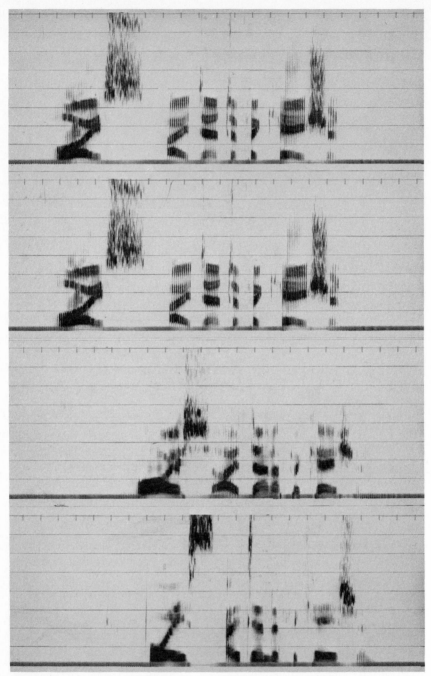

Figure 14-5 "Voice identification," as uttered by (a) first male subject; (b) first male subject recorded a second time; (c) second male subject; (d) female subject (Courtesy Voice Identification, Inc., Somerville, NJ).

1. The examiner must be allowed all the time necessary to reach a decision.
2. The examiner must be properly and thoroughly trained.
3. The examiner must have extensive experience.
4. The examiner must be allowed not to make a positive determination when the evidence available does not warrant it.
5. The examiner must be allowed to listen to the voice while examining the spectrograms.

Role of the Voiceprint Today

While the use of the voiceprint in law enforcement and related areas is gaining ground quite rapidly, it is obvious that it does not yet come close to playing the important role that fingerprinting does. For one thing, fingerprinting has more than 60 years of accumulated experience on which to base its claim to reliability in identifying individuals. In this regard, voiceprinting is still in its infancy.

Another reason that the use of voiceprinting is largely restricted to special cases and certain areas is that it is expensive—at least compared to fingerprinting. A sound spectrograph costs as much as $15,000, which puts it beyond the budget for many police departments.

The Michigan state police have used voiceprints quite extensively. In a number of homicide cases, the killer has called the police and given a false request for help, thus bringing the police to the scene of an ambush. In a case in Scranton, Pennsylvania, the caller told the police he had killed a woman and gave the location of the body. However, he gave as his name that of an innocent acquaintance. The investigation which followed eliminated the acquaintance from suspicion, and the true perpetrator was identified by the voiceprint method. He was found guilty and sentenced to prison.

In writing about the Voice Scan Spectrograph, which he developed, Kersta cites two other notable examples of the voiceprint's usefulness. One concerns a delicate international incident, the other a plane crash in which the voiceprint help to reconstruct an unintelligible message.

International Incident

The voiceprint identification technique was used to substantiate the claim of the Israeli Government that it had intercepted a radiotelephone conversation between President Nasser of Egypt and King Hussein, in which Nasser requested Hussein to back Egyptian claims that United States and British planes assisted the Israelis. The voice alleged to be that of Nasser on the Israeli Government release was compared to comparable phonetic elements from previously identified broadcasts of President Nasser. The findings, supported by an exhibit of 25 phone-elements from each recording, proved the voice was that of Nasser.

Reconstructing Unintelligible Messages

The voiceprint technique has also been used in reconstructing unintelligible messages, among which importantly were several from crashing airplanes. An example of this application was the crash of the Pacific Air Lines plane in flight between Las Vegas and San Francisco. The deciphering of the last message revealed that the co-pilot reported that he and the pilot were shot. Subsequent investigations supported the message when a gun was found and a penetration hole in the frame of the pilot's seat. The ownership of the gun was traced to a passenger who had lost considerable money at Las Vegas and had purchased a large flight insurance policy.

In Police Work

Problems of voice identification enter into many aspects of law enforcement, in all of which the voiceprint can be called into play. Crimes involving the telephone (such as threatening or obscene calls), gambling, and extortion are obvious instances where voiceprints may help identify an unknown caller.

A taped recording of the demands made by a kidnapper or an associate would provide an excellent basis for identifying the voice of the caller. When a suspect is arrested, a recording of his or her voice could be used for comparison with that of the taped call demanding the ransom. A voice comparison would certainly bolster the prosecutor's case when a trial takes place.

Obscene calls, bomb threats, and false fire reports are all likely situations. Some police departments are recording the emergency calls they receive for possible later analysis. A voiceprint of the caller's voice could be made and used for comparison purposes with the voice of a suspect recorded upon arrest.

Investigators recording wiretap conversations, which is a common practice, could use the taped voices for comparison with suspects recorded after arrest. Extortion attempts by telephone could be recorded and used for comparison with the voice of the suspect when he or she is arrested.

The voiceprint diagrams or spectrograms are examined visually side by side in much the same way as fingerprints are compared. It takes a little practice to recognize similarities in the spectrograms of the two voices (i.e. known and unknown). After the experience of examining some 75 to 100 voiceprints, one should be able to recognize similarities of the spectrograms' patterns. In fact, Kersta used high school students in his early research, which should certainly tend to prove that comparing voice spectrograms is not a difficult feat.

Engineers at the Air Force Systems Command are working on the voiceprint arrangement for controlling access to limited-entry areas. Persons who are to be cleared to enter a given area record four preselected phrases which become an identity record in a computer memory. After the individual triggers the system using either a keyboard or a card similar to a credit card, the computer switches to his or her recorded phrases, and a voice asks the person to repeat one of them. If the match is immediate, the door opens; if it is not, the computer asks the applicant to repeat another of the previously recorded phrases. In tests 99 percent of the legitimate applicants were granted entry. Professional mimics were able to fool the system in fewer than 1 percent of their attempts.

Talking Rogues Gallery

The Nassau County Police Department of Mineola, New York, is planning a program called the "Talking Rogues Gallery project." After an arrestee has his or her history, fingerprints, and photograph taken, he or she is to be brought to an acoustically sound-proofed room where a voice recording will be made. The arrestee will be asked to give his or her name and address and to utter a few short, selected sentences. This procedure is to "record those persons arrested for crimes where it is felt that the system [of voiceprinting] will have the most chance for success." The voice recording will be used in conjunction with a projected life-size color slide of the individual on the screen. A witness will be able to view the individual and hear him or her at the same time. It is easy to imagine how readily a person who has been the victim of the "confidence game" can make an identification.

This kind of approach to voiceprinting may well point the direction of future developments. It is clear that voiceprinting is now gaining wide acceptance. But most authorities believe that there remains the need for the massive accumulation of facts and figures proving beyond doubt that voiceprints do, in fact, indicate irrefutable individuality. This, of course, takes years, as was seen in the development of fingerprinting.

At the present state of the art, voiceprinting needs to develop data concerning the effect of such varied factors as nasal or oral surgery, dentures, mimicking, illness, emotional state, and many other conditions that might alter an individual's voice patterns.

At the same time, the student of criminalistics need not wait until voiceprinting is a routine practice in every police station before gaining at least a general knowledge of its techniques and applications. There is no question that it has already established itself as an important part of the science of criminalistics, and all indications are that it will be more important in the future.

15

Instruments of Investigation

With the highly sensitive instruments now available, the forensic scientist is able to measure and characterize the properties of very small quantities of materials with great precision.

The remarkable sensitivity of some of these instruments can be grasped from the following example. A typical dose of the tranquilizer Valium is 5 mg, which is five one-thousandths of a gram or about two ten-thousands of an ounce—barely enough to see. Detecting its presence in a drop of blood or a bit of tissue of a body weighing 150 lb (the equivalent of 2400 oz through which the Valium has spread) is like mixing 1 part of alcohol with 20 million parts of water and being able to taste the alcohol. Nowadays, with the analytical instruments available in many crime laboratories, it is routine practice to do so.

In this chapter, you will look at the important scientific instruments for measuring and characterizing small quantities of materials and see how they are applied to police investigations. The instrumental techniques to be studied are chromatography, X-ray, infrared, ultraviolet and emission spectrometry, mass spectrometry, neutron activation analysis, and scanning electron microscopy. (See Table 15-4.)

Before the more complex instruments are discussed, some of the important routine instruments that are a must for any forensic laboratory should be mentioned.

1. Analytical balances. These are capable of measuring the weight of objects as small as 0.0001 g or about 0.000004 oz, roughly the weight of a single human hair (Fig. 15-1).
2. Micrometer calipers are used to measure the thickness of a substance such as a sheet of paper, and a vernier caliper is used to

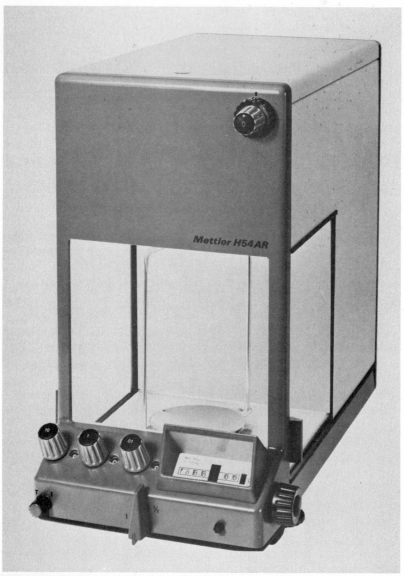

Figure 15-1   Analytical balance (Mettler Instrument Corp., Hightstown, NJ).

measure inside and outside diameters. These can measure thicknesses as small as 0.01 of a millimeter (or about 0.0004 in).

3. Microscopes are used to examine evidence and to perform various analytical tests. A stereoscopic (three-dimensional) binocular microscope (Fig. 11-2) is used to examine tool marks, cloth, various types of writing and paper, fibers, hairs, and other materials collected in a vacuum sweeper filter, etc. Its range of magnification is from about 10 to 100. The high-powered miscroscope (Fig. 15-2) is used in examination of hairs and fibers, blood, semen, metals, etc. The normal range of magnifications is from about 100 to 1000.

4. Ultraviolet light sources. These are hand-held or table-mounted lamps with special bulbs that emit light in the ultraviolet range. They are generally of two types, depending on the energy of

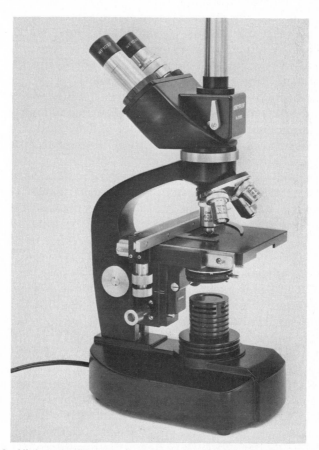

Figure 15-2   High-magnification microscope. Top center tube is for camera attachment for making photomicrograph (Mettler Instrument Corp., Hightstown, NJ).

ultraviolet light emitted: long wavelength (corresponding to the familiar blacklight lights) and short wavelength (higher-energy) ultraviolet light.

When irradiated with ultraviolet light, many substances will have a color different from that viewed with ordinary light. They are said to fluoresce. Some substances that may not be visible will become visible under ultraviolet light. It can be used to compare materials such as glass, lipstick, inks, etc., or to detect substances such as urine (yellow), semen (white), secret ink, and ink eradicator.

Chromatography

As you have seen, evidence often presents itself as a mixture of materials—heroin, for example, may contain quinine, sugar, and a number of other adulterants. A sample of urine, which contains traces of a drug, may also contain metabolites of the drug, in addition to naturally occurring body materials, such as urea, water, and various sugars, proteins, and carbohydrates.

To identify these materials and to measure how much of each is present, it is often necessary to separate them and to examine each as a single component. There are a number of ways of doing this. The most versatile, sensitive, and widely used of these methods fall into the category known as chromatographic separations.

In chromatographic separations, the entire mixture is dissolved in a suitable solvent. The resulting solution is then passed over a finely divided, solid adsorbent (*Note:* The solvent is called the mobile phase and the adsorbent the stationary phase. In some applications the latter may not be a solid. See Table 15-1), which is usually packed in a long glass tube (See Fig. 15-3).

As the solvent carries them down the tube past the adsorbent, the components of the solution tend to stick to the solid particles. At the same time, the continued flow of solvent past them tends to pull them off the solid and redissolve them. The different components of the mixture become "stuck" to the solid and held to it with different strengths. This occurs because they each have a unique chemical structure. These determine how strongly they will be held to the solid particles. As a result, they pass through at different rates.

At the end of the tube, they have been separated from one another and may be collected. Further analysis is relatively easy, since they are now pure substances. As they exit from the tube, they pass over a detecting device which registers their presence in the form of an electric signal, which is transmitted to a recorder that marks their presence on a chart.

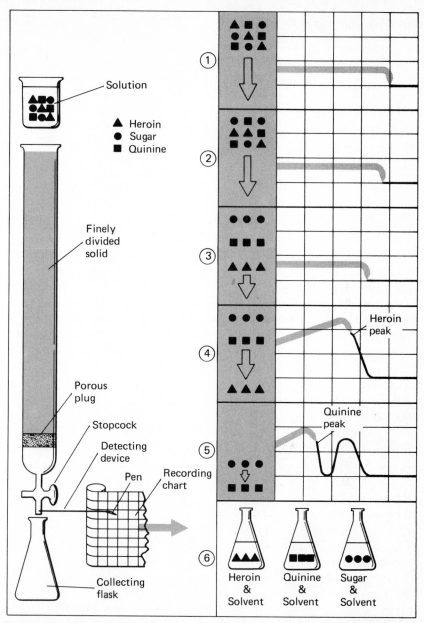

Figure 15-3 Chromatographic separation: Solution containing solvent and three dissolved substances is poured from beaker (top left) into buret packed with finely divided solid absorbent (left). Detection device below stopcock measures and records separated substances, which are then collected in flask (bottom left). Stages of separation and the progressive graphic record made by the detecting device are at right.

Gas Chromatography

In some variations of chromatography, the substances to be analyzed are heated to a high enough temperature so that they vaporize entirely. They are then carried over the finely divided solid by the flow of an inert carrier gas, such as helium. This variation is known as gas-solid or more simply gas chromatography (GC). See Fig. 15-4. It is particularly useful in the analysis of arson evidence where one is looking for accelerants, such as gasoline, which are very easily vaporized. (See Fig. 12-1.)

Thin-layer Chromatography

Another widely used chromatographic technique is known as thin-layer chromatography (TLC). In TLC a thin layer of the stationary phase is coated on one side of a glass or metal plate (a microscope slide, for example). The sample is applied near the bottom of the plate in the form of a small spot. The plate is then placed in a container with a small amount of an appropriate liquid (mobile phase), so that the liquid level is below the spot. The liquid wets the station-

Figure 15-4   Gas chromatograph, Perkin-Elmer model 900 (Courtesy New York Police Department Forensic Laboratory).

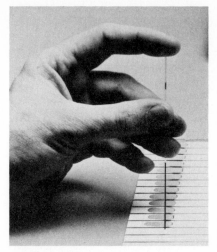

Figure 15-5 *Left:* placing of mixtures to be analyzed on multicolumn chromato-graphic plate; *right:* chromatographic plate in container with mobile phase. Note that separation of mixture has occurred in each column (Courtesy Kontes Glass Co., Vineland, NJ, and Quantum Industries, Fairfield, NJ).

ary phase and is carried up it by capillary action. (The solid is actually made up of fine particles separated by microscopically small empty channels. It is the action of the liquid filling up these empty channels that causes it to spread upward. The same sort of effect is observed if a drop of liquid falls on a newspaper or shirt. The drop will spread for some distance as it is absorbed by the material.)

As the liquid passes the spots, it carries the components along with it. They become more and more separated as they are carried farther and farther up the plate (see Figs. 15-5, 15-6, and 15-7).

Pyrolysis Variation

An important chromatographic technique known as pyrolysis gas chromatography was used recently to show that the chewing gum found in the throat of a murdered child matched the gum found both at the crime scene and on the suspect. This variation involves heating the sample to such a high temperature that it decomposes, breaking up into small fragments. This mixture of fragments is then sent through the GC and separated. Since each substance will always break into the same characteristic fragments, comparison of the pyrolysis chromatograms for the different samples enables one to determine whether the samples are from the same source. See Fig. 6-11.

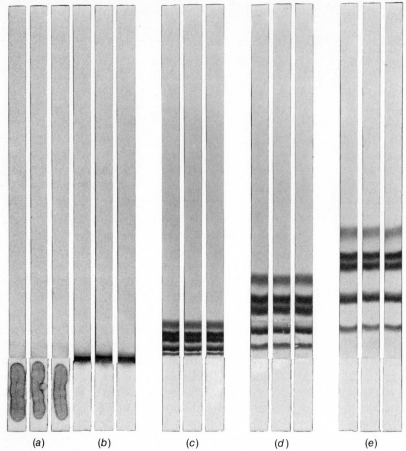

(a)   (b)   (c)   (d)   (e)

Figure 15-6 Chromatography is a means of comparing substances to see if they are identical. Stages from left to right are: (a) three mixtures identical in composition are placed on three columns of a multicolumn chromatographic plate; (b) then the solvent starts separating the substances in the mixtures; (c), (d), and (e) as development time increases, the substances show greater separation as they move further up the plates. Note the similarity from column to column, which is to be expected since the mixtures are identical in composition (Courtesy Kontes Glass Co., Vineland, NJ).

Normally, these analyses would be expected to be carried out at the laboratory by trained technicians or scientists. However, there are commercial field kits available which employ TLC for the preliminary analysis of such evidence as marijuana and inks.

There are other variations of chromatographic techniques, based on the nature of the stationary and mobile phases. (Table 15-1.)

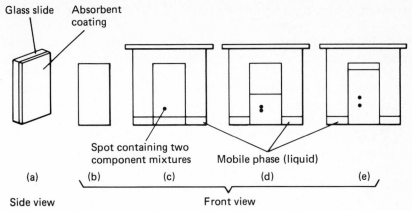

Glass slide   Absorbent coating

Spot containing two component mixtures

Mobile phase (liquid)

(a)   (b)   (c)   (d)   (e)

Side view   Front view

Figure 15-7   Thin-layer chromatography.

TABLE 15-1: Some Types of Chromatography

Name	Type of Solvent or Mobile Phase	Type of Stationary Phase	Method of Fixing the Stationary Phase
Gas-liquid	Gas	Liquid	Absorbed on a porous solid held in a tube or absorbed on the inner surface of a capillary tube.
Gas-solid	Gas	Solid	Held in a tubular column.
Partition	Liquid	Liquid	Absorbed on a porous solid held in a tubular column.
Thin layer	Liquid	Liquid or solid	Finely divided solid held on a glass plate. Liquid may be absorbed on particles.
Gel	Liquid	Liquid	Held in the interstices of a polymeric solid.
Column	Liquid	Solid	Finely divided solid held in a tubular column.
Paper	Liquid	Liquid	Held in the pores of a thick paper.

Spectrometry

Spectrometers and spectrographs analyze light after it passes through a solid, liquid, or gaseous sample or as it is emitted from a substance which has been raised to a high energy (as by heating it to a very high temperature).

In order to understand how these techniques work, certain characteristics of light must be kept in mind.

Visible, or white light, is made up of light having all the colors of the rainbow (red, orange, yellow, green, blue, indigo, and violet). When they are all mixed in equal amounts, the light appears colorless, i.e., white. A glass prism has the property of being able to separate this mixture into its component colors (see Fig. 15-8). Each of the colors is a type of light, distinguished from others by its effect on the eye, i.e. by their different colors (red, orange, etc.). Scientists often refer to colors in terms of wavelength, a property which is directly related to color. Light can be thought of as being made up of waves traveling through space, much like the ripples created in a lake when a pebble is dropped into it. The wavelength is the distance between successive crests (see Fig. 15-9).

Thus, red light has a different wavelength from green light, green light a different wavelength from purple light, and so on. There are many more types of light (differing in their wavelengths) than can be seen with the naked eye. For instance, radio waves are a form of light different from visible light (and therefore being characterized by different wavelengths) in that they cannot be seen by the human eye. However, they can be detected with some other device, for example, radio receivers. They are similar to other forms of light in that they travel from a source (in this case a radio transmitter) through space with the same speed (the speed of light, which is equal to 186,000 miles per second).

Some other types of light are X-rays, cosmic rays, ultraviolet

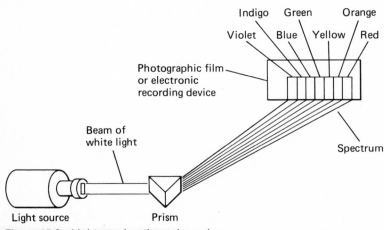

Figure 15-8   Light passing through a prism.

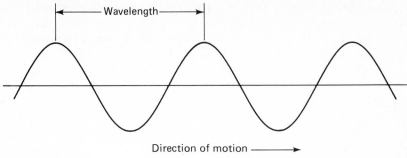

Figure 15-9

(UV) rays, and infrared (IR) rays. They all differ with respect to their characteristic wavelength and, therefore, in the way they may be sensed (or detected). It should be noted that each of these types refers to a range of wavelengths; e.g. visible light ranges in wavelength from about 0.00004 (violet) to 0.00075 (red) cm. Table 15-2 lists the types of light and their corresponding wavelengths.

TABLE 15-2: Types of Light and Corresponding Wavelengths

Name	Range of Wavelengths (in Centimeters)*
Cosmic rays	Less than 10^{-12} (one-millionth of one-millionth)
Gamma rays	10^{-11} to 10^{-9} (one-hundredth of a billionth to one-billionth)
X-rays	10^{-9} to 10^{-6} (one-billionth to one-millionth)
Ultraviolet (UV)	10^{-6} to $4(10^{-5})$ (one-millionth to four hundred-thousandths)
Visible	$4(10^{-5})$ to $7.5(10^{-5})$ (4 to 7.5 hundred-thousandths)
Infrared (IR)	$7.5 (10^{-5})$ to 10^{-2} (7.5 ten thousandths to one-hundredth)
Microwaves	A few tenths of a centimeter to a few meters
Radio waves	A few meters and up

* 1 cm = 0.01 m = 0.3937 in.

Spectrometric Analysis

When infrared light is directed at a thin sample of material, it will pass through the substance more or less unchanged. It is the "more or less" that is important. A precise analysis of the intensity (or brightness) of the light will show that in passing through the sample, the different wavelengths of infrared light have been absorbed to varying degrees by the sample. In other words, the light incident on the sample is partially absorbed by it. Only a fraction is transmitted through it. Precisely which wavelengths are absorbed and to what degree depends on the structure of the material in the sample. *Structure* is used in the chemical sense. All substances are made up of small submicroscopic particles called atoms which are chemically bound to one another, to form the basic units of matter, called molecules. Molecules are the smallest unit of the substance that will have all its chemical and physical properties.

The atoms in molecules are held together by strong forces known as chemical bonds. The structure, then, is determined by what atoms are present in the molecule and by how they are bonded to one another. An infrared spectrophotometer is a device that passes the different wavelengths of infrared light through a sample and electronically measures and records the intensity (or brightness) of light that is transmitted at each wavelength. (See Fig. 15-10.) The percentage of incident light that passes through is called the "transmittance." These measurements are automatically recorded in the form of a graph (or infrared spectra) of the substance. Even if two different materials contain the identical atoms, the infrared spectra of the two substances will be different since their chemical structures will be different (i.e. in the two substances the arrangement or bonding of the atoms to one another will still be different).

The chemical structure and infrared spectrum of heroin hydrochloride are shown in Fig. 15-11. The letters represent the atoms located at these points:

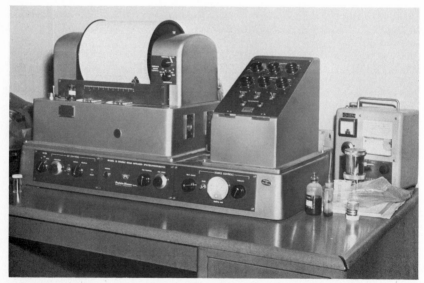

Figure 15-10   Perkin-Elmer model 21 infrared spectrophotometer (Courtesy New York Police Department Forensic Laboratory).

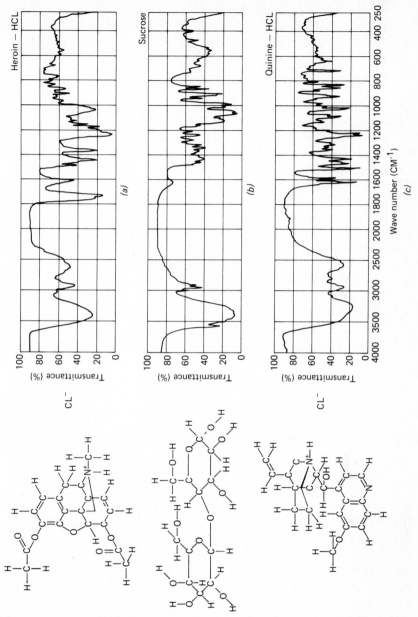

Figure 15-11 (a) Chemical structure and infrared spectra of heroin hydrogen chloride; (b) chemical structure and infrared spectra of sucrose; (c) chemical structure and infrared spectra of quinine hydrogen chloride.

C represents an atom of carbon
O represents an atom of oxygen
N represents an atom of nitrogen
H represents an atom of hydrogen
Cl represents an atom of chlorine

The lines between two atoms represent the bonds holding these two atoms together. This representation is called a "chemical structure" or "structural formula." A sample of heroin is made up of millions of these molecules. As the infrared light passes through the sample, each molecule absorbs some of the light. It is the sum of the absorption by all these molecules that is actually measured. Note that in the infrared spectra the amount of light of a particular wavelength transmitted is shown on the verticle (or Y axis) while the reciprocal of the wavelength is shown on the horizontal (X axis). (The reciprocal of the wavelength is just 1/wavelength.) Thus, for instance, you see that infrared radiation of 1450 wavenumbers is transmitted to the extent of about 20 percent by the sample. Now compare the structural formula and corresponding infrared spectrum of sucrose (sugar) in Fig. 15-11b and quinine hydrochloride in Fig. 15-11c. The percent transmittances at the same wavenumber, 1450, are 50 and 35 percent respectively. It is this wavelength-to-wavelength difference in the spectra that makes the infrared spectrum of each substance unique.

Clearly the structure and the spectra for all three are different from one another. Every pure substance possesses a unique structure and will therefore have a unique infrared spectrum. The infrared spectrum of each compound is so unique that it is often termed the *chemical fingerprint* of the substance. The infrared spectra of thousands of compounds are recorded for reference in handbooks. Thus, if presented with an unknown liquid, solid, or gas, one can measure its infrared spectrum and then compare it with those in handbooks until the identical one is found. If one merely wishes to ascertain whether two samples (paints, for example) are the same, one merely needs to record their infrared spectra and see if they match.

Infrared spectroscopy can be very useful in hit-and-run cases. For instance, one can examine the paint chips found on the victim and often determine the type of paint used. This can be helpful in determining the manufacturer of the car, whether the car was repainted, and if the chips on the victim are identical with the paint on the car. Consider the following case history:[1]

[1] P. G. Rodgers et al., "The Classification of Automotive Paint by Diamond Window Infrared Spectrophotometry, *Journal of Forensic Sciences*, vol. 9, 1976.

In a hit-and-run incident, a red vehicle was struck and damaged. A sample of the victim's paint, taken from the damaged area, revealed a three-layer paint system:

Red-brown metallic [alkyd melamine—Fig. 15-12*a*]
Gray [nitrocellulose + talc—Fig. 15-12*b*]
Black [nitrocellulose + talc + clay—Fig. 15-12*c*]

No foreign paint was found in the damaged area of the victim's car.

Shortly afterward a suspect vehicle was brought to the laboratory garage for examination. Approximately 100 flecks of paint were removed from the dented front bumper. Of these, about ten would have combined to dot the letter *i*. All but one "large" fleck were single-layered red-brown metallic paint. A spectrum obtained from several of these red-brown fragments is shown in Fig. 15-12*d*. A comparison with Fig. 15-12*a* leaves little doubt about chemical similarity. The "large" fragment was mainly red-brown metallic paint with a trace of gray adhering to the underside. Since it was not possible to separate the gray layer, a composite spectrum was run (Fig. 15-12*e*). The intrusion of talc absorption bands (from the gray layer) in the alkyd melamine spectrum is apparent (see Fig. 15-12*a* and *b*). That is, the flecks from the suspect vehicle had both red-brown metallic and gray in them. Therefore, their spectrum (Fig. 15-12*e*) was a composite of Fig. 15-12*a* and *b*. Thus a detailed chemical comparison of the paint, layer by layer, was presented in the ensuing courtroom testimony. In other words, using a microscopic amount of evidence from the suspect's vehicle, it was shown conclusively that it came from the paint on the victim's vehicle.

An added advantage of the technique is that it is nondestructive and requires very small amounts of material. The amount of material used to obtain the spectra shown in Fig. 15-11*a*, *b*, and *c* was about 3 mg (0.0001 oz). For those with large budgets, it is even possible to couple an infrared spectrophotometer with a computer. One can store the infrared spectra of thousands of compounds in the computer memory. The computer can be programmed to rapidly compare the infrared spectra of the unknown compound with those in its memory banks until it finds a match, and then print out the name of the unknown compound. One of the problems of applying the technique to police work is that one rarely deals with pure materials.

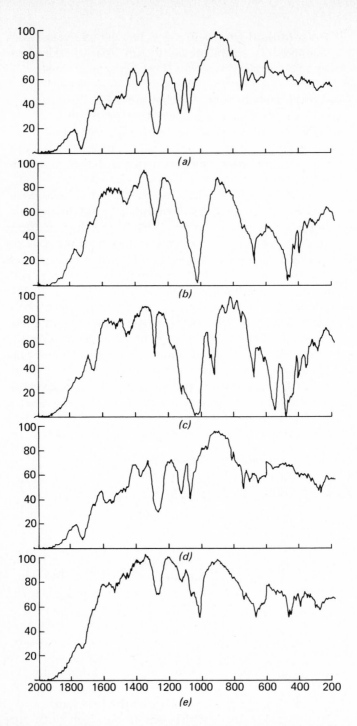

Figure 15-12 (a) Metallic red-brown topcoat; (b) gray undercoat; (c) black primer, individual layers from paint sample from victim's car; (d) metallic red-brown top-coat; (e) composite of red-brown/gray chip—individual layer and composite from foreign flecks found on suspect's bumper.

If one merely wants to show that two samples of material are the same, then usually a comparison of their infrared spectra is sufficient. However, if one wants to know what substances are present in the mixture, the problem is a good deal more difficult, but still solvable. The resultant spectrum will be the sum of the individual spectra. For example, Fig. 15-12e can be thought of as being obtained by adding the spectra in parts a and b. The difficulties increase as the number of components in the mixture increases.

In the illustration used in the section on chromatography, a mixture of heroin, quinine, and sugar was separated. If one measured the infrared spectrum of the initial mixture, for example as it was confiscated from a pusher, the resulting spectrum would essentially be the sum of Fig. 15-11a, b, and c. It would be very difficult to sort out which peaks and valleys belonged to which compound. It still would be useful, for example, in comparing this evidence to another sample picked up from another pusher. If they matched, this would tend to show they came from the same supplier. However, after separating these components by chromatography, it is a simple matter to evaporate the solvent, measure the infrared spectrum of each of the pure compounds, and compare them to known standards for heroin, quinine, and sugar, thereby proving exactly what was present. The two techniques will also tell how much of each component was present in the mixture.

Other Types of Spectrometers

Other types of spectrometers operate in a like fashion and are used for similar purposes. The most notable is ultraviolet (UV) spectroscopy. This is generally not as specific for identifying a substance but is often used to give information as to what class of drug might be present, for example, whether an amphetamine or a barbiturate is present.

So far, absorption spectrometers have been considered, i.e. devices where the amount of light that a material absorbs as the light is passed through the material is measured. Another class of spectrometers is also used extensively for identifying materials. These are generally, although not always, destructive in that the sample which is analyzed is not recoverable after the analysis.

One of the oldest of these techniques, in terms of being used in forensic problems, is the emission spectrograph (Fig. 15-13). The technique involves bringing the sample into a high-voltage arc of electricity created between two carbon electrodes. (Some instruments heat the sample to a high temperature to introduce this energy, others use a laser beam, and still others employ a beam of electrons.) This introduces large amounts of energy into the sample

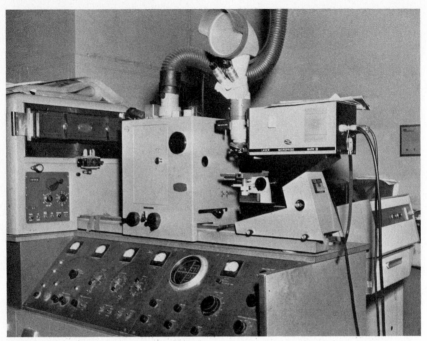

Figure 15-13 Emission spectrograph with laser microprobe (Courtesy New York Police Department Forensic Laboratory).

which is reemitted in the form of individual wavelengths of light. This light is made to strike a photographic film. When the film is then developed, one observes a series of lines on the film, indicative of the emitted wavelengths.

Each element will emit different wavelengths of light (recorded as a series of lines) that are unique to that element. This photographic record is then compared to that of reference spectra in order to identify the elements present in the sample. This technique is particularly useful in the analysis of paints, metals, and minerals. X-ray fluorescence and atomic absorption spectrometry are other important, sensitive emission techniques.

The use of X-ray fluorescence spectrometry to solve forensic problems is increasing. One may rapidly analyze a microscopic portion of the evidence and accurately determine what elements are present with great sensitivity. Diverse types of evidence such as suspected poisons, drugs, paints, and documents have been analyzed. An important recent case solved through the application of these techniques involved a huge oil spill in the Atlantic Ocean.[2]

[2] "Oil Spill Identification System," Document ADA 00380/LK, National Technical Information Service, Springfield, VA.

Using infrared and fluorescence spectroscopy (in addition to other techniques such as thin-layer chromatography, gas chromatography, etc.) government scientists showed that more than 40,000 gallons of oil which spilled into the Atlantic Ocean in July 1975 had come from a certain Liberian vessel. The oil had blackened 50 miles of Florida coastline and cost nearly $400,000 to clean up. The oil from the spill was "fingerprinted" by means of these tests and matched with the "fingerprints" of samples taken from the hold of the suspect ship. The investigation led to the arrest of the master of the vessel.

Mass Spectrometry

Mass spectrometry, like the other spectrometric techniques, is useful for identifying an unknown substance. However, its principle of operation is quite different from those spectrometric techniques already discussed. In mass spectrometry, the substance is injected into an instrument where it is bombarded by high-energy electrons. They have the effect of breaking the molecule into many fragments, each fragment containing some of the atoms that made up the original molecule. Exactly how the molecule breaks up and what fragments are formed depends on the chemical structure of the substance and can thus be used to characterize the substance.

The instrument performs such an analysis and records the fragments that are formed in a graph depicting the weights of the fragments formed. (Each atom in a molecule has a certain weight. The weight of the molecule is equal to the sum of the weights of the atoms that make up the molecule. Likewise, when the molecule is broken up into fragments, each fragment has its own weight depending on what atoms are in it. Imagine holding up a jigsaw puzzle and then striking it with sufficient force to cause the pieces to fly apart. The pattern of pieces produced will be uniquely characteristic of that particular jigsaw puzzle and can be used to identify and distinguish it from other jigsaw puzzles.)

The result is another type of "chemical fingerprint" of the material. Figure 15-14 is a reproduction of an actual mass spectrum of an extract of the stomach contents of a victim of drug overdose. The results were obtained with a Dupont 21-490 Mass Spectrometer System in less than 5 minutes. They show peak 1 to be due to the presence of triamterene (an antihypertensive), peak 2 to be due to the presence of acetylcarbromal (a sedative), and peak 3 to be due to benztropine (an antidepressant). The ability to perform such a rapid analysis can be the difference between life and death in the case of drug overdose or can result in a positive identification of the components of some street drug.

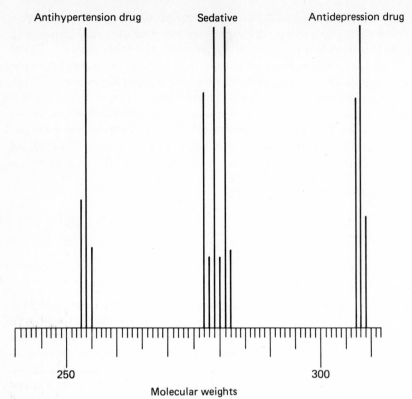

Figure 15-14   Mass spectrum of stomach extract.

As with other spectrometric techniques, success in identification is greatly enhanced if pure substances are used. This has given rise to instruments combining a gas chromatograph (GC) and a mass spectrometer (MS) where the pure components coming out of a GC are fed directly into an MS and identified, much as one compares fingerprints with those on file. One can use a computer to compare the results of MS with a file stored in its memory to effect a rapid identification. Probably the main obstacle to the presence of such a combination in every crime laboratory is their price, currently about $150,000.

Neutron Activation Analysis

There are a number of examples of naturally occurring radioactive materials, uranium and radium being the first two that come to mind. They give off characteristic energy known as radiation (they are said to be radioactive). This radiation is principally of three types —alpha rays (helium nuclei), beta rays (electrons), and gamma rays (X-rays).

Which radiation is given off and its precise energies are uniquely characteristic of the element. Therefore, a measurement of these properties can be used to identify the element. Very sensitive devices known as scintillation counters are used for making these measurements. Substances that are not normally radioactive may be made radioactive by bombarding them with subatomic particles called neutrons. The substance becomes radioactive and then gives off its characteristic radiation. This process is summarized by the following:

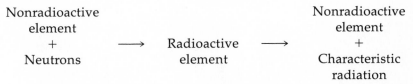

Neutrons are produced in the core of a nuclear reactor. Therefore, the sample to be analyzed is inserted in a container which is placed in a nuclear reactor for an appropriate length of time. Here, it is bombarded by neutrons and becomes radioactive. Then it is removed, and the rays emitted are measured. The technique is extremely sensitive; very little material is needed (a few hairs, for example). One analysis may identify a number of elements simultaneously, even though they are present in extremely small amounts. This is the great value of neutron activation analysis (NAA) (Fig. 15-15).

The ability to precisely detect trace elements is the major strength of NAA. Two chips of red paint made by the same manufacturer but in different batches may or may not be fairly similar with respect to their major and minor ingredients, but will almost certainly differ with respect to their trace elements. Also, as generally applied NAA is nondestructive—you get back all the material you started with. Table 15-3 lists some elements that can be detected by NAA and their lower limits of detection. The reader should be aware that the substances found are present in quantities which are less than one-billionth of one-millionth of a pound.

NAA has been used to compare hair, paints, glass, soil, and paper as well as a number of other items of evidence in investigation. It has been used to detect whether a person has discharged a firearm. This involves analyzing swabbings taken from a person's hand for barium and antimony. These metals are deposited on the hand as a result of the explosion of the primer and powder charge in the bullet. The technique has great potential but requires the availability of a nuclear reactor, which is a serious limitation.

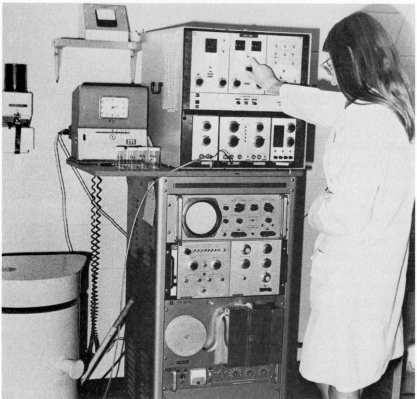

Figure 15-15 Neutron activation analysis. *Top:* capsule containing sample to be analyzed is placed in pneumatic tube through which it is brought to the core of the nuclear reactor (not shown); *bottom:* scientist analyzing radioactive sample that has been placed in the scintillation counter at lower left (Courtesy Union Carbide Corp., Tuxedo, NY).

TABLE 15-3: Sensitivities*

Element	Micrograms
Oxygen (O)	100.
Fluorine (F)	1.
Sodium (Na)	.02
Magnesium (Mg)	.06
Aluminum (Al)	.0009
Silicon (Si)	.5
Sulfur (S)	20.
Chlorine (Cl)	.004
Potassium (K)	.2
Calcium (Ca)	.2
Scandium (Sc)	.0003
Titanium (Ti)	.005
Vanadium (V)	.0001
Chromium (Cr)	0.1
Manganese (Mn)	.0002
Cobalt (Co)	.001
Nickel (Ni)	.2
Copper (Cu)	.005
Zinc (Zn)	.05
Gallium (Ga)	.01
Arsenic (As)	.0001
Selenium (Se)	.01
Bromine (Br)	.001
Rubidium (Rb)	.1
Strontium (Sr)	.08
Yttrium (Y)	1.0
Columbium (Cb or Nb)	.01
Molybdenum (Mo)	.04
Ruthenium (Ru)	.08
Rhodium (Rh)	.0001
Palladium (Pl)	.01
Silver (Ag)	.001
Cadmium (Cd)	1.0
Indium (In)	.00002
Tin (Sn)	.07
Antimony (Sb)	.007
Tellurium (Te)	.02
Iodine (I)	.001
Cesium (Cs)	.001
Barium (Ba)	.1
Lanthanum (La)	.002
Cerium (Ce)	.9
Praseodymium (Pr)	.005
Neodymium (Nd)	.03
Samarium (Sm)	.004
Europium (Eu)	.00004
Gadolinium (Gd)	.006
Terbium (Tb)	.01
Dysprosium (Dy)	.0001
Holmium (Ho)	.002
Erbium (Er)	.003
Thulium (Tm)	.09
Ytterblum (Yb)	.01
Lutetium (Lu)	.0004
Hafnium (Hf)	.005
Tantalum (Ta)	.005
Tungsten (W)	.009

Table continues overleaf

TABLE 15-3 (cont'd.)

Element	Micrograms
Rhenium (Rh)	.002
Osmium (Os)	.2
Iridium (Ir)	.00001
Platinum (Pt)	.05
Gold (Au)	.0001
Mercury (Hg)	.05
Thorium (Th)	.001
Uranium (U)	.0001

* Representative of the sensitivities possible for short irradiations are the values shown below for some of the elements.

TABLE 15-4: Types of Analysis for Various Kinds of Evidence

Evidence	Typing	Gas Chromotagraphy	TLC	Chemical Tests	IR Spectrometry	X-ray Spectrometry	Microscope
Drugs		✓	✓	✓	✓	✓	✓
Glass						✓	✓
Hairs	✓						✓
Fibers		✓		✓	✓	✓	✓
Tool marks							✓
Ink			✓	✓	✓		✓
Metal pieces				✓		✓	✓
Paint		✓	✓	✓	✓	✓	✓
Documents				✓	✓		✓
Soil				✓		✓	✓
Tobacco				✓			✓
Jewelry						✓	
Blood	*✓	✓		✓	✓		
Saliva, urine hair*, sweat, nails	✓			✓			
Semen	✓			✓			
Arson		✓			✓		
Explosive remnants		✓	✓	✓	✓	✓	✓
Bombs and other explosive devices		✓	✓	✓	✓	✓	✓
Cloth					✓		✓
Fingerprints				✓		✓	✓
Gunshot powder residues				✓		✓	✓
Erased serial numbers				✓			
Bullets							✓
Cartridges							✓

Scanning Electron Microscopy

Scanning electron microscopy (SEM) has provided the means to gain an unparalled microscopic view of materials. Ordinary microscopes can enlarge materials by a factor of about 1000. By focusing a beam of electrons, instead of light, on the item of interest, three-dimensional enlargements of up to about 150,000 times can be obtained with commercially available instruments, although the usual magnification used in forensic work is less than 10,000 times.

UV Spectrometry	NAA	AA	Ion Microprobe Analysis	Emission Spectrometry	Standards in Reference Library	Thermal Analysis	
✓	✓	✓	✓	✓	✓		
	✓		✓	✓			
	✓	✓	✓				
✓					✓	✓	
✓			✓	✓	✓		
	✓	✓	✓	✓	✓		
✓	✓	✓	✓	✓	✓	✓	
✓	✓	✓	✓	✓	✓		
	✓	✓	✓	✓		✓	
	✓	✓	✓	✓	✓		
					✓		
	✓	✓	✓	✓	✓		
						✓	
✓	✓	✓	✓	✓	✓		
					✓		
	✓	✓	✓	✓	✓		
	✓	✓	✓	✓	✓		
					✓		

* Also can tell whether it is human or animal in origin.

One can examine in great detail minute portions of the material. The technique is especially useful in comparing materials like paints, fibers, wood, metals, and paper. One can work with evidence samples in the order of a hundred thousandths of an inch in size. These instruments can also operate as emission spectrometers (a technique known as microprobe analysis). One can obtain precise information about the elemental composition of the material at exactly the location one has looked at when it was operated as a SEM.

With SEM, it is possible to analyze extremely small portions of the item. This is important if one is examining a document, a rare painting, a sculpture, or a rare coin. The amount of material affected by the microprobe analysis is so small as to be invisible and therefore will not affect the worth of the object. This technique has been used to prove certain rare gold coins to be forgeries. Another case involved the Vinland map, purportedly an ancient map proving that the Vikings discovered America prior to Columbus. Since the document might have been authentic, it was necessary to take microscopic samples for analysis. About 50 samples of ink, each weighing approximately a billionth of a gram, were analyzed by the scanning electron microscope and microprobe analysis. They showed that the ink pigment contained a form of titanium that did not come into use until centuries after the map was supposedly drawn. The conclusion: It was a skillful forgery.

It may be important simply to be able to see the fine detail present on some bit of evidence so as to compare it with a standard. The scanning electron microscope is ideal for this purpose, since it provides an enlarged three-dimensional image with great depth of field. An example is the comparison of the scales on samples of hair from two different individuals (see Fig. 6-7).

A combination of SEM and x-ray fluorescence spectrometry is currently being tested for the identification of gunshot powder residues on the hands of a person suspected of discharging a weapon (see Chap. 4, p. 82).

X-ray Analysis

X-rays—short wavelength, high energy light—have long been used as an aid in the investigation of crimes. The most familiar application is identical to that used by doctors to x-ray broken bones. Materials differ with respect to their ability to block x-rays. This difference can be used to take an x-ray photograph of hidden objects. The technique has been extended to develop latent prints on skin and other porous surfaces where normal techniques are unsuccessful. (See Fig. 3-10.)

A second important and traditional use of x-rays is known as x-ray diffraction analysis. It is generally used to identify the materials in crystalline solids such as metals, paints, and powders. The x-rays are directed at a powdered sample of the material. They are deflected, or diffracted, by the crystals in particular directions that are recorded electronically or on photographic film. The pattern is characteristic of the material and can be compared with standard reference patterns for identification.

Summary

In this chapter a variety of scientific methods for analyzing evidence have been discussed. The future use of analytical instrumentation in police work depends largely on developments in the sciences from which the knowledge and techniques derive. Sometimes the transition from pure science to forensic science is slow. There are techniques and instruments being used today in the pure sciences that could be usefully adapted to the field of criminalistics, but so far they have not been. Their application depends on the awareness and interest of people who are involved in both fields and also upon the financial resources available to law enforcement agencies. Much progress is being made. Surely science will continue to advance, and sooner or later these advances will find worthwhile and exciting applications in the forensic laboratory.

The Crime Laboratory

Crime laboratories play an increasingly important role in the investigation of murder, theft, arson, and other crimes, mainly because forensic science has developed sharper and more sophisticated tools and techniques for analyzing, processing, and comparing evidence in all its forms. The crime laboratory has the equipment and the trained personnel to tackle many jobs that a local law enforcement agency is not equipped to do. Some crime laboratories utilize investigators because they find that the combination of practical police experience and theoretical laboratory knowledge produces a formidable working team.

There are approximately 140 crime laboratories in the United States (see the list in Appendix B). In 1968, in an effort to improve the nation's criminal justice system, the federal government created the Law Enforcement Assistance Administration (LEAA), which provides grants that enable crime laboratories throughout the country to upgrade and expand their resources and their services. As a result, the work of the crime laboratory has become a more significant part of criminal investigation. At the same time, laboratory case loads have mounted and the shortage of trained personnel has become acute. Many crime laboratories struggle to maintain high standards in the face of budgetary restrictions and work pressures. One solution that has been adopted is for many counties to share the services and expenses of a regional laboratory (see Fig. 16-4).

Purpose of the Crime Laboratory

The primary purpose of the crime laboratory is to answer the following questions about evidence:

What is it and where did it come from?
Can it be associated indisputably with a suspect?
Is it identical with that found at the scene of a crime?
What are the chances of this identity being accidental?

The modern crime laboratory is better able to answer these questions now than ever before. Modern instruments enable one to corroborate the answers by making the comparisons between the evidence and the standard using a number of different techniques. The more independent tests one can present to a jury, the stronger the evidence.

A Model Crime Laboratory

The Federal Bureau of Investigation has one of the largest and best equipped crime laboratories in the world, employing more than 300 scientists and technicians. In a recent year, the FBI laboratory undertook 460,000 examinations of 290,000 specimens of evidence. Some of these investigations—33 percent—were done for agencies other than the FBI. It is worth remembering that the FBI laboratory is available to process evidence for local and state law enforcement agencies. See Appendix A, Sending Evidence to the FBI Laboratory.

As important as the analysis of evidence may be, without proper recognition, collection, preservation, and transfer to the laboratory, the evidence is worthless. This is the function of the crime scene processing division.

Crime Scene Processing Division

These individuals are trained in sketching and photographing the crime scene, in recognizing and collecting all types of evidence whether this involves vacuuming the area for retrieval of microscopic evidence, lifting latent prints, or making casts of impressions (footprints, tool marks, etc.) found at the scene. They will know how to properly package, label, and transmit the evidence to the laboratory. Usually, these individuals do not have degrees in the sciences. They may perform preliminary tests using field kits, for example, in determining whether a particular powder may be cocaine or another drug. While numerous regional crime laboratories have the resources and personnel to carry on top-quality work in many fields, the FBI laboratory stands out as a model. Here is how it is organized into groups working in the major areas of forensic science.

Figure 16-1 Criminalist marking evidence in a forensic laboratory (Courtesy *Law and Order* magazine, New York, NY).

Physics and Chemistry Section

This is the heart of a major crime laboratory. It is certainly the place where the most sophisticated and expensive equipment is found. This group has the heaviest case loads. Such subspecialties as drug analysis, toxicology, and serology usually are included here (see Fig. 16-2). It analyzes such diverse evidence as glass, minerals and soil, prints, dyes, inks, hairs, and fibers. These individuals most likely have college degrees in chemistry or biology and more and more frequently advanced degrees in their specialties. They are often identified by the title of "criminalist," indicating they can analyze a number of different kinds of evidence, but usually they have one specialty.

Firearms Investigations and Identification

This group is often mistakenly referred to as the ballistics division. Their responsibilities extend beyond the analysis and comparison of bullets (and cartridge casings) as this name implies. They will identify and test weapons, determine the distance from which a weapon was fired, determine whether an individual fired a weapon, and often distinguish bullet wounds from other types of wounds (as well as ascertaining whether they are entrance or exit wounds). They may also be called upon to make tool mark comparisons. Usually,

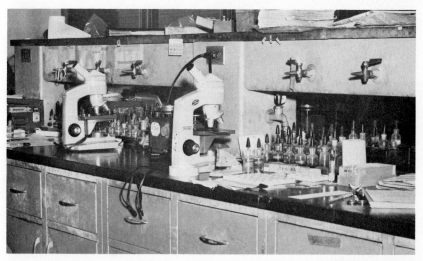

Figure 16-2   Narcotics laboratory section of New York Police Department. Note reagents in eye dropper bottles, microscopes, and spot plates—all used in the drug identification process (Courtesy New York Police Department Narcotics Laboratory).

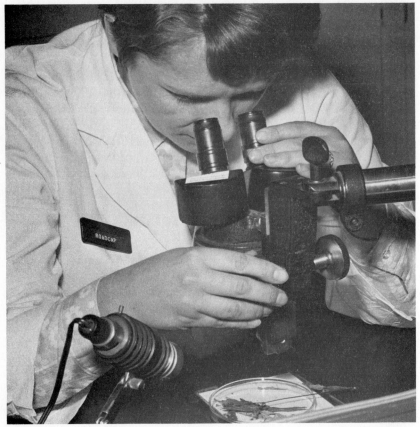

Figure 16-3   Criminalist examining evidence with stereoscopic microscope (Courtesy Pennsylvania State Police).

they are not scientists per se but individuals with special training in this type of work.

Bomb Disposal

These individuals can disarm explosive devices, as well as process the scene of an explosion for evidence. Often, they received their initial training in the military. This is supplemented by special courses such as are given by the FBI.

Polygraph and Voiceprint Identification

These personnel are usually skilled interrogators with a knack for dealing with and understanding people. They have special training in the operation of the associated instruments. More importantly, they are trained to administer and interpret these tests.

Document Examination

All types of related evidence—typewritten analysis, paper analysis, ink analysis, handwriting analysis, etc.—are processed here. The individuals must be versed in many areas of science and draw heavily from other divisions such as physics and chemistry, and photography.

Additional Services

The FBI performs some additional services. In its radio engineering division, it deals with electronic devices. These include illegal transmitters, voice analysis equipment, and devices illegally attached to telephone lines, to mention a few.

The cryptanalysis division deals with the decoding of messages, writings, etc. The FBI also maintains an extensive file of inks, fingerprints, hairs and fibers, tire treads, and typewriter standards, for comparison with samples of evidence. These reference libraries are extremely important because the analysis of evidence in most cases amounts to comparing the evidence to some standard. The techniques for performing these comparisons are becoming very sophisticated.

Crime Laboratory Personnel

Depending on the particular laboratory, the personnel may be police or civilian, with or without a baccalaureate degree in the sciences. One characteristic of these laboratories is the increased reliance on exotic instrumentation and techniques. Generally, to the people who work there, this means more training and education. A degree in chemistry seems most desirable. For example, the New Jersey state police crime laboratory in West Trenton employed a professional staff of forty-four in 1972. Of these, thirty-five were chemists, four with the Ph.D. degree.

In most laboratories, only certain individuals are assigned or trained to process crime scenes. In others, all the technicians are trained in processing crime scenes. Studies have shown actual laboratory personnel are involved in gathering less than 10 percent of the evidence reaching the laboratory. In all cases, there are rigorous procedures for transmitting and storing evidence so that the chain of evidence is unbroken.

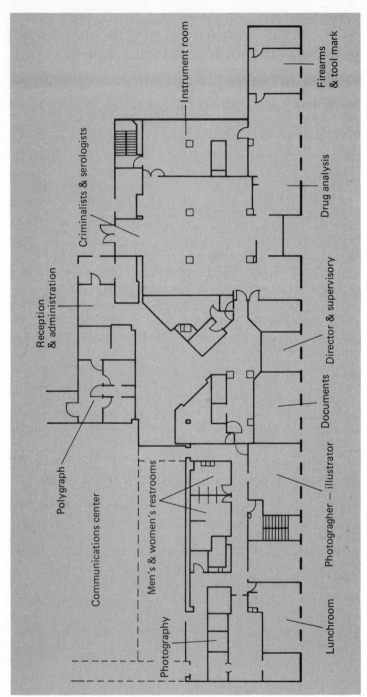

Figure 16-4 Schematic of the new Western Washington State laboratory (Courtesy Western Washington State crime laboratory).

In Perspective

The powerful techniques for the processing of evidence made available to law enforcement agencies by the crime laboratories are certainly impressive. The authors would not have done their jobs properly if this point were not made. But this can be overemphasized, or, more properly, blown out of perspective. It is very infrequent that an individual is convicted solely on the basis of forensic evidence. There is no substitute for the exercise of plain common sense during an investigation. Often, it is the determination, persistence, alertness, and hard work of the investigator that results in a conviction.

The clever investigator will know what to look for and what questions can be answered by the correct processing of evidence when it is sent to the laboratory. These answers may provide vital leads, indicating what direction the investigation should take, who is suspect, who is innocent, what vehicle was used, whether the truth is being told by a witness, etc.

In a detailed investigation of the procedures used by law enforcement agencies in processing crime scenes, it was found that of all serious crimes committed during the study period (murders, burglaries, automobile thefts, thefts, robberies, rapes, assaults with battery—neglecting cases of minor assaults and crimes involving less than $50), only 4 cases of a possible 1400 resulted in a laboratory examination. Over 1300 of the cases were judged to have data suitable for laboratory review. Of all the evidence analyzed by this laboratory during the same time, 92 percent involved drugs and narcotics. The high demand narcotics analysis puts on crime laboratory personnel is typical. It even tends to crowd out the analysis of other types of evidence since there is a shortage of facilities, personnel, and money in most laboratories. Table 16-1 indicates the frequency with which different types of evidence occur in different categories of crimes. These data are based on a 3-month study in 1969 in a medium-sized western city. A total of 749 cases were involved in compiling these data.[1]

If each of these numbers is multiplied by 100, then the result would represent the percentage of cases in that particular type of crime that involved the kind of evidence in question. Some examples will clarify this point. Using fingerprints as an illustration: they occurred as evidence in 45 percent of the automobile theft cases, 30 percent of the rape cases, 40 percent of the murder cases, and 41 percent of all the cases studied.

[1] Brian Parker and Joseph Peterson, "Physical Evidence Utilization in the Administration of Criminal Justice," LEAA Grant NI-032, Washington, D.C., U.S. Dept. of Justice, 1972.

TABLE 16-1: Physical Object Category Rate of Occurrence Compared with Suspected Offense Classes

Physical Object Category	Number of Categories per Number of Cases in Each Category											
	Burglary Res.	Burglary Non-res.	Auto	Sub total	Auto Theft	Theft	Robbery	Rape	Assault Battery	Murder	All Others	Total
Tool marks	.39	.68	.54	.46	.39	.24	.10	.0	.2	.4	.32	.43
Fingerprints	.41	.46	.41	.42	.45	.45	.29	.3	.4	.4	.27	.41
Organic substance	.35	.19	.10	.28	.31	.18	.14	.5	.2	.4	.14	.27
Glass	.16	.38	.32	.23	.15	.06	.00	.2	.2	.2	.50	.21
Paint	.21	.23	.09	.20	.24	.12	.00	.5	.0	.2	.32	.20
Track	.23	.31	.04	.22	.10	.09	.10	.3	.2	.2	.18	.20
Clothing	.17	.09	.16	.15	.20	.09	.19	.8	.2	.2	.18	.16
Wood	.20	.32	.03	.20	.04	.00	.05	.0	.0	.0	.09	.16
Dust	.20	.13	.06	.17	.13	.09	.10	.3	.0	.2	.05	.15
Cigarette	.09	.19	.07	.11	.29	.18	.38	.5	.0	.2	.14	.15
Paper	.07	.19	.10	.10	.31	.12	.19	.2	.0	.0	.18	.13
Soil	.14	.09	.04	.12	.23	.03	.05	.2	.2	.4	.05	.12
Fibers	.15	.14	.04	.13	.01	.03	.14	.0	.0	.0	.05	.11
Tools	.05	.22	.09	.09	.09	.09	.19	.2	.4	.4	.05	.10
Grease	.05	.16	.04	.07	.09	.12	.00	.2	.0	.0	.05	.07
Document	.05	.16	.03	.07	.10	.06	.05	.0	.0	.0	.05	.07
Container	.05	.04	.06	.05	.09	.12	.00	.0	.2	.2	.41	.07
Construction material	.08	.11	.03	.08	.04	.00	.00	.0	.0	.0	.14	.07
Metal	.03	.10	.04	.05	.05	.09	.00	.2	.0	.2	.14	.05
Hair	.06	.05	.01	.05	.03	.03	.10	.5	.6	.0	.09	.05
Blood	.02	.06	.00	.03	.05	.03	.14	.2	.0	.6	.23	.05
Inorganic Substance	.03	.09	.00	.04	.03	.00	.00	.0	.0	.0	.14	.04
Miscellaneous	.09	.07	.12	.09	.14	.09	.05	.2	.2	.2	.09	.10

The work of the forensic laboratory, of course, aids the police investigator. However, the answers provided must be fitted together by the investigator, like the pieces of a jigsaw puzzle, to form a logical whole. It is not wise to believe that the more expensive the instrument, the better the quality of the evidence processing. There may be simpler, less expensive methods for arriving at the same conclusions. These may be more easily explained to a jury of laypeople. There is no instrument that can replace clear thinking. The following case history, "A Forensic Jig-Saw," provides an excellent illustration of the interplay between the investigation of a crime and the crime laboratory.

Some time ago the body of a young girl was found partly concealed behind a hawthorn hedge at the end of a rough track leading into some fields. Her clothing was in disarray and only one of her shoes was found.

She had last been seen the previous evening waiting for a bus near her home, two miles from where she was found. The cause of death was given as asphyxia due to pressure on the neck. There were also scratches on the body which could have been caused by barbed wire or the hawthorn hedge. The remains of a girl's black shoe and some underwear were found in a field two days later, seven miles away. They had been burnt but the ashes remained and these included metal components which matched those present on the shoe found near the girl's body.

Scientific examination of the scene, the girl's clothing and post mortem samples yielded valuable scientific evidence involving biological, chemical and tyre mark examinations and led to the laboratory examination of over 10,000 saliva samples, 15 cars, 50 samples of car paint, 35 samples of car carpets, 10 samples of car seats and numerous tyres.

The position of the body and the absence of soil on the clothing suggested that a vehicle had been used and that the body had been carried from the vehicle to where it was found.

This case was unusual in that correct interpretation of contact trace materials could be used to describe the vehicle involved as well as to predict the probable blood group of the assailant.

THE SCIENTIFIC EVIDENCE 1. A large number of superimposed tyre marks were present in the field particularly around the field gate, adjacent to where the body was found, and in the track leading into the field.

These marks, which included tractor, bicycle and car tyre marks, were preserved by covering the track and the gate area of the field with polythene sheeting. The most recent tyre marks indicated that the vehicle came up the track, entered and turned round in the field, getting bogged down at one point and departed back down the track. These latter marks were examined in detail— measurements of turning circle, track and tyre width were taken and photographs and plaster casts were prepared at the tracks which had been identified as having been left by each of the four wheels of this last vehicle to pass where the body was found. Over 1 cwt (50.8 kg) of plaster of paris was used.

TYRES The vehicle responsible for leaving the marks had a turning circle of approximately 37 ft and a rear track measurement of 51 in. The front track width could not be measured accurately because of cornering considerations. It was concluded that the vehicle had two 165 size Dunlop SP41 radial tyres on the rear axle and two 560 or 590 size Fisk Premier cross ply tyres on the front axle. The turning circle was within the range of a large percentage of popular cars and not of great significance. Also the rear track width could not be attributed to a specific model of car. The Dunlop tyres on the rear axle were a fairly common tyre but the Fisk tyres on the front axle were relatively rare.

Many footwear marks were found near the body. These were recorded by photographs and plaster casts. All these marks were later eliminated, the vast majority belonging to the person who discovered the body.

BLOOD GROUPING 2. Tests carried out subsequent to the post mortem examination showed that sexual intercourse had taken place and that despite the very occasional anomalies encountered in secretor groupings, there was justification for predicting that the person who had had intercourse with the girl was a blood group B secretor. The deceased was a blood group O secretor.

This discovery led to the police taking over 10,000 saliva samples collected from people living locally and any other male persons who were acquainted with the deceased or who were interviewed by the police. Grouping tests were carried out in duplicate. The proportion of these people who were blood group B secretors was 5.9 per cent which is very close to the generally quoted figure of 6 per cent for the British population.

CARPET 3. The loose fibre debris from five of the deceased's articles of clothing included some 30 similar dark red textile fibres. Their widespread distribution suggested they could have been recently transferred to the deceased's clothing. The fibres were coarse textured viscose rayon, some as coarse as 50 denier whilst others were 18 denier. It seemed likely that they had originated from carpets rather than clothing but it was established that they could not have originated from the carpets in the deceased's own home. Some of the fibres had microscopic amounts of a black rubber material at one end which suggested they could have originated from a non-woven car carpet with a black rubber backing.

Inquiries from textile and carpet manufacturers indicated that the fibres were crimped viscose and that fibres of these two deniers and with a black rubberized backing material were manufactured for motor cars under a particular trade mark until 1964. Samples from car carpet manufacturers which showed the best agreement had been manufactured in 1962 for the Austin A60 range of cars.

LEATHER SEAT 4. The loose debris from the girl's jumper included two very small (0.02 in) fragments of leather each having a pale blue painted surface. This material could not have originated from the deceased's leather coat. It seemed possible that these fragments could have come from a car seat where the upper surface of leather was peeling off in places. Most modern mass produced cars seats are not made of real leather and thus if these fragments were from a car it was likely to be from a narrow range of older vehicles.

REPAINTED SURFACE 5. The loose debris from the deceased's skirt included a small flake of red paint about 1 mm² in area. This comprised three distinct layers, two differing shades of red on a cream undercoat. Attempts to clean the flake for microscopic examination resulted in detachment of the uppermost layer. Small particles of grey material, thought possibly to be body filler, were observed adhering to the underside of the cream layer. This was in addition to a general 'rusty' surface discolouration. The observed sequence of colours did not correspond to any of the arrangements usually encountered in mass-produced vehicles. The general appearance and properties of the 'crime' flake suggested that it had originated from a fairly old vehicle which had been partly or completely repainted.

THE VEHICLE These findings were presented on the reasonable assumption that one or more of them could assist in the identification of the vehicle in which the deceased had been carried. The most likely type of vehicle was a pre 1964 BMC type of the Austin A60 size —although it was known that no car had been manufactured with this particular combination of colours. This suggested that the car had been resprayed and could perhaps contain certain parts from other vehicles. Some diligent police work resulted in many samples of car paint, car seat upholstery, car carpets and car tyres being submitted to the laboratory for comparison purposes. One set of samples related to a 1960 MG Magnette car recovered from a scrap yard. The body of this car had been partly painted over black on top of red and the number plates had been painted over black. It had blue leather seats and dark red carpets. The tyres were not on the vehicle but fortunately three of the four could be recovered.

The samples from the clothing (fibres, leather and paint) all matched the samples from this car in composition and fine detail and the tyre tracks from the field corresponded, even down to the presence of a repair plug, in one of the tyres. One of the carpets had an 8.5 in long head hair on it similar to those of the deceased. Extensive enquiries showed when and by whom the car had been purchased and when it had been scrapped. The previous owner had painted the car with two different colours of red paint, and had transferred to it some carpets from an Austin A60. The original colour of the car had been light blue with grey carpets.

A saliva sample from the car owner showed that he was a blood group B secretor and he was charged with the girl's murder nearly four months after the girl's body had been discovered.

CAREFUL EXAMINATIONS This case demonstrates the value of careful scientific examination of trace material combined with painstaking and prolonged enquiries. Some parts of the evidence had been preserved by chance in that the car body shell and tyres were still present in the scrap yard. Other material was preserved by prompt police action in covering the tyre tracks with polythene sheeting and in cordoning off the area where the body was found.[1]

---

[1] R.P.G. Gregory "A Forensic Jig-Saw," *Chemistry in Britain*, vol. 11, no. 12, pp. 436–37, December 1975.

The Expert Witness and Testifying in Court

What is an expert witness and how does he or she attain that status? There are no hard-and-fast rules governing the qualification of expert witnesses. As a matter of fact, each expert must qualify as such every time he or she takes the witness stand at a different trial. Generally, standards are as high as possible. The expert must be a person with above-average education and experience in a technical or scientific field. Membership in a professional society is not, in itself, a qualifying factor, nor is authorship of a book or an article. The standards of qualification embrace achievement and recognition in a particular field as well as personal character, integrity, and reputation.

Not all experts make good witnesses. Many testifying for the first time try too hard to impress the court with their knowledge, thus giving the defense the chance to find loopholes and contradictions in their testimony. Like everybody else, they need practice to become effective witnesses. For this reason, the Federal Bureau of Investigation maintains a corps of experts, with years of experience in specific areas of criminalistics, who stand ready to testify when the need arises. They are said to be among the most professional expert witnesses in the world.

One of the easiest ways to qualify as an expert witness is before a grand jury, where the qualifying is done by a prosecutor or district attorney. The defense attorney is not present; neither is the defendant (in most instances). A grand jury witness is not subject to cross-examination, as he or she would be in the courtroom. Jurors sometimes ask questions, but usually the expert will have little trouble answering them.

Testifying in Court

When you're called to take the witness stand, the first part is easy. In the familiar procedure often seen on television and in the movies, the clerk of the court will ask you to put your left hand on the Bible and to raise your right hand. (See Fig. 17-1.)

"Do you solemnly swear to tell the truth, the whole truth, and nothing but the truth?"

You answer, "I do."

You will then be asked to sit down and give your name and address (for security reasons, give your working address, not your home address).

Figure 17-1   Interior of a courtroom, in which the final decision of guilt or innocence is made.

Now the district attorney or prosecutor begins the preliminary line of questioning.

"What is your occupation?"

"How long have you been so employed?"

"What is your title?"

"Briefly describe your duties."

So far there is no problem.

Then, the prosecutor turns to the substance of the case before the court. There is nothing to worry about here either. You will have discussed your testimony with the prosecutor before the case came to trial. As a member of the law enforcement team, you are the prosecutor's witness, helping build the chain of evidence upon which the case depends. Your testimony, however, must be impartial. You are there only to state the true facts. Whether they prove guilt or innocence is for the jury to determine. He or she makes things as easy as possible for you. Just be yourself, answer all questions honestly (and briefly), and you will do very well.

Now comes the tricky part. The defense attorney rises and addresses you. He or she may seem friendly or hostile, casual or intensely involved. Whatever the appearance, watch out! The defense attorney, by training, profession, and legal obligation, is there for only one purpose—to secure the acquittal of his or her client. He or she will try to find all the flaws, loopholes, inconsistencies, and logical fallacies in your testimony. This may be done in any number of ways. You, on the other hand, must remain calm—confident of your ability and the truth of your testimony.

This is why it takes practice, skill, and a cool head to be a good witness in a court of law. This chapter comes at the end of the book because testifying in court is the climax of investigatory procedures. It is in court that the techniques of sound police work and scientific procedures really help to determine the course of justice. You and other witnesses for the prosecution must present your findings with integrity and unshakeable authority if this is to be the case.

Here is some advice about appearing as a witness in court. Of course, you will not be called to testify in every case you investigate. In fact, a large percentage of cases never come to trial, mainly because the accused pleads guilty when faced with the evidence or makes a deal about the sentence by plea bargaining with the district attorney. But many of the most important cases do go to trial, and it is conceivable that every individual who had anything to do with the case—police officer, fingerprint expert, document analyst, firearms examiner, detective, and police investigator—could be called to testify. If all the people involved in an investigation kept this fact in mind while working on a case, their testimony would be greatly improved. All the warnings throughout this book about the careful handling, labeling, and filing of evidence are designed to help prosecution witnesses build a chain of credible evidence in court.

How to Be an Effective Witness

Here are twenty-two suggestions to help you become an effective witness (Fig. 17-2).

1. Dress neatly and conservatively.
2. Seat yourself comfortably in the witness chair with as much poise as possible.
3. Make every effort to act relaxed, in command of yourself and the situation.
4. Answer questions slowly, distinctly, and loudly enough that the judge, jury, and all in the courtroom can hear you.
5. Answer only what you are asked. Do not enlarge upon any statement. Do not volunteer information.
6. Do not attempt to answer a question you do not understand.
7. Do not hesitate to ask to have a question repeated.

Figure 17-2   Helpful hint in testifying: a sloppy appearance detracts from your testimony.

8. Do not improvise if your memory is faulty. Tell the court you do not remember.

9. Do not get excited.

10. Do not argue.

11. Do not use police jargon, abbreviations, or technical terms that the average person would not understand.

12. Do not repeat obscene language without prior warning to the court.

13. Admit, if asked, that you have discussed the case with the prosecuting official.

14. Answer all questions respectfully by saying "Yes, Your Honor" or "No, Your Honor."

15. Be as brief as possible in your answers.

16. Think about the question before attempting to give an answer.

17. Be confident of your opinion.

18. Look at the defense attorney and jury when answering questions.

19. If you take out your notes in court, be prepared to be cross-examined about them.

20. Be objective in your testimony and avoid giving the impression of prejudice or that you are trying only to prove guilt. Your only role is to present the facts.

21. Be accurate and factual in all your replies.

22. Review the case before you take the stand. You should have a grasp of the details as well as the broad outline.

Now consider these points in detail.

Dress

It is important that your clothes reinforce the image of credibility and probity that you, as a witness, are trying to project in court, especially to the jurors. "Dress conservatively" is the way most lawyers would put it. For men, this means a dark suit and white shirt; for women, a dress or suit not necessarily funereal but not too attention-getting either. In other words, avoid the temptation to overdress because you are going to be the center of attention. *Remember:* You are on the stand to state facts or render a serious opinion as an expert, not to show off in dress or any other way.

Uniformed police officers must abide by the custom of the court on the question of whether to wear their gun on the witness stand. If the gun is worn, care should be taken—the accused may go beserk and try to grab it.

Behavior

You may be nervous—in fact, you probably will be! But make every effort to appear calm. Tell yourself that you are here to do an important job in a reasonable and mature way. Signs of anxiety or tension, such as twisting in the chair, shifting your position, folding and unfolding your hands, may quickly detract from your creditility. Assume an air of quiet confidence. It will add a measure of authority to your testimony.

Answering Questions

First things first. *You are under oath.* If you lie, you commit a crime. Do not be embarrassed to tell the defense attorney, if asked, that you have discussed the case with the prosecutor. This is standard procedure.

Respond to questions alertly, but do not hurry with your answers. Pause a moment to give the prosecutor a chance to object to the question, if this is necessary. It goes without saying that your answers must be clearly enunciated and loud enough for everyone in court to hear. Your voice carries its own tone of conviction and confidence. Do not be shy! And avoid a droning monotone when explaining an event or situation. Change the tone and pitch of your delivery as you would in normal conversation. Speaking in a normal, pleasant voice not only influences the jury but also helps to ease your nervousness.

If a defense attorney asks a question that confuses you, perhaps because of its length, do not hesitate to ask that the question be repeated. More often than not, it will turn out well for your credibility as a witness.

Never Volunteer Information

This is extremely important. There is a natural inclination to tell all you know about a happening when being questioned. But this is precisely what the defense attorney wants you to do, because the added information may provide the opportunity to discredit your testimony. It is the defense attorney's job, what he or she is being paid for. And it is your job to defuse such tactics by sticking strictly to the answer called for by the question.

Handling Harassment

The mandate to be calm gets tougher if the defense attorney begins to bully you with rapid-fire questions, snide remarks, broad innuendos about your honesty or competence, or highly excited charges. This is the time to keep your cool, realizing that the defense is merely acting out a charade intended to damage you as a witness. If the defense attorney goes too far, of course, the prosecutor will properly object, and the judge will warn the defense. By maintaining a reasonable attitude—not rising to the defense's bait, in other words—you will gain the jury's respect as a professional.

Nothing But the Truth

In addition to the fact that you are under oath, there is a compelling reason for always telling the truth on the witness stand. It is, quite simply, that any lies will probably be discovered in the course of the trial. Thus you will be discredited as a witness and will suffer damage to your reputation as a law enforcement officer.

Now it is likely that you are saying to yourself that the idea of lying in court, under oath, is unthinkable, especially since you appear as part of your job, not seeking any gain for yourself but only to establish the chain of evidence that you have helped put together. Sometimes, however, witnesses lie almost inadvertently. Usually, it is to protect their egos as, for example, in admitting that they had made a mistake or that they cannot remember a certain detail. If you have made a mistake in the course of the investigation or in your testimony, admit it. If you cannot remember, say so. There is a temptation often to improvise when memory is vague. This is a mistake, which an alert defense attorney will use against you.

Jargon

Your whole mission on the witness stand is to help the jury understand the case about which it will cast its verdict. Thus, you must try to avoid the kind of language that persons unfamiliar with police work may not understand. Do not say, for instance, "DOA" when you mean "dead on arrival." Do not use police slang or technical terms either. Talk to the court in direct, simple words, making sure your meaning is clear. You score no points for your learning, scholarship, or command of the English language. You confuse the jury when you use police abbreviations and "in" language. Spell out everything as clearly as possible.

Obscenity

In repeating the quotes of those involved in a crime—a sex case, for example—it might be necessary for you to use obscene words in open court. It is a good idea to advise the judge that such words are going to be forthcoming. This is a matter of courtesy, a way of showing your respect, as is your use of the phrases "Your honor," "yes, sir," and "no, sir."

Visual Aids for Drama and Understanding

There is nothing that commands the attention of a jury more than a witness using visual aids, especially hard visible evidence such as the murder weapon. Allowing the jury to see the evidence or some tangible representation of it, like a photograph, will have a decided effect upon its verdict. (See Fig. 17-3 and 17-4.) This is why in the preceding chapters the importance of marking physical evidence for identification has been stressed. The evidence must be secured from the time of finding until its appearance at the trial. There is little dispute that can be raised by a defense attorney who is shown the initials of the officer on physical evidence.

The following will give you some general idea of the exhibits that may be introduced during a trial.

> *Physical evidence*
>   Weapons
>   Clothing
>   Letters
>   Bank statements
> *Photographs*
>   Fingerprint comparisons
>   Ballistic comparisons
>   Tool mark comparisons
>   Handwriting comparisons
>   Shoe print and tire tread comparisons

Figure 17-3　Visual presentations assist investigation and prosecution.

Voiceprint comparison charts
Instrumentation spectra
Slides or movies
Three-dimensional models

There are many practical reasons for using visual aids. The statement "A picture is worth a thousand words" holds true in the courtroom. During the famous Brink's robbery trial in Boston in 1956, a complete model of the building and the surrounding streets was used to great effect, helping jurors visualize how the crime was committed.

Imagine a pathologist or medical examiner testifying on the witness stand in technical medical terminology about the cause of death of a homicide victim. Now imagine the same doctor using an enlarged outline of the human form showing the wounded areas and describing the cause of death. It is much easier for the jurors to understand the doctor when they can see what she or he describes.

In many cases, a conviction is obtained as a direct result of the excellent testimony of a convincing witness. The best criminal lawyer cannot offset the identification of a suspect's fingerprints on a murder weapon. This means that the testimony of the expert and the nature of the evidence are what convinces the jury of the guilt of the accused. Once a jury is convinced of that guilt, it usually cannot be misled by dramatic defense tactics.

The impression you make on the witness stand depends on

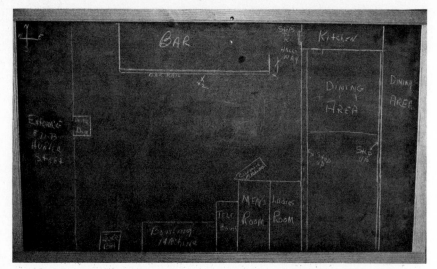

Figure 17-4   Blackboard sketch used during trial of "double homicide."

many factors. This chapter has discussed those over which you have some control. By anticipating the pitfalls that inevitably confront an inexperienced witness, you rest assured that your testimony will reflect credit on yourself and the law enforcement department you represent.

Appendix A

Sending Evidence to the FBI Laboratory

Local law enforcement agencies may call upon the facilities of the Federal Bureau of Investigation for the analysis of evidence. Below are instructions from the FBI concerning the proper procedures for doing so. Also included are a sample letter from a local agency requesting help, a sample report of the FBI Laboratory, an FBI report of the Identification Division, a complete chart containing information to be used in submitting evidence to the FBI laboratory, and regulations concerning the shipping of live ammunition.

I. Collection of physical evidence (five things to keep in mind)
   A. Obtain it legally:
      1. Warrant.
      2. Consent.
      3. Incidental to arrest.
   B. Describe it in notes:
      1. Location, circumstances, how obtained.
      2. Date, chain of custody.
      3. How identified.
   C. Identify it properly:
      1. Use initials, date, case number.
      2. Preferably on evidence itself. Liquids, soils, and tiny fragments must be placed in suitable container, sealed, and marked on the outside.
   D. Package it properly. One case to one box:
      1. Use suitable containers such as round pill boxes, plastic vials, glass or plastic containers, strong cardboard cartons.
      2. Seal securely against leakage.
      3. Package each item separately—avoid even appearance of leakage or contamination.
      4. If wet or bearing blood, air-dry before packaging (except arson cases where hydrocarbons are present).
   E. Maintain chain of custody—keep it short:
      1. Same person or persons should find, seal, initial, and send evidence, if possible.

307

The method shown below permits access to the invoice letter without breaking the inner seal. This allows the person entitled to receive the evidence to receive it in a sealed condition just as it was packed by the sender.

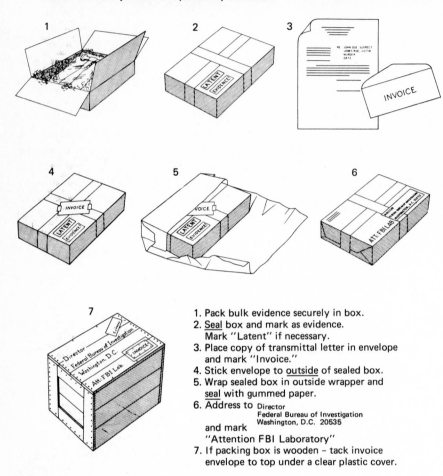

1. Pack bulk evidence securely in box.
2. <u>Seal</u> box and mark as evidence.
   Mark "Latent" if necessary.
3. Place copy of transmittal letter in envelope and mark "Invoice."
4. Stick envelope to <u>outside</u> of sealed box.
5. Wrap sealed box in outside wrapper and <u>seal</u> with gummed paper.
6. Address to Director
   Federal Bureau of Investigation
   Washington, D.C. 20535
   and mark
   "Attention FBI Laboratory"
7. If packing box is wooden – tack invoice envelope to top under a clear plastic cover.

Figure A-1 Proper sealing of evidence.

USE OFFICIAL LETTERHEAD

Police Headquarters
Right City, State (Zip Code)
March 17, 19--

Director
Federal Bureau of Investigation
U. S. Department of Justice
Washington, D. C. 20535

<u>ATTENTION: FBI LABORATORY</u>

Dear Sir:

RE: GUY PIDGIN, SUSPECT
EMPALL MERCHANDISE MART
BURGLARY

Sometime during the early morning of March 16, 19--,
someone entered the Empall Merchandise Mart through an unlocked
side window and made an unsuccessful attempt to rip open the
safe. The outer layer of metal on the safe door had been pried
loose from the upper right corner and bent outward ripping the
metal along the top and down the side of the safe about 12" each
way. The burglar may have been scared away because the job was
not completed. Investigation led us to one Guy Pidgin who denies
complicity. He voluntarily let us take his shoes and trousers
and a crowbar that was under his bed in his rooming house.

I am sending by railway express a package containing
the following evidence in this case:

1. One pair of shoes obtained from Guy Pidgin
2. A pair of grey flannel trousers obtained from
    Guy Pidgin
3. One 28" crowbar obtained from Guy Pidgin
4. Safe insulation taken from door of safe at Empall
    Merchandise Mart
5. Piece of bent metal approximately 12" x 12" taken
    from door of safe at Empall Merchandise Mart. In
    order to differentiate the two sides cut by us,
    we have placed adhesive tape on them.
6. Chips of paint taken from the side of safe
7. Fingerprint card for Guy Pidgin
8. Ten transparent lifts

It will be appreciated if you will examine the shoes
and trousers to see if there is any safe insulation on them and
to see if there are any paint chips on them that match the paint
taken from the safe. Also, we would be interested to know whether
it is possible to determine if the crowbar was used to open the
safe. Examine items 5 and 8 to determine if latent fingerprints
are present. If present, compare with item 7.

This evidence which should be returned to us, has not
been examined by any other expert.

Very truly yours,

James T. Wixling
Chief of Police

Figure A-2 Sample letter sent to FBI laboratory by local law enforcement agency.

2. Maintain in locked vault, cabinet, or room until shipped.
3. Send by railway express, air express, registered mail, registered air mail, or personal delivery to laboratory or identification division (there is no way to trace parcel post, certified mail, or regular mail).

II. How to request an FBI laboratory or fingerprint examination: (See Fig. A-2.)
  A. All requests should be made by letter, *in duplicate.*

  To: Director
  Federal Bureau of Investigation
  Washington, D.C. 20535

  Marked: "ATTENTION: FBI Laboratory" or "ATTENTION: FBI Identification Division, Latent Fingerprint Section" in accordance with the following:

  1. If evidence is for laboratory or combined laboratory-fingerprint examination, it should be marked "ATTENTION: FBI Laboratory."
  2. If evidence is *exclusively* for fingerprint examination, mark "ATTENTION: FBI Identification Division, Latent Fingerprint Section."

  B. Use additional copies of this letter of request as "Invoices" for separate shipment of evidence (see Part III,B).
  C. Information in letter should include:
    1. Complete names of all suspects and victims for indexing purposes.
    2. Nature of violation or type of crime (character of case).
    3. Date and place of crime.
    4. Brief facts of case insofar as they pertain to the requested examinations—such as whether soil is from filled area, whether evidence was weathered or otherwise altered, whether preservative was added to blood, or whether evidence is in the form in which it was at time of crime. Include photographs if you feel they will assist.
    5. How evidence is being sent (herewith or under separate cover—see Part III).
    6. List of evidence correlated with notes on wrappings of individual items, if appropriate.
    7. What examinations or comparisons are to be conducted.

8. Whether to be compared with evidence in other *specific* cases.
9. Reference to previous correspondence in this or related case, if any.
10. Disposition that should be made of the evidence.
11. If submitted for laboratory examination, include statement certifying that same evidence has not and will not be subjected to examination by other experts for the prosecution in the same scientific field.* This statement is not required regarding fingerprint evidence.
12. Include statement as to whether any civil action has been specifically indicated by interested parties.
13. Whether expeditious examination is needed. *Caution:* This treatment should not be *routinely* requested.

III. Dependent on size and type, evidence may be submitted:
    A. *Herewith.*
       1. Certain small items of evidence, such as a fraudulent check or latent lifts, may be submitted along with the letter of request. This method is limited to items not endangered by transmission in an envelope.
       2. Letter of request would state "Submitted herewith are the following items of evidence."
    B. *Under separate cover.* Generally used for shipment of numerous and/or bulky items of evidence. Letter of request would state "Submitted under separate cover by (method of shipment) are the following items of evidence."
       1. Submit letter of request, in duplicate, by appropriate mailing method. (See Part II on contents of letter.)
       2, Pack bulky evidence securely in box.
       3. *Seal* box and mark as evidence. Mark "Latent" if necessary.
       4. Place copy of transmittal letter (letter of request) in envelope and mark "Invoice."
       5. Attach envelope containing invoice to *outside* of sealed box.
       6. Wrap sealed box in outside wrapper and *seal* with gummed paper. Attach any necessary labels.
       7. Address to: Director
                        Federal Bureau of Investigation
                        Washington, D.C. 20535

* Exceptions are made on a case-by-case basis if this is a significant obstacle to an orderly prosecution.

and marked to attention of appropriate FBI division. (See II,A, 1 and 2 of this section.)

8. If packing box is wood, tack invoice envelope to top under a clear plastic cover.

IV. Steps an officer should take before calling an FBI laboratory or latent fingerprint expert to testify:
   A. Ascertain whether the expert is a necessary witness. Is his or her testimony material? Can report be stipulated to by defense?
   B. Advise the Bureau when and where the trial is to be held as far in advance as possible in order to avoid conflicts with other commitments.
   C. Advise regarding the expected duration of the trial and the exact date on which the expert will be needed.
   D. Arrange for a conference between the prosecutor and the expert prior to the time the expert takes the stand, and arrange for the expert's early release after testifying.
   E. Furnish the names of opposing experts, if any, and ascertain whether the prosecutor contemplates using any other experts.

FBI experts will furnish testimony regarding evidence they have examined. In the interest of economy, however, their testimony should not be requested if it is to be duplicated by another prosecution expert. (It is realised that exceptions to this general policy may be required, in a given instance.) Likewise, in the case of pretrial action (preliminary or grand jury hearings, for example), testimony should not be requested if legal considerations permit the substitution of FBI evidence reports.

REPORT
of the

FBI

LABORATORY

FEDERAL BUREAU OF INVESTIGATION
WASHINGTON, D. C. 20535

To: Mr. James T. Wixling
Chief of Police
Right City, State (Zip Code)

March 22, 19--

FBI FILE NO. 95-67994

LAB. NO. PC-C4800 RF PD ST

Re: GUY PIDGIN, SUSPECT;
EMPALL MERCHANDISE MART;
BURGLARY

YOUR NO.

Examination requested by: Addressee

Reference: Letter dated 3/17/--

Examination requested: Microscopic - Instrumental Analyses - Toolmarks

Specimens:

Q1	Right shoe belonging to GUY PIDGIN (your item 1)
Q2	Left shoe belonging to GUY PIDGIN (your item 1)
Q3	Pair of gray flannel trousers belonging to GUY PIDGIN (your item 2)
Q4	28" crowbar belonging to GUY PIDGIN (your item 3)
Q5	Piece of bent metal from door of safe (your item 5)
K1	Insulation from safe door at EMPALL MERCHANDISE MART (your item 4)
K2	Paint from front and side of safe at EMPALL MERCHANDISE MART (your item 6)

Also Submitted: 1 fingerprint card and ten transparent lifts (your items 7 and 8)

This examination has been made with the understanding that the evidence is connected with an official investigation of a criminal matter and that the Laboratory report will be used for official purposes only, related to the investigation or a subsequent criminal prosecution. Authorization cannot be granted for the use of the Laboratory report in connection with a civil proceeding.

C M Kelley

Clarence M. Kelley
Director

Figure A-3 *Above:* sample report of the FBI Laboratory; *page 314:* result of examination, sent in response to request by local law enforcement agency.

Result of examination:

The insulation from the safe at the EMPALL MERCHANDISE MART, K1, is a vermiculite type used by several leading safe manufacturers.

Particles of vermiculite safe insulation similar to K1 were found in and on the shoes, Q1 and Q2, on the crowbar, Q4, and in the debris removed from the gray trousers, Q3. The particles of safe insulation on or in Q1, Q2, Q4 and Q3 either came from the safe represented by K1 or from another safe containing the same kind of insulation as K1.

The paint chips, K2, from the safe consisted of five layers of paint:

(1) Dark green enamel
(2) Light green enamel
(3) Gray enamel
(4) Black lacquer
(5) Red primer

The Q3 trousers contained chips of paint consisting of five layers of paint similar in colors, layer structure, texture and composition to the K2 paint and could have come from the same source as K2 or another surface painted in a similar manner with similar paint.

The Q4 crowbar has smears of green paint on it similar to the top two layers of paint of K2 and the smears could have come from the same source as K2.

The Q5 piece of metal had no toolmarks of value for comparison with the Q4 crowbar.

The evidence in this case is being returned to you under separate cover by registered mail. The "Also Submitted" items will be the subject of a separate report.

FEDERAL BUREAU OF INVESTIGATION
Washington, D. C. 20537
REPORT
of the
IDENTIFICATION DIVISION
LATENT FINGERPRINT SECTION

YOUR FILE NO.

FBI FILE NO.   95-67994

LATENT CASE NO. A-73821

March   22, 19--

<u>REGISTERED</u>

TO: Mr. James T. Wixling
    Chief of Police
    Right City, State (Zip Code)

RE: GUY PIDGIN;
    EMPALL MERCHANDISE MART
    RIGHT CITY, STATE
    MARCH 16, 19--
    BURGLARY

REFERENCE: Letter March 17, 19--
EXAMINATION REQUESTED BY: Addressee
SPECIMENS: Piece of bent metal, Q5
         Ten transparent lifts
         Fingerprints of Guy Pidgin, FBI #213762J9

        Four latent fingerprints of value were developed
on the piece of metal, Q5. Seven latent fingerprints of
value appear on three lifts marked "safe door" and five
latent fingerprints of value appear on two lifts marked
"side window." No additional latent prints of value appear
on the remaining lifts.

        Twelve of the latent fingerprints are not identical
with the fingerprints of Guy Pidgin, FBI #213762J9. For the
results of the additional comparisons conducted see the
attached page.

        Photographs of the unidentified latent fingerprints
have been prepared for our files and will be available for
any additional comparisons you may desire.

Clarence M. Kelley

Clarence M. Kelley, Director

Figure A-4   Sample report of the FBI Identification Division, Latent Fingerprint Section, sent in response to request by local law enforcement agency.

SHIPPING OF LIVE AMMUNITION
REGULATIONS FOR SHIPMENT OF SMALL-ARMS
AMMUNITION (CLASS C EXPLOSIVES) EXCERPTED FROM
"HAZARDOUS MATERIALS REGULATIONS OF THE
DEPARTMENT OF TRANSPORTATION"
(Tariff #29)-Effective 1/14/75

§173.00 Definitions of class C explosives. (a) Explosives, class
C, are defined as certain types of manufactured articles which contain class A, or class B explosives, or both, as components but in
restricted quantities, and certain types of fireworks. These explosives are further specifically described in this section.

(b) *Small arms ammunition* is fixed ammunition consisting of a
metallic, plastic composition, or paper cartridge case, a primer and
a propelling charge, with or without bullet, projectile, shot, tear
gas material, tracer components, or incendiary compositions, or
mixtures and is further limited to the following:

(1) *Ammunition* designed to be fired from a pistol, revolver,
rifle, or shotgun held by the hand or to the shoulder.

(2) *Ammunition* of caliber less than 20 millimeters with incendiary, solid, inert or empty projectiles (with or without tracers),
designed to be fired from machine guns or cannons.

(3) *Blank cartridges* including canopy remover cartridges,
starter cartridges, and seat ejector cartridges, containing not more
than 500 grains of propellant powder, provided that such cartridges shall be incapable of functioning en masse as a result of
the functioning of any single cartridge in the container or as a result of exposure to external flame.

(4) Twenty millimeter ammunition other than specified in
§173.53 (q).

§173.101 *Small-Arms ammunition. (a) Small-arms ammunition
must be packed in pasteboard or other inside boxes, or in partitions designed to fit snugly in the outside container, or must be packed in metal
clips. The partitions and metal clips must be so designed as to protect
the primers from accidental injury. The inside boxes, partitions and
metal clips must be packed in securely closed strong outside wooden or
fiberboard boxes or metal containers.* Blank Industrial Power Load
cartridges, similar to the 22 long rim-fire cartridge, may be packed
in bulk in securely closed fiberboard boxes.

(b) Small-arms ammunition in pasteboard or other inside
boxes, in addition to containers prescribed in paragraph (a) of this
section, may be shipped when packed in the same outside container with nonexplosive and nonflammable articles; or with small-

arms primers or percussion caps in quantity not to exceed 5 pounds. The weight of the small-arms ammunition packed with other articles must not exceed 55 pounds in outside fiberboard box, or 75 pounds in outside wooden box. The outside package must be a securely closed strong wooden or fiberboard container.

(c) *Each outside package must be plainly marked "SMALL-ARMS AMMUNITION."*

(d) Outside containers of cartridges with tear gas material must in addition to marking prescribed herein be marked "Tear Gas Cartridges" and must be labeled with "Tear Gas" label. (See §173.409 (a) (3) of this part for label.)

(e) No restrictions, other than proper description, packing and marking for small-arms ammunition and additional marking and labeling for tear gas cartridges are prescribed in this part for the transportation of small-arms ammunition and tear gas cartridges.

(f) Shipments of small-arms ammunition, including broken lots which have lost their identity (lot number identification), may be shipped loosely packed in securely closed strong wooden boxes or metal boxes, in carload or truckload lots, when shipments are made by or for the Departments of the Army, Navy or Air Force of the United States Government to depots or manufacturing plants for reprocessing or demilitarization. Seriously deteriorated ammunition or ammunition damaged to the point of exposing incendiary or tracer composition, spillage of propellant powder, or ammunition with other hazardous defects must not be shipped. Each outside package must be plainly marked "Small-Arms Ammunition."

§173.101a Cartridges, practice ammunition. (a) Cartridges, practice ammunition must be packaged in pasteboard or other *inside* boxes, or in partitions designed to *fit snugly in the outside packaging or must be packed in metal clips.* The partitions and metal clips must be so designed as to protect the primers from accidental injury. The *inside boxes*, partitions, and metal clips *must be packaged in securely closed strong outside wooden or fiberboard boxes or metal packagings.*

(1) Each package must be plainly marked "Cartridges, Practice Ammunition."

Chart to Be Used in Submitting Evidence to the FBI Laboratory

| Specimen | Identification | Amount Desired | | Preservation | Wrapping and Packing | Transmittal | Miscellaneous |
		Standard	Evidence				
Abrasives, including carborundum, emery, sand, etc.	On outside of container. Type of material. Date obtained. Name or initials.	Not less than one ounce	All	None	Use containers, such as ice-cream box, pillbox, or plastic vial. Seal to prevent any loss.	Registered mail or RR or air express	Avoid use of envelopes.
Acids	Same as above	One pint	All to one pint	None	Plastic or all-glass bottle. Tape in stopper. Pack in sawdust, glass, or rock wool. Use bakelite- or paraffin-lined bottle for hydrofluoric acid.	RR express only	Label acids, glass, corrosive.
Adhesive tape	Same as above	Recovered roll	All	None	Place on waxed paper or cellophane.	Registered mail	Do not cut, wad, or distort.
Alkalies—caustic soda, potash, ammonia, etc.	Same as above	One pint liquid One pound solid	All to one pint All to one pound	None	Plastic or glass bottle with rubber stopper held with adhesive tape	RR express only	Label alkali, glass, corrosive.
Ammunition (Cartridges)	Same as above			None	"Shipping of Live Ammunition," p. 45 and p. 132. Note: Outside shipping container must be made of wood or fiberboard, per Department of Transportation regulations.	RR or air express	Unless specific exam of cartridge is essential, do not submit. Shipping is costly.

Specimen	Identification	Amount	Handling/Wrapping	Packaging	Transmittal	Miscellaneous
Anonymous letters, extortion letters, bank robbery notes	Initial and date each document unless legal aspects or good judgment dictates otherwise.	All	Do not handle with bare hands.	Place in proper enclosure envelope and seal with "Evidence" tape or transparent cellophane tape. Flap side of envelope should show (1) wording "Enclosure(s) to Bureau from (name of submitting office)," (2) title of case, (3) brief description of contents, and (4) file number, if known. Staple to original letter of transmittal.	Registered mail	Advise if evidence should be treated for latent fingerprints.
Blasting caps	On outside of container. Type of material, date obtained, and name or initials.	All		Should not be forwarded until advised to do so by the Laboratory. Packing instructions will be given at that time.		
Blood: 1. Liquid Known samples	Use adhesive tape on outside of test tube. Name of donor, date taken, doctor's name, name or initials of submitting agent or officer	$1/6$ ounce (5 cc) collected in sterile test tube	Sterile tube only. NO REFRIGERANT.	Wrap in cotton, soft paper. Place in mailing tube or suitably strong mailing carton.	Air mail, special delivery, registered	Submit immediately. Don't hold awaiting additional items for comparison.
2. Drowning cases	Same as above	Two specimens: one from each side of heart	Same as above	Same as above	Air mail, special delivery, registered	Same as above

Chart to Be Used in Submitting Evidence to the FBI Laboratory (Continued)

Specimen	Identification	Standard	Amount Desired Evidence	Preservation	Wrapping and Packing	Transmittal	Miscellaneous
3. Small quantities: a. Liquid Questioned samples	Same as above as applicable		All to 1/6 ounce (5 cc)	Allow to dry thoroughly on nonporous surface.	Same as above	Air mail, special delivery, registered	Collect by using eyedropper or clean spoon, transfer to non-porous surface. Allow to dry and submit in pillbox.
b. Dry stains Not on fabrics	On outside of pillbox or plastic vial. Type of specimen date secured, name or initials.		As much as possible	Keep dry.	Seal to prevent leakage.	Registered mail	
4. Stained clothing, fabric, etc.	Use tag or mark directly on clothes. Type of specimens, date secured, name or initials.		As found	If wet when found, dry by hanging. Use no heat to dry. No preservative.	Each article wrapped separately and identified on outside of package. Place in strong box packed to prevent shifting of contents.	Registered mail or air or RR express	
Bullets (not cartridges)	Initials on base, nose or mutilated area		All found	None. Unnecessary handling obliterates marks.	Pack tightly in cotton or soft paper in pill, match or powder box. Label outside of box as to contents.	Registered mail	
Cartridges (live ammunition)	Initials on outside of case near bullet end	See Note re "Shipping of Live Ammunition"	All found	None	Same as above	RR express or air express	Live ammunition cannot be sent through U.S. mails. See "Shipping of Live Ammunition."

Specimen	Identification	Standards	Wrapping	Packing	Transmittal	Remarks
Cartridge cases (shells)	Initials preferably on inside near open end or on outside near open end.	All	None	Same as above	Registered mail	
Charred or burned	On outside of container indicate fragile nature of evidence, date obtained, name or initials.	All	None	Pack in rigid container between layers of cotton.	Registered mail	Added moisture, with atomizer or otherwise, not recommended.
Checks (fraudulent)	See anonymous letters.	All	None	See anonymous letters.	Registered mail	Advise what parts questioned or known. Furnish physical description of subject.
Check protector, rubber stamp and dater stamp sets, known standards. Note: Send actual device when possible.	Place name or initials, date, name of make and model, etc., on sample impressions.	Obtain several copies in full word-for-word order of each questioned checkwriter impression. If unable to forward rubber stamps, prepare numerous samples with different degrees of pressure.	None	See anonymous letters or bulky evidence wrapping instructions.	Registered mail	Do not disturb inking mechanisms on printing devices.
Clothing	Mark directly on garment or use string tag. Type of evidence, name or initials, date.	All	None	Each article individually wrapped with identification written on outside of package. Place in strong container.	Registered or RR or air express	Leave clothing whole. Do not cut out stains. If wet, hang in room to dry before packing.
Codes, ciphers, and foreign language material	As anonymous letters	All	None	As anonymous letters	As anonymous letters	Furnish all background and technical information pertinent to examination.

Chart to Be Used in Submitting Evidence to the FBI Laboratory (Continued)

Specimen	Identification	Amount Desired Standard	Amount Desired Evidence	Preservation	Wrapping and Packing	Transmittal	Miscellaneous
Drugs: 1. Liquids	Affix label to bottle in which found including name or initials and date.		All to one pint	None	If bottle has no stopper, transfer to glass-stoppered bottle and seal with adhesive tape.	Registered mail or RR or air express	Mark "Fragile." Determine alleged normal use of drug and if prescription, check with druggist to determine supposed ingredients.
2. Powders, pills, and solids	On outside of pillbox. Name or initials and date.		All to ¼ pound	None	Seal to prevent any loss by use of tape.	Registered mail or RR or air express	
Dynamite and other explosives	Consult the FBI Laboratory and follow their telephonic or telegraphic instructions.						
Fibers	On outside of sealed container or on object to which fibers are adhering	Entire garment or other cloth item	All	None	Folded paper or pillbox. Seal edges and openings with tape.	Registered mail	Do not place loose in envelope.
Firearms	Mark inconspicuously as if it were your own. String tag gun, noting complete description on tag. Investigative notes should reflect how and where gun marked.		All	Keep from rusting.	Wrap in paper and identify contents of package. Place in cardboard box or wooden box.	Registered mail or RR or air express	Unload all weapons before shipping.

Specimen	Identification	Standard	Amount desired	Preservative	Wrapping and packing	Transmittal	Remarks
Flash paper	Initials and date	One sheet	All	Fireproof, vented location away from any other combustible materials. If feasible, immerse in water.	Individual polyethylene envelopes double wrapped in manila envelopes. Inner wrapper sealed with paper tape.	Five sheets (8 × 10¹/₂) surface mail parcel post. Over 5 sheets telephonically consult FBI Laboratory.	Mark inner wrapper "Flash Paper Flammable."
Fuse, safety	Attach string tag or gummed paper label, name or initials, and date.	One foot	All	None	Place in manila envelope, box, or suitable container.	Registered mail or RR or air express	
Gasoline	On outside of all-metal container, label with type of material, name or initials, and date.	One quart	All to one gallon	Fireproof container	Metal container packed in wooden box	RR express only	
Glass fragments	Adhesive tape on each piece. Name or initials and date on tape. Separate questioned and known.	All	All	Avoid chipping.	Wrap each piece separately in cotton. Pack in strong box to prevent shifting and breakage. Identify contents.	Registered mail or RR or air express	Mark "Fragile."
Glass particles	Name or initials, date on outside of sealed container	3″ piece of broken item	All	None	Place in pillbox, plastic or glass vial; seal and protect against breakage.	Registered mail	Do not use envelopes.
Gunshot Residue Tests: 1. Paraffin	On outside of container. Type of material, date, and name or initials.	All	All	Containers must be free of any nitrate-containing substance. Keep cool.	Wrap in waxed paper or place in sandwich bags. Lay on cotton in a substantial box. Place in a larger box packed with absorbent material.	Registered mail	Use "Fragile" label. Keep cool.

Chart to Be Used in Submitting Evidence to the FBI Laboratory (Continued)

Specimen	Identification	Amount Desired		Preservation	Wrapping and Packing	Transmittal	Miscellaneous
		Standard	Evidence				
2. On cloth	Attach string tag or mark directly. Type of material, date, and name or initials.		All	None	Place fabric flat between layers of paper and then wrap, so that no residue will be transferred or lost.	Registered mail	Avoid shaking.
Hair	On outside of container. Type of material, date, and name or initials.	Dozen or more full length hairs from different parts of head and/or body	All	None	Folded paper or pillbox. Seal edges and openings with tape.	Registered mail	Do not place loose in envelope.
Handwriting and hand printing, known standards	Name or initials, date, from whom obtained, and voluntary statement should be included in appropriate place.	See footnote.*		None	See anonymous letters.	Registered mail	
Matches	On outside of container. Type of material, date, and name or initials.	One to two books of paper. One full box of wood.	All	Keep away from fire.	Metal container and packed in larger package to prevent shifting. Matches in box or metal container packed to prevent friction between matches.	RR express or registered mail	"Keep away from fire" lable

* Duplicate the original writing conditions as to text, speed, slant, size of paper, size of writing, type of writing instruments, etc. Do not allow suspect to see questioned writing. Give no instructions as to spelling, punctuation, etc. Remove each sample from sight as soon as completed. Suspect should fill out blank check forms in cases (FD-352). In hand printing cases, both upper- (capital) and lower-case (small) samples should be obtained. In forgery cases, obtain sample signatures of the person whose name is forged. Have writer prepare some specimens with hand not normally used. Obtain indicated handwriting when feasible.

Type of specimen	Identification	Standard amount desired	Minimum amount	Preservative	Wrapping and packing	Transmittal	Remarks
Medicines (See drugs.)							
Metal	Same as above	One pound	All to one pound	Keep from rusting.	Use paper boxes or containers. Seal and use strong paper or wooden box.	Registered mail or RR or air express	Melt number, heat treatment, and other specifications of foundry if available.
Oil	Same as above	One quart together with specifications	All to one quart	Keep away from fire	Metal container with tight screw top. Pack in strong box using excelsior or similar material.	RR express only	*Do not use dirt or sand for packing material.*
Obliterated, eradicated, or indented writing	See anonymous letters.		All	None	See anonymous letters.	Registered mail	Advise whether bleaching or staining methods may be used. Avoid folding.
Organs of body	On outside of container. Victim's name, date of death, date of autopsy, name of doctor, name or initials.		All to one pound.	None to evidence. Dry ice in package not touching glass jars.	Plastic or all-glass containers (glass jar with glass top)	RR or air express	"Fragile" label. Keep cool. Metal top containers must not be used. Send autopsy report.
Paint:							
1. Liquid	On outside of container. Type of material, origin if known, date, name or initials.	Original unopened container up to 1 gallon if possible	All to 1/4 pint	None	Friction-top paint can or large-mouth, screw-top jars. If glass, pack to prevent breakage. Use heavy corrugated paper or wooden box.	Registered mail or RR or air express	
2. Solid (paint chips or scrapings)	Same as above	At least 1/2 sq. inch of solid, with all layers represented	All. If on small object send object.	Wrap so as to protect smear.	If small amount, round pillbox or small glass vial with screw top. Seal to prevent leakage. Envelopes not satisfactory.	Registered mail or RR or air express	Do not pack in cotton. Avoid contact with adhesive materials.

Chart to Be Used in Submitting Evidence to the FBI Laboratory (Continued)

Specimen	Identification	Standard	Amount Desired Evidence	Preservation	Wrapping and Packing	Transmittal	Miscellaneous
Plaster casts of tire treads and shoe prints	On back before plaster hardens. Location, date and name or initials.	Send in shoes and tires of suspects. Photographs and sample impressions are usually not suitable for comparison.	All shoe prints; entire circumference of tires.	Allow casts to cure (dry) before wrapping.	Wrap in paper and cover with suitable packing material to prevent breakage. Do not wrap in unventilated plastic bags.	Registered mail or RR or air express	Use "Fragile" label. Mix approximately four pounds of plaster to quart of water.
Powder patterns (See gunpowder tests.)							
Rope, twine, and cordage	On tag or container. Type of material, date, name or initials.	One yard	All		Wrap securely.	Registered mail	
Safe insulation or soil	On outside of container. Type of material, date, name or initials.	1/2 pound	All to one pound		Use containers, such as pillbox or plastic vial. Seal to prevent any loss.	Registered mail or RR or air express	Avoid use of glass containers and envelopes.
Shoe print lifts (impressions on hard surfaces)	On lifting tape or paper attached to tape. Name or initials and date.	Photograph before making lift of dust impression.	All	None	Prints in dust are easily damaged. Fasten print or lift to bottom of a box so that nothing will rub against it.	Registered mail	Always rope off crime scene area until shoe prints or tire treads are located and preserved.
Tools	On tools or use string tag. Type of tool identifying number, date, name or initials.		All		Wrap each tool in paper. Use strong cardboard or wooden box with tools packed to prevent shifting.	Registered mail or RR or air express	

Specimen	Identification	Amount desired	Method of preserving or collecting	Protection of evidence	Packing and wrapping	Manner of shipping	Remarks
Tool marks	On object or on tag attached to or on opposite end from where tool marks appear. Name or initials and date.	All	Send in the tool. If impractical, make several impressions on similar material as evidence using entire marking area of tool.	Cover ends bearing tool marks with soft paper and wrap with strong paper to protect ends.	After marks have been protected, wrap in strong wrapping paper, place in strong box, and pack to prevent shifting.	Registered mail or RR or air express	
Typewriting, known standards	Place name or initials, date, serial number, name of make and model, etc., on specimens.		Obtain at least one copy in full word-for-word order of questioned typewriting. Also include partial copies in light, medium, and heavy degrees of touch. Also carbon paper samples of every character on the keyboard.	None	See anonymous letters.	Registered mail	Examine ribbon for evidence of questioned message thereon. For carbon paper samples either remove ribbon or place in stencil position.
Urine or water	On outside of container. Type of material, name of subject, date taken, name or initials.	All	Preferably all urine voided over a period of 24 hours	None. Use any clean bottle with leak-proof stopper.	Bottle surrounded with absorbent material to prevent breakage. Strong cardboard or wooden box.	Registered mail	
Wire (See also tool marks.)	On label or tag. Type of material, date, name or initials.	All (Do not kink.)	Three feet (Do not kink.)		Wrap securely.	Registered mail	Do not kink wire.
Wood	Same as above	All	One foot		Wrap securely.	Registered mail	

NOTE: This chart is not intended to be all-inclusive. If evidence to be submitted is not found herein, consult the specimen list for an item most similar in nature and submit accordingly.

Appendix B

A Crime Laboratory Directory

Many names of laboratories included in this directory were taken from existing lists in the forensic science literature. A master list was compiled and submitted to Law Enforcement Assistance Administration's system of State Planning Agencies, which, in turn, consulted with criminalists in the respective states in making necessary additions and deletions. Criteria used in determining if a facility would be labeled a criminalistics laboratory were the following:

1. A criminalistics laboratory should, at the minimum, have capabilities in the area of wet-chemical analysis, microscopy, and photography.
2. The laboratory must employ on a permanent basis at least one scientist with training in the physical sciences.
3. The laboratory should have responsibility for the collection and analysis of physical evidence in its jurisdiction and have staff who deliver expert testimony in court.
4. In this particular listing, identification bureaus, coroner's and medical examiner's offices, and laboratories dedicated to the analysis of narcotics and dangerous drugs were not included.

National Directory of Criminalistics Laboratories

(This listing was compiled by Joseph Peterson, Ph.D., for the National Institute of Law Enforcement and Criminal Justice)

ALABAMA

Director
Alabama State Department of
  Toxicology and Criminal Investigation
P.O. Box 231
Auburn, Alabama 36830

Director
Alabama Toxicology Department
P.O. Box 2591
Birmingham, Alabama 35233

Director
Alabama Toxicology Department
P.O. Box 580
Huntsville, Alabama 35804

Director
Department of Toxicology and Criminal
  Investigation
Court House
Church and Royal Streets
Mobile, Alabama 36602

Director
State Health Department
Montgomery, Alabama 36104

ALASKA

Director
General Laboratory Studies
Toxicology and Drug Analysis
Alaska Medical Laboratories
P.O. Box 4-1539
Anchorage, Alaska 99503

ARIZONA

Director
Criminalistics Laboratory
Phoenix Police Department
17 South 2nd Avenue
Phoenix, Arizona 85003

Director
Criminalistics Laboratory
Department of Public Safety
2016 W. Encanto Boulevard
Phoenix, Arizona 85005

Director
City-County Criminalistics Laboratory
P.O. Box 1071
Tucson, Arizona 85716

UNIVERSITY PROGRAM

Chairman
Department of Police Science
  Administration
Northern Arizona University
P.O. Box 6014
Flagstaff, Arizona 86001

ARKANSAS

Director
Criminalistics Laboratory
Arkansas State Police
Little Rock, Arkansas 72201

CALIFORNIA

Director
Criminalistics Laboratory
Kern County Sheriff's Office
P.O. Box 2208
Bakersfield, California 93303

Director
Criminalistics Laboratory El Cajon
  Police Department
100 Fletcher Parkway
El Cajon, California 92020

Director
Criminalistics Laboratory
Huntington Beach Police Department
P.O. Box 70
Huntington Beach, California 92648

Note: The laboratories and facilities listed here do not necessarily represent all criminalistics capability in the respective states. Hospitals, medical examiners and coroner's officers, and some other laboratories may offer additional support to law enforcement agencies.

CALIFORNIA *(Cont'd.)*

Director
Criminalistics Laboratory
Long Beach Police Department
400 West Broadway
Long Beach, California 90802

Director
Criminalistics Laboratory
Los Angeles Police Department
150 North Los Angeles Street
Los Angeles, California 90012

Director
Criminalistics Laboratory
Los Angeles County Sheriff's Office
501 N. Main Street
Los Angeles, California 90012

Director
Criminalistics Laboratory
Contra Costa County Sheriff's Office
P.O. Box 391
Martinez, California 94553

Director
Criminalistics Section
Oakland Police Department
455 7th Street
Oakland, California 94607

Director
Criminalistics Laboratory
Alameda County Sheriff's Office
P.O. Box 787
Pleasanton, California 94566

Director
Criminalistics Laboratory
San Mateo County Sheriff's Office
Hall of Justice
Redwood City, California 94063

Director
Criminalistics Laboratory
Riverside County Sheriff's Department
P.O. Box 512
Riverside, California 92502

Director
Sacramento County Crime Laboratory
Office of the District Attorney
4400 "V" Street
Sacramento, California 95817

State of California
Bureau of Criminal Identification and
   Investigation
Criminalistics Laboratory
P.O. Box 1859
Sacramento, California 95809

Director
San Bernardino County Sheriff's
   Department
P.O. Box 569
San Bernardino, California 92403

Crime Laboratory
San Diego Police Department
801 West Market Street
San Diego, California 92101

Director
Criminalistics Laboratory
San Diego County Sheriff's Office
222 W. "C" Street
San Diego, California 92101

Director
Criminalistics Laboratory
San Francisco Police Department
850 Bryant Street
Room 435
San Francisco, California 94103

Director
United States Army Crime Laboratory
515th Military Police Detachment
APO San Francisco, California 96343

Director
Criminalistics Laboratory
Department of District Attorney
Santa Clara County
875 San Pedro Street
San Jose, California 95110

Director
Criminalistics Laboratory
Santa Ana Police Department
Santa Ana, California 92702

CALIFORNIA *(Cont'd.)*

Director
Criminalistics Laboratory
Orange County Sheriff's Office
P.O. Box 449
Santa Ana, California 92702

Director
Criminalistics Laboratory
Ventura County Sheriff's Office
501 POLI Street
Ventura, California 93001

UNIVERSITY PROGRAMS

Director
Forensic Science Program
School of Criminology
University of California
Berkeley, California 94720

Director
Department of Police Science and
  Administration
California State College at Los Angeles
5151 State College Drive
Los Angeles, California 90032

Director
Department of Police Science and
  Administration
Sacramento State College
6000 Jay Street
Sacramento, California 95819

COLORADO

Director
Criminalistics Laboratory
Colorado Bureau of Investigation
1550 Lincoln Street
Denver, Colorado 80204

Director
Criminal Investigation and Forensic
  Sciences Laboratory
West 6th Avenue and Cherokee
Denver, Colorado 80204

Director
Criminalistics Laboratory
Denver Police Department
13th and Champa Street
Denver, Colorado 80204

CONNECTICUT

Director
Criminalistics Laboratory
Hartford Police Department
155 Morgan Street
Hartford, Connecticut 06103

Director
State Bureau of Identification
Connecticut State Police
100 Washington Street
Hartford, Connecticut 06106

UNIVERSITY PROGRAM

Director
Forensic Science Program
Division of Criminal Justice
University of New Haven
West Haven, Connecticut 06516

DELAWARE

Director
Criminalistics Laboratory
Delaware State Police
Box 430
Dover, Delaware 10101

DISTRICT OF COLUMBIA

Director
Police Laboratory
Metropolitan Police Department
300 Indiana Avenue, N.W.
Washington, D.C. 20001

Director
Criminalistics Laboratory
Federal Bureau of Investigation
Ninth and Pennsylvania Avenue, N.W.
Washington, D.C. 20535

DISTRICT OF COLUMBIA (*Cont'd.*)

Director
Alcohol, Tobacco and Firearms
  Laboratory
Internal Revenue Service
Washington, D.C. 20224

Director
Secret Service Laboratory
1800 G Street, N.W.
Washington, D.C. 20226

Director
U.S. Postal Service Crime Laboratory
1100 L Street, N.W.
Washington, D.C. 20260

Director
Forensic Sciences Division
Armed Forces Institute of Pathology
Washington, D.C. 20012

Director
Regional Criminalistics Advisor
AID-OPS/LA
Department of State
Crime Laboratory
Washington, D.C. 20523

Director
Questioned Document Laboratory
Department of Army
Washington, D.C. 20013

UNIVERSITY PROGRAMS

Director
Forensic Science Center
Reiss Science Building
Georgetown University
Washington, D.C. 20007

Director
Department of Forensic Science
The George Washington University
Washington, D.C. 20006

FLORIDA

Director
Criminalistics Laboratory
City Police Department
Jacksonville, Florida 32201

Director
Dade County Crime Laboratory
1320 N.W. 14th Street
Miami, Florida 33125

Director
Criminalistics Laboratory
Florida Department of Law Enforcement
P.O. Box 654
Tallahassee, Florida 32302

Director
Crime Laboratory, P.B.I.A.
P.O. Box 670
West Palm Beach, Florida 33402

Director
Criminalistics Laboratory
Region IV
P.O. Box 1737
Sanford, Florida 32771

PROPOSED UNIVERSITY PROGRAM

Director
Criminalistics Project
Chemistry Department
Florida Technological University
Box 25000
Orlando, Florida 32816

GEORGIA

Director
Georgia State Crime Laboratory
Department of Public Safety
P.O. Box 1456
Atlanta, Georgia 30301

Director
Laboratory Branch ATF
Federal Office Building
P.O. Box 926
Atlanta, Georgia 30301

GEORGIA (*Cont'd.*)

Director
U.S. Army Criminal Investigation
  Laboratory
Fort Gordon, Georgia 30905

Director
Georgia State Crime Laboratory
Chatham County Branch
Box 523
Savannah, Georgia 31402

HAWAII

Director
Crime Laboratory
Honolulu Police Department
1455 S. Beretania Street
Honolulu, Hawaii 96814

IDAHO

Director
Idaho Department of Health
  Laboratories Division
2120 Warm Springs Avenue
Boise, Idaho 83702

ILLINOIS

Director
Criminalistics Division
Chicago Police Department
1121 South State Street
Chicago, Illinois 60605

Director
Illinois Bureau of Identification
Highway 51
DeSoto, Illinois 62924

Director
Northern Illinois Police Laboratory
1677 Old Deerfield Road
Highland Park, Illinois 60035

Director
Criminalistics Laboratory
Illinois Bureau of Identification
515 East Woodruff Road
Joliet, Illinois 60035

Director
Illinois Bureau of Identification
299-1/2 Court Street
Pekin, Illinois 61554

Director
Illinois Bureau of Identification
c/o Pump Handle Inn
2620 11th Street
Rockford, Illinois 61101

Director
Illinois Bureau of Identification
333 15th Street
Rock Island, Illinois 61201

Director
Criminalistics Laboratory
Illinois Bureau of Identification
415 Iles Park Place
Springfield, Illinois 62703

Director
Du Page County Crime Laboratory
Du Page County Sheriff's Office
P.O. Box 300, 205 Reber Street
Wheaton, Illinois 60187

UNIVERSITY PROGRAM

Director
University of Illinois
Administration of Criminal Justice
Box 4348
Chicago, Illinois 60680

INDIANA

Director
Criminalistics Laboratory
City Police Department
Bloomington, Indiana 47401

Director
Criminalistics Laboratory
Fort Wayne Police Department
Fort Wayne, Indiana 46802

Director
Forensic Sciences Division
Indiana State Police Department
100 N. Senate Avenue
Indianapolis, Indiana 46204

INDIANA (Cont'd.)

Director
Criminalistics Laboratory
Indianapolis Police Department
Indianapolis, Indiana 46201

UNIVERSITY PROGRAM

Director
Department of Police Administration
Indiana University
Room 120, Sycamore
Bloomington, Indiana 47401

IOWA

Director
Iowa Crime Laboratory
E. 7th and Court Streets
Des Moines, Iowa 50319

KANSAS

Director
Criminalistics Laboratory
Bureau of Investigation
State of Kansas
Topeka, Kansas 66612

Director
Forensic Laboratory
Wichita Police Department
115 East William
Wichita, Kansas 67202

PROPOSED UNIVERSITY PROGRAM

Director
Administration of Justice
Wichita State University
1845 Fairmont
Wichita, Kansas

KENTUCKY

Director
Criminalistics Laboratory
State Police Division
1250 Louisville Road
Frankfort, Kentucky 40601

LOUISIANA

Director
Criminalistics Laboratory
Department of Public Safety
Louisiana State Police
P.O. Box 1791
Baton Rouge, Louisiana 70806

Director
Criminalistics Laboratory
Calcasiu Sheriff's Laboratory
Lake Charles, Louisiana 70823

Director
Criminalistics Laboratory
Police Department
Box 51480
New Orleans, Louisiana 70150

Director
Acadiana Criminalistics Laboratory
P.O. Box 643
New Iberia, Louisiana 70560

Director
Northwestern Regional Criminalistics
  Laboratory
Box 4
Shreveport, Louisiana 71102

MAINE

Director
State Police Crime Laboratory
36 Hospital Street
Augusta, Maine 04330

Director
Maine Department of Health and
  Welfare
State House
Augusta, Maine 04330

UNIVERSITY PROGRAMS

Director
Criminal Justice Program
University of Maine
Augusta, Maine 04330

MAINE *(Cont'd.)*

Director
Criminal Justice Program
University of Maine
Bangor, Maine 04401

MARYLAND

Director
Criminalistics Laboratory
Baltimore Police Department
601 E. Fayette Street
Baltimore, Maryland 21202

Director
Criminalistics Laboratory
Hagerstown Jr. College
Hagerstown, Maryland 21740

Director
Criminalistics Laboratory
Maryland State Police
Pikesville, Maryland 21205

Director
Criminalistics Laboratory
Montgomery County Police Department
108 S. Perry Street
Rockville, Maryland

Director
Criminalistics Laboratory
Prince George's County Police
  Department
410 Addison Road
Seat Pleasant, Maryland 20027

Director
Criminalistics Laboratory
Ocean City Police Department
Snow Hill, Maryland 21863

Director
Criminalistics Laboratory (Baltimore
  County P.D.)
Bosley Avenue and Kenilworth Drive
Towson, Maryland 21204

MASSACHUSETTS

Director
Criminalistics Laboratory
Boston Police Department
154 Berkeley Street
Boston, Massachusetts 02116

Director
Criminalistics Laboratory
Department of Public Safety
1010 Commonwealth Avenue
Boston, Massachusetts 02215

UNIVERSITY PROGRAM

Director
Chemistry Department
Boston State College
625 Huntington Avenue
Boston, Massachusetts 02120

MICHIGAN

Director
Criminalistics Laboratory
City Police Department
Records and Identification Bureau
Dearborn, Michigan 48125

Director
Scientific Bureau
Detroit Police Department
1300 Beubien Street
Detroit, Michigan 48226

Director
Michigan State Police
Scientific Laboratory
714 South Harrison Road
East Lansing, Michigan 48828

Director
Chemist-Crime Laboratory
Prosecuting Attorney's Office
105 Courthouse
Flint, Michigan 48208

Director Criminalistics Laboratory
Police Headquarters
333 Monroe Avenue, N.W.
Grand Rapids, Michigan 49502

MICHIGAN (*Cont'd.*)

Director
Criminalistics Laboratory
Police Department
Identification Bureau
Highland Park, Michigan 48203

Director
Michigan State Police
Crime Laboratory
304 Garden Street
P.O. Box 1115C
Holland, Michigan 49423

Director
Division of Crime Detection
Bureau of Laboratories
Lansing Police Department
Lansing, Michigan 48933

Director
Michigan Department of Health
3500 N. Logan Street
Lansing, Michigan 48914

Director
Criminalistics Laboratory
Michigan State Police
186 S. Main Street
Plymouth, Michigan 48170

Director
Crime Laboratory
Oakland County Sheriff's Department
Pontiac, Michigan 48056

Director
Michigan State Police
Crime Laboratory
30950 Van Dyke
Warren, Michigan 48089

UNIVERSITY PROGRAM

Director
School of Police Administration and
   Public Safety
Forensic Sciences Program
Michigan State University
East Lansing, Michigan 16802

MINNESOTA

Director
Criminalistics Laboratory
Bureau of Criminal Apprehension
Minnesota Department of Public Safety
1246 University Avenue
St. Paul, Minnesota 55104

Director
Criminalistics Laboratory
Police Department
101 East 10th Street
St. Paul, Minnesota 55101

MISSISSIPPI

Director
Criminalistics Laboratory
Jackson Police Department
P.O. Box 17
Jackson, Mississippi 39205

Director
Criminalistics Laboratory
Department of Public Safety
P.O. Box 6097
Jackson, Mississippi 39208

MISSOURI

Director
LEAC Crime Laboratory
Southeast Missouri State College
Cape Girardeau, Missouri 63701

Director
St. Louis County Crime Laboratory
226 S. Central
Clayton, Missouri 63105

Director
Northwest Missouri Regional
   Criminalistics Laboratory
2100 North Noland Road
Independence, Missouri 64051

Director
Criminalistics Division
Missouri State Highway Patrol
1710 East Elm Street
Jefferson City, Missouri 65101

MISSOURI *(Cont'd.)*

Director
Region 9 Crime Laboratory
Missouri Western College
Newman Road
Joplin, Missouri 64802

Director
Region 2 Crime Laboratory and
   Identification Center
321 East Chestnut Expressway
Springfield, Missouri 65802

Director
Criminalistics Laboratory
St. Louis Police Department
1200 Clark Street
St. Louis, Missouri 63103

NEBRASKA

Director
Criminalistics Laboratory
Law Enforcement and Safety Bureau of
   Criminal Investigation and
   Identification
14th and Burnham
Lincoln, Nebraska 68509

Director
Criminalistics Laboratory
Omaha Police Department
Omaha, Nebraska

NEVADA

Director
Criminalistics Laboratory
Clark County Sheriff's Office
200 East Carson Street
Las Vegas, Nevada 89101

Director
State Criminalistics Laboratory
790 Sutro Street
Reno, Nevada 89507

Director
Criminalistics Laboratory
Washoe County Sheriff's Office
Box 2915
Reno, Nevada 89505

UNIVERSITY PROGRAM

Director
University Criminalistics Laboratory
University of Nevada
Department of Law Enforcement
Reno, Nevada 89507

NEW HAMPSHIRE

Director
Criminalistics Laboratory
Department of Public Safety
John O. Morton Building
Concord, New Hampshire 03301

NEW JERSEY

Director
Chemist-Newark Police Laboratory
Police Academy
10008-18th Avenue
Newark, New Jersey 07106

Director
Criminalistics Laboratory
New Jersey State Police
P.O. Box 68
West Trenton, New Jersey 08625

NEW MEXICO

Director
Criminalistics Laboratory
Department of Pathology
University of New Mexico School of
   Medicine
Albuquerque, New Mexico 87109

Director
New Mexico State Police
State Crime Laboratory
P.O. Box 1628
Santa Fe, New Mexico 87501

NEW YORK

Director
Criminalistics Laboratory
New York State Police
Building No. 22
State Campus
Albany, New York 12226

NEW YORK (*Cont'd.*)

Director
Buffalo Police Crime Laboratory
74 Franklin Avenue
Buffalo, New York 14202

Herbert L. MacDonnell
Consulting Criminalist
P.O. Box 1111
Corning, New York 14830

Director
Criminalistics Laboratory
Suffolk County Police Department
Veterans Memorial Highway
Hauppauge, New York 11787

Director
Nassau County Police Department
Scientific Investigation Bureau
1490 Franklin Avenue
Mineola, New York 11501

Director
Criminalistics Laboratory
New York City Police Department
235 E. 20th Street
New York, New York 10003

Director
Criminalistics Laboratory
Department of Public Safety
Police Division
209 Niagara Street
Niagara Falls, New York 14303

Director
Public Safety Laboratory
Monroe County
150 Plymouth Avenue South
Rochester, New York 14614

Director
Syracuse Police Laboratory
Public Safety Building
511 South State Street
Syracuse, New York 13202

Director
Criminalistics Laboratory
Westchester County
Grasslands Reservation
Valhalla, New York 10595

Director
Laboratory for Forensic Sciences
87 Nepperha Avenue
Yonkers, New York 10701

Director
New York Regional Laboratory
Bureau of Narcotics and Dangerous
  Drugs
90 Church Street
New York, New York 10007

UNIVERSITY PROGRAM

Director
Forensic Science Program
John Jay College of Criminal Justice
315 Park Avenue South
New York, New York 10010

NORTH CAROLINA

Director
Charlotte Crime Laboratory
Law Enforcement Center
825 East 4th Street
Charlotte, North Carolina 28202

Director Crime Laboratory
State Bureau of Investigation
421 North Blount
Raleigh, North Carolina 27601

OHIO

Director
Criminalistics Laboratory
Hamilton County
3223 Eden Avenue
Cincinnati, Ohio 45219

Director
Criminalistics Laboratory
Cleveland Police Department
2001 Payne Avenue-Room 301
Cleveland, Ohio 44114

Director
Criminalistics Laboratory
Cuyhoga County Coroner's Office
1212 Adelbert Road
Cleveland, Ohio 44106

OHIO (*Cont'd.*)

Director
Criminalistics Laboratory
Columbus Police Department
Columbus, Ohio 43215

Director
Ohio State Highway Patrol
Investigation and Laboratory Section
Columbus, Ohio 43224

Director
Criminalistics Laboratory
Dayton Police Department
335 West 3rd Street
Dayton, Ohio 45401

Director
N.W. Ohio BCI&I Laboratory
405 Pine Street
Fremont, Ohio

Criminal Identification and
    Investigation Bureau
Northeast Ohio Regional Crime
    Laboratory
Kent State University
Kent, Ohio 44240

Director
Criminalistics Laboratory
Ohio Bureau of C.I.I.
P.O. Box 365
London, Ohio 43140

Director
BCI Regional Laboratory
Administration Building
30335 Oregon Road
Perrysburg, Ohio 43601

Director
Criminalistics Laboratory
Toledo Police Department
525 Erie Street
Toledo, Ohio 43601

Director
Worthington Police Department
789 High Street
Worthington, Ohio 43085

Director
Crime Laboratory and Records
Police Department
Youngstown, Ohio 44501

OKLAHOMA

Director
Oklahoma State Bureau of Investigation
Laboratory Division
4363 N.W. 10th Street
Box 7-F, Farley Station
Oklahoma City, Oklahoma 73107

Director
Criminalistics Laboratory
Oklahoma City Police Department
Oklahoma City, Oklahoma 73125

OREGON

Director
Crime Laboratory
Eugene Police Department
777 Pearl Street
Eugene, Oregon 97401

Director
Oregon State Police Crime Detection
    Laboratory
364-$^{1}/_{2}$ West 7th
Eugene, Oregon 97401

Director
Oregon State Police Crime Detection
    Laboratory
P.O. Box 1648
Medford, Oregon 97501

Director
Oregon State Police Crime Detection
    Laboratories
Blue Mountain Community College
P.O. Box 1519
Pendleton, Oregon 9701

Director
Crime Detection Laboratory
Oregon State Police
University of Oregon Medical School
3181 S.W. Sam Jackson Park Road
Portland, Oregon 97201

OREGON (*Cont'd.*)

Director
Criminalistics Laboratory
Portland Police Department
222 S.W. Pine Street
Portland, Oregon 97204

PENNSYLVANIA

Director
Bethlehem Criminalistics Laboratory
Pennsylvania State Police
2930 Allentown-Schoenersville Road
P.O. Box 2005
Bethlehem, Pennsylvania 19001

Director
Regional Criminalistics Laboratory
Pennsylvania State Police, Troop "A"
P.O. Box 38
Greensburg, Pennsylvania 15601

Director
Criminalistics Laboratory
Pennsylvania State Police
21st and Herr Street
Harrisburg, Pennsylvania 17013

Director
Buck's County Criminalistics Laboratory
2659 Trenton Road
Levittown, Pennsylvania 10056

Director
Forensic Chemist
Office of the District Attorney
Delaware County
Media, Pennsylvania 19063

Director
Police Chemical Laboratory
Room 305
Police Headquarters
Franklin Square
Philadelphia, Pennsylvania 19106

Director
Pittsburgh-Allegheny County
Crime Laboratory
401 Courthouse
Pittsburgh, Pennsylvania 15219

Director
Criminalistics Laboratory
Pennsylvania State Police
475 Wyoming Avenue
Wyoming, Pennsylvania 18644

UNIVERSITY PROGRAMS

Director
Division of Police and Public
  Administration
Harrisburg Area Community College
3300 Cameron Street Road
Harrisburg, Pennsylvania 17110

Director
Forensic Chemistry Program
Department of Chemistry
University of Pittsburgh
Pittsburgh, Pennsylvania 15213

Director
212 Whitmore Laboratory
Pennsylvania State University
University Park, Pennsylvania 16802

SOUTH CAROLINA

Director
Criminalistics Laboratory
South Carolina Law Enforcement
  Division
P.O. Box 1166
Columbia, South Carolina 29202

Director
Pathology and Chemistry Department
Medical University of South Carolina
Charleston, South Carolina 29401

PUERTO RICO

Director
Criminal Laboratory
Puerto Rico Police
G.P.O. Box 938
Hato Rey, Puerto Rico 00919

Director
U.S. Customs Laboratory
P.O. Box 2112
Old San Juan Station
San Juan, Puerto Rico 00903

RHODE ISLAND

Director
Laboratories for Scientific Criminal
  Investigation
University of Rhode Island
Kingston, Rhode Island 02881

Director
Rhode Island State Police Mobile Crime
  Lab
Rhode Island State Police Headquarters
P.O. Box 185
North Scituate, Rhode Island 02857

Director
Rhode Island Division of Criminal
  Identification
Providence Courthouse
250 Benefit Street
Providence, Rhode Island 02903

SOUTH CAROLINA

Director
Criminalistics Laboratory
South Carolina Law Enforcement
  Division
P.O. Box 1166
Columbia, South Carolina 29202

Director
Pathology and Chemistry Department
Medical University of South Carolina
Charleston, South Carolina 29401

SOUTH DAKOTA

Director
Crime Laboratory
Division of Criminal Investigation
State Capital Building
Pierre, South Dakota 57501

TEXAS

Manager
Crime Laboratories Bureau
Texas Department of Public Safety
Box 4143
Austin, Texas 78765

Headquarters Laboratory-Austin
Field Laboratories   -Dallas
                         -Tyler
                         -Houston
                         -Corpus Christi
                         -Midland
                         -El Paso
                         -Lubbock
                         -Waco

Director
Dallas County Criminal Investigation
  Laboratory
Southwestern Institute of Forensic
  Sciences
5230 Medical Center Drive
Box 35728
Dallas, Texas 75235

Director
Criminalistics Laboratory
Fort Worth Police Department
1000 Throckmorton Street
Fort Worth, Texas 76102

Director
Police Laboratory
Houston Police Department
61-Riesner Street
Houston, Texas 77002

Director
Criminalistics Laboratory
San Antonio Police Department
Box 9346
San Antonio, Texas 78204

UTAH

Director
Crime Laboratory
Davis County Sheriff's Office
Davis County Courthouse
Farmington, Utah 84025

Director
Crime Laboratory
Cache County Sheriff's Office
Logan, Utah 84321

UTAH (Cont'd.)

Director
Crime Laboratory
Ogden Police Department
Ogden, Utah 84401

Director
Crime Laboratory
Weber County Sheriff's Office
Ogden, Utah 84401

Director
Division of Health
44 Medical Drive
Salt Lake City, Utah 84113

UNIVERSITY PROGRAM

Director
Police Science Department
Weber State College
Ogden, Utah 84401

VERMONT

Director
Vermont State Police Laboratory
Redstone
Montpelier, Vermont 05602

VIRGINIA

Director
Northern Virginia Police Laboratory*
4250 North Fairfax Drive
Arlington, Virginia 22203

Director
Tidewater Regional Crime Laboratory*
711 Crawford Street
Portsmouth, Virginia 23704

Director
Division of Consolidated Laboratory
  Services
Bureau of Forensic Science
404 N. 12th Street
Richmond, Virginia 23219
  Parent Laboratory-Richmond
  Regional Laboratories-Norfolk
                          Roanoke
                          Fairfax

WASHINGTON

Director
Crime Laboratory
Bellevue Police Department
111-116 S.E.
Bellevue, Washington 98004

Director
Crime Laboratory
Seattle Police Department
Room 219
Public Safety Building
Seattle, Washington 98104

Director
King County Crime Laboratory
King County Courthouse
516 3rd Avenue
Seattle, Washington 98104

Director
Drug Control Assistance Unit
Spokane Regional Laboratory
Room 1120 Public Safety Building
Spokane, Washington 99201

Director
Crime Laboratory
Tacoma Police Department
County-City Building
Tacoma, Washington 98402

UNIVERSITY PROGRAMS

Director
Police Science Department
106 Van Doren
Washington State University
Pullman, Washington 99163

* To become integral parts of State Bureau of Forensic Science

WASHINGTON (*Cont'd.*)

Director
Department of Law Enforcement
  Studies
Spokane Community College
Mission Avenue Campus
Spokane, Washington

WEST VIRGINIA

Director
Criminalistics Laboratory
West Virginia State Police
725 Jefferson Road
South Charleston, West Virginia 25303

WISCONSIN

Director
Glendale Crime Laboratory
5909 N. Milwaukee Parkway
Glendale, Wisconsin 53209

Director
Crime Laboratory
Sheriff's Department
Kenosha, Wisconsin 53141

Director
Wisconsin State Crime Laboratory
4706 University Avenue
Madison, Wisconsin 53705

Director
Bureau of Laboratories
Health Department
Municipal Building
841 North Broadway
Milwaukee, Wisconsin 53203

WYOMING

Director
Criminalistics Laboratory
P.O. Box 3228
Laramie, Wyoming 82970

Based upon previously discussed criteria, the following states have no active criminalistics laboratories: Montana, North Dakota, Tennessee

Glossary

A-B-O system   One of a number of classification systems for the typing of human blood.

absorbent   Material that has the ability to hold other substances on its surface. Powdered charcoal being used to remove gases with offensive odors from the atmosphere is an example.

absorption-elution (also absorption-inhibition)   Procedure for determining blood group from dried blood stains using the red blood cell antigen.

accelerant   Substance that burns easily. Added to materials so that they will catch fire.

accidental whorl   Combination of any two fingerprint patterns exclusive of the plain arch.

acetone   Colorless, volatile, flammable organic liquid. Used to dissolve substances. Often found as an ingredient in nail polish remover.

addict   Individual who for psychological or physical reasons needs repeated doses of a drug.

alkaloid   Class of organic compounds, often exhibiting druglike action, e.g., nicotine, morphine, quinine.

alpha rays   One of three types of radiation (rays) given off by radioactive materials. They are actually composed of electrically charged helium particles.

aminata mushroom   Extremely poisonous type of wild mushroom that closely resembles certain edible mushrooms.

amphetamine   Drug that stimulates the central nervous sytem, used chiefly to lift the mood or to control the appetite.

anagen   Phase of the hair cycle during which synthesis of the hair takes place.

analgesic   Substance that relieves pain.

anthropometry   The measurement of the size and proportions of the human body.

antibody   Protein produced by the body to overcome the toxicity of some antigen.

anticholinesterase agents   Certain chemicals that interfere with the functioning of the enzyme cholinesterarase in the junction between two nerves.

antigen   Substance that stimulates the production of antibodies in the body.

antioxidant   Chemical that prevents a substance from combining with oxygen.

arson The deliberate burning of a house or property.

articulators Organs of the vocal system that move and adjust themselves to form a sound.

ASA rating American Standards Association rating. A numercial rating given to photographic film indicating its sensitivity to light. The higher the number, the more sensitive (faster) the film.

atom The smallest particle from which all matter is formed.

automatic pistol Firearm having a mechanism that ejects the empty shell, puts in a new one, and prepares the pistol to be fired again. It will continue firing as long as the trigger is pressed.

autopsy Inspection and dissection of a body to determine the cause of death.

axillary From the armpit.

bacterial Pertaining to bacteria, microscopic organisms.

ballistics Science that studies the motion of projectiles.

barbiturate Any of a group of barbituric acid derivatives used as sedatives and hypnotics.

Barr bodies X-chromosome present in female cells.

bar voiceprint Type of recording made with a voice spectrograph, which displays the intensity of sound by the degree of darkness.

Bertillon system System of identifying persons by a record of individual physical measurements and peculiarities. Devised by Alphonse Bertillon.

beta rays One of three types of radiation (rays) given off by radioactive materials. Consists of electrons (negatively electrically charged particles).

bhang Indian name for the common low-potency form of marijuana.

bifurcation A division or forking, as in a fingerprint.

biochemistry Study of body's chemistry.

black powder Earlier form of gun powder containing sulfur, charcoal, and potassium nitrate.

blood enzymes Protein material carried in the blood and required for normal body activity.

body secretions Liquid material produced in various parts of the body, e.g., saliva, semen.

bore Diameter of a barrel, measured from land to land in a rifled firearm; expressed in thousandths of an inch, or millimeters.

borosilicate glass Pyrex glass.

breathalizer Device that analyzes the amount of alcohol in the breath, thereby determining its concentration in the blood.

breech Rear portion of the bore of a gun, sometimes referred to as the throat or chamber.

bullet Part of a cartridge propelled out by powder charge.

caliber   Diameter of the bore of a gun measured from land to land.

Cannabis sativa   Scientific name for marijuana plant.

cannelure   Groove in a bullet, containing lubrication.

capillary action   Movement by which liquids rise in narrow-bored tubes or channels.

carbon black   Finely divided form of charcoal.

cartridge   Case containing explosive charge and bullet.

cast   Object formed by pouring a metal, plaster, etc., into a mold and letting it harden.

catagen   Brief portion of the hair growth cycle in which the growth ANAGEN stops and the arresting starts.

Caucasian   Individual from one of the five principal races of humankind.

cellulose acetate   Yarns, fibers, or textiles made from a combination of cellulose and acetic acid.

central nervous system depressant   Substance that depresses or slows down the action of the part of the nervous system made up of the spinal cord and brain.

centrifuge   Laboratory instrument that rotates at high speed and that by centrifugal force separates materials of different densities.

charas   Indian name for hashish, the pure resin removed from the marijuana plant. It is very potent.

chemical structure   The particular arrangement of atoms in a molecule.

chromatin   Part of cell nucleus containing genes and chromosomes.

chromatography   General technique for separating the components of a mixture from one another.

comatose   To be unconscious or in a stupor.

compression marks   Impressions made on a surface by striking it as with a hammer.

contour voiceprint   Recording resembling a contour map made with a voice spectrograph.

core   Innermost center of a loop or whorl fingerprint pattern.

cortex   Layer of hair lying between cuticle and medulla.

cosmic rays   Very high energy, short wavelength radiation originating in outer space.

criminalistics   The application of scientific techniques to the solution of crime.

cryptanalysis   The deciphering of codes.

crystalline   Solid substance having a high degree of internal order.

cuticle   Outermost layer of a hair.

delta   Focal point of a loop or whorl. A whorl must have two or more deltas.

de-lustering agent   Substance added to decrease the shininess of an object.

density   The weight of an object divided by its volume.

dependence   The physical and/or psychological need for a drug brought on by its repeated use. Physical need is characterized by withdrawal symptoms like nausea, chills, etc. Psychological need is characterized by the desire to escape from reality.

depressant   A sedative or drug that lowers body activity.

diaphragm   Aperture device for adjusting the amount of light passing through a camera lens.

dilate   To widen, as in the widening of the irises of the eye caused by the use of certain drugs.

distillation   Process used to separate volatile liquids from the less volatile components of a mixture. This involves heating the mixture to vaporize it and cooling the mixture to reliquify it.

divergence   Point of separation of two fingerprint ridges running parallel.

DOA   Dead on arrival.

document   Written or printed paper.

double loop whorl   Fingerprint pattern containing two separate and distinct sets of shoulders.

ejector   Part of a weapon that causes the cartridge case to be ejected from the weapon after firing.

electrolytic method   Technique involving the connecting of two metals to the terminals of a battery and the placing of these in a suitable liquid or paste so that electricity can flow through this circuit (as in the developing of erased serial numbers).

electron microscope   Special type of microscope using electrons instead of light, and capable of enormous magnifications. Two basic types which are in use, transmission and scanning electron microscopes, provide three dimensional images.

electrophoresis   Analytical technique that separates and identifies the components of a mixture by placing it in an electric field.

emulsion side   Light-sensitive side of film or photographic papers.

epidermis   Outer layer of the skin.

ethyl alcohol   Grain alcohol, ethanol, alcohol. The type of alcohol found in alcoholic beverages.

eumelanin   Type of pigmentation found in hair and skin.

evidence   Anything that proves the facts at issue in a court of law, in particular concerning how, why, when, where, or by whom a crime was committed.

expert witness   individual possessing exceptional qualifications, knowledge, or skill in a particular field, and who is recognized as such by the court.

extractor Part of a weapon that removes the cartridge case from the firing chamber.

fingerprints Skin pattern formation of ridges found on the first joint of each finger.

firing pin Part of a weapon that strikes the primer of the cartridge, thereby setting off the process that causes the powder charge to explode.

fixer Chemical solution used in processing photographic film and paper. Also known as hypo.

flammable fluids Liquids that are easily ignited.

fluorescence Property of some materials enabling them to give off a light of different color than the light that shines on, or irradiates them.

forensic Pertaining to, or used in a court of law.

forgery An object or document altered or falsely rendered that is then claimed to be genuine.

friction marks Marks made by one object on another due to the drawing or scraping of one of them across the other.

fuels Additives that burn readily.

fusi Air pockets present in the cortex.

gallic acid Crystalline solid used mainly in tanning and in ink dyes.

galvanic skin reflex (GSR) Involuntary increased passage of electricity through electrodes placed on the skin as the result of tension, anxiety, response to threat, etc.

galvanometer Instrument used for measuring electric currents.

gamma rays One of three types of radiation given off by radioactive materials. They are the same as x-rays.

ganja Indian name for a form of marijuana of medium potency made from a mixture consisting of the small leaves and resinous material.

gas chromatography (GC) Type of chromatography in which the mixture to be separated is vaporized and swept over a solid or liquid absorbent.

gelatin side Light-sensitive side of film, commonly referred to as emulsion side.

gene Biological unit of heredity carried on chromosomes, which are structures in the cell.

grand jury Jury whose function is to inquire into an alleged violation of the law in order to determine whether the evidence is sufficient to warrant trial by a petty jury.

graphite Common soft, native form of carbon used in pencil leads, as a lubricant, etc.

grooves Portions of a rifle that are cut out in a spiral fashion in order to impart a spin to a bullet as it exits from the barrel.

gyroscopic stability Property imparted to a bullet due to its spiral motion, which keeps it from turning end over end.

hackle marks Small chips in the edges of a glass fracture caused by the rubbing together of the edges along radial fractures. This action results in the chipping off of tiny pieces of glass.

hallucinogens Chemical agents capable of producing extreme mental distortions.

handgun Firearm that can be held and fired with one hand.

hashish a narcotic derived from parts of Indian hemp.

headstamp Manufacturer's identifying markings impressed on the end of a cartridge case.

helixometer Instrument for measuring the twist in a gun.

Henry system System used in classifying fingerprints.

hydrocarbons Organic compounds formed from the elements carbon and hydrogen.

hydrosphygmograph Instrument that measures the quantity of blood in a part of the body by the pressure exerted on a fluid contained in a closed chamber, thus enabling the pulse rate to be recorded.

hypo Chemical solution, primarily made up sodium thiosulfate, used in processing photographic film and paper. Also known as fixer.

immunity Property of being protected or not susceptible to a particular disease.

immunohematology Science that deals with matters related to blood grouping.

incendiary Pertaining to the use of devices that ignite.

infrared rays (IR) Part of the invisible spectrum of radiation having wavelengths between about 0.8 to 1000 millionths of a meter.

intoxication Drunkenness.

isoagglutinin procedure Method for determining blood groups from dried blood stains using antibodies in dried serum.

jacketed bullet Bullet, usually lead, covered with some other metal like copper, steel, or nickel.

keratin Protein found in the dead outer skin layer and in horns, hair, feathers, hoofs, nails, etc.

lands Narrowest diameter in the bore of a gun.

lattes crust test Procedure for determining blood groups from dried stains using the clumping of known cells to small dried crusts of blood.

LEAA Law Enforcement Assistance Administration—Federal agency whose purpose is to improve law enforcement procedures.

leucocytes White blood cells, which help to maintain immunity to infection and protection against bacteria.

lifting tape Transparent adhesive used to permanently transfer a "dusted" fingerprint from its original surface.

magazine Quickly replaceable metal receptacle for a number of cartridges, for insertion in an automatic weapon.

Magna-Brush A trademark device that develops fingerprints on surfaces through the use of colored powders.

mass spectrometry Analytical technique used to identify what compounds are present in a mixture. The technique involves breaking the molecules apart into characteristic fragments that are detected and used to make the identification.

medulla The core of a hair.

melanin Dark pigment occurring in hair, skin, etc.

metabolism All the chemical and physical processes occurring in the body, through which life is maintained.

Mexican mud Slang term for a brand of heroin from Mexico.

modus operandi (MO) Characteristic methods used by individuals in the commission of crimes and by which they may be classified.

molecular structure The particular three dimensional arrangement of atoms whereby one atom is connected to another in a molecule, much like the parts in a tinker toy set.

molecule Smallest unit of matter representing the smallest particles into which matter can be divided without losing its properties.

Molotov cocktail An incendiary device often consisting of a narrow-necked glass bottle filled with gasoline, with a wick inserted in the neck. The wick is lighted and then the bottle is thrown.

Mongoloid Individual from one of the five principal races of humankind coming from Asia.

muzzle Exit end of a gun barrel.

narcotic Medically: a substance that induces sleep, stupor, or drowsiness.

narcotic analgesic Drug that induces sleep or drowsiness and relieves pain.

Negroid An individual from one of the five principal races of humankind.

neurotoxin Poison that interferes with the action of the nerves.

neutralization In chemistry, the mixing of an acidic solution with an equivalent amount of basic solution, resulting in a solution that is neutral, neither acidic nor basic.

oxidizer Substance that gives off oxygen to another substance, causing it to burn.

pathologist Scientist trained in the causes and nature of diseases or other abnormal body conditions.

phaemelanin Red-brown pigment that colors the hair and skin of redheads.

pharmacopeia Book containing a list of drugs with directions for their use and preparation.

photochromic Changing color when exposed to light, as in sunglasses or windowglass.

photoelectric cell Device that generates electricity when exposed to light.

photomicrograph Photograph made through the lens of a microscope.

pigmentation Coloring material.

pipette Laboratory device designed to deliver a precise amount of material.

plain arch One of the basic fingerprint patterns, containing neither a delta nor a core.

plain whorl Fingerprint pattern containing a core and two deltas.

plea bargaining Arrangement in which a defendant agrees to plead guilty to a reduced crime or in return for a reduced sentence.

polarized light Modified form of light that can be blacked out by passage through a polaroid filter.

potentiation When two drugs are given together and one increases the effect of the other. The first is said to potentiate the second, e.g., when epinephrine is given with procaine, a local anesthetic, the effect of the procaine is intensified because the epinephrine constricts the blood vessels, thus slowing down the removal of the procaine from the area.

prism Transparent, geometrical solid having three faces and two sides. The latter are triangular while the faces are rectangular.

psychopathic liar Person who is driven to lie because of mental disease.

psychotic To be suffering from mental derangement.

pyrolysis Decomposition, due to heat, of a material in the absence of oxygen.

pyromaniac Mentally deranged person whose illness compels him or her to set fires.

quinine Drug used to treat malaria.

rap sheet An individual's record of arrests.

reagent Chemical used to carry out a particular reaction.

reciprocal In mathematics, the reciprocal of a number is equal to one divided by the number, e.g., the reciprocal of 2 is $1/2$ or 0.5.

refractive index of a substance A number that is equal to the speed of light in space divided by the speed of light in the substance.

revolver Pistol in which a barrel containing cartridges is rotated to present each one in succession to be fired by the hammer.

rh system Rhesus factor—a factor that can be identified in blood and used to classify it.

scribe Device for making a mark on some object.

semiautomatic pistol Firearm in which the firing of the weapon automatically causes the next cartridge to be pushed from a magazine into the firing chamber. The pistol is fired each time the trigger is pulled.

shotgun Type of rifle used for firing small shot or pellets through an unrifled barrel.

solvent Substance that will dissolve another substance. For example, water is a solvent for sugar.

spectrometer Instrument that passes light of different wavelengths through a material and records the intensity of the light that passes through.

spectrum The visual or electronic display of light.

standard A reference material.

stimulant Substance that increases state of activity or alertness.

striae Fine scratches or grooves as in gun barrels.

subpoena To summon as a witness in court.

telogen Resting stage of the hair cycle.

therapeutic A level of drug deemed to be of medicinal value.

toxicology Study of the harmful effect of drugs.

tranquillizer Drug that reduces activity or sedates.

ultraviolet light (UV) Type of light occurring beyond the blue end of the spectrum.

viscose Special form of cotton pulp.

volatile solvent Solvent that vaporizes easily.

wad cutter Type of bullet with a flat nose used for target shooting.

wetting agent Substance added, for example to ink, to increase its ability to wet paper.

white collar crime Nonviolent type of crime such as embezzlement, fraud, computer theft.

x-ray High energy form of radiation.

zipgun A crude homemade gun that often makes use of a pipe or car antenna for a barrel.

Bibliography

"Admissability of Standard Writings," *FBI Law Enforcement Bulletin*, May 1966.

Allison, Harrison C.: *Personal Identification*, Holbrook Press, Boston, 1972.

"The Approximate Age of a Document," *FBI Law Enforcement Bulletin*, February 1966.

Barrett, James: *Textbook of Immunology*, 2d ed., Mosby, St. Louis, 1974.

Battle, Brendan P. and Paul B. Weston: *Arson*, Arco, New York, 1954.

"Blood, Fiber and Hair Evidence in Crimes *vs* Person," *FBI Law Enforcement Bulletin*, June 1958.

"Blood, Hair and Fiber Analysis," *FBI Law Enforcement Bulletin*, March 1950.

Bryan, D. E. and V. P. Guinn: "Forensic Activation Analysis—Trace-Level Elements in Commercial Paints," *Transactions of the American Nuclear Society*, vol. 9, 1966.

Burke, John J.: "Testifying in Court," *FBI Law Enforcement Bulletin*, September 1975.

Burton, John: *Glass*, Chilton, Philadelphia, 1967.

"Charred Documents Frequently Provide Valuable Evidence," *FBI Law Enforcement Bulletin*, February 1961.

Classification of Fingerprints, U.S. Government Printing Office, Washington, D.C., 1947.

Coleman and Weston: "A Case Concerning NAA of Glass," *Journal of Forensic Sciences*, vol. 8, 1968.

Conway, J. V. P.: *Evidential Documents*, Charles C. Thomas, Springfield, IL, 1972.

"Corpus Delecti Is Established by Blood Evidence," *FBI Law Enforcement Bulletin*, August 1957.

"Correctly Obtaining Known Samples Aids the Document Examiner," *FBI Law Enforcement Bulletin*, July 1962.

Culliford, Bryan: *The Examination and Typing of Bloodstains in the Crime Laboratory*, U.S. Department of Justice, Law Enforcement Assistance Administration, Washington, D.C., 1971.

Davies, Geoffrey: *Forensic Science*, American Chemical Society, Washington, D.C., 1975.

Davis, John E.: *An Introduction to Tool Marks, Firearms and the Striagraph*, Charles C. Thomas, Springfield, IL, 1958.

"Document Examiner Bases His Decision on Scientific Study," *FBI Law Enforcement Bulletin*, January 1963.

"Don't Overlook Evidentiary Value of Glass Fragments," *FBI Law Enforcement Bulletin*, February 1973.

Erskine, Addine: *The Principles & Practice of Blood Grouping*, Mosby, St. Louis, 1973.

"Expert Testimony in Court Governed by Many Factors," *FBI Law Enforcement Bulletin*, April 1960.

Fakhari, N. R., *et al.*: "Absorption and Elution on Plates," *International Police Review*, February 1971.

"FBI Laboratory Makes Tool Mark Examinations," *FBI Law Enforcement Bulletin*, September 1950, revised January 1975.

Ferguson, R. W.: *Drug Abuse Control*, Holbrook Press, Boston, 1975.

Ferguson, Robert J. and Allan L. Miller: *The Polygraph in Court*, Charles C. Thomas, Springfield, IL, 1973.

"Fiber and Fabric Analysis," *FBI Law Enforcement Bulletin*, December 1953.

"Forensic Emphasis Shifts to Broader Role," *Chemical Engineering News*, February 1973.

Guinn, V. P., ed.: *Proceedings of the First International Conference of Forensic Activation Analysis*, Report GA-8171, Gulf Energy & Environmental Systems, Conf. 660937.

"Gunpowder and Shot Pattern Test," *FBI Law Enforcement Bulletin*, September 1970.

"Gunpowder Tests," *FBI Law Enforcement Bulletin*, August 1949.

Hall, Jay Cameron: *Inside the Crime Lab*, Prentice-Hall, Englewood Cliffs, NJ, 1974.

Hammesfahr, James E. and Clair Strong: *Creative Glass Blowing*, W. H. Freeman, San Francisco, 1968.

"Handwriting Habits Are Basic Factors in Identification," *FBI Law Enforcement Bulletin*, March 1963.

Hendry, Sgt. Ed. B.: "Restoring a Heavily Rusted Weapon—No Problem If You Know How," *Fingerprint and Identification Magazine*, September 1975.

Henry, Sir E. R.: *Classification and Uses of Fingerprints*, Chicago Medical Book, Chicago, 1934.

Hoffman, C. M., *et al.*: "Comparison of Forensic Soil Specimens by Neutron Activation Analysis," in J. R. Devoe, ed., *Modern Trends in Activation Analysis*, USAEC Report Conf. 681003, 2 vols., NBS Special Pub. 312, U.S. Government Printing Office, 1969.

Horgan, John J.: *Criminal Investigation*, McGraw-Hill, New York, 1974.

Hormachea, Carroll: *Sourcebook in Criminalistics*, Reston, Reston, VA, 1974.

Inbau, Fred, Andre Moenssens, and Louis Vitullo: *Scientific Evidence in Criminal Cases*, Foundation Press, Mineola, NY, 1973.

Irwin, Samuel: "Drugs of Abuse, An Introduction to Their Action and Potential Hazards," *The Student Association for the Study of Hallucinogens*, Madison, WI, 1973.

Issitt, Peter and Charla Issitt: *Applied Blood Group Serology*, 2d ed., Spectra Biological, Oxnard, CA, 1975.

Jürgen, Thorwald: *Crime and Science: The New Frontier in Criminology*, Harcourt, Brace, Jovanovich, New York, 1967.

Kersta, L. G.: *Fingerprint and Identification Magazine*, July 1963.

Kind, Stuart and Michael Overman: *Science Against Crime*, Doubleday, Garden City, NY, 1972.

Kirk, Paul L.: *Crime Investigation*, Wiley, New York, 1974.

————: *Density and Refractive Index*, Charles C. Thomas, Springfield, IL, 1971.

————: *Fire Investigation*, Wiley, New York, 1969.

Leonard, V. A.: *The Police Detective Function*, Charles C. Thomas, Springfield, IL, 1970.

Lloyd, J. B. K., K. Hadley, and B. R. G. Roberts: "Pyrolysis Gas Chromatography Over Hydrogenated Graphitized Carbon-Black Differentiation of Chewing Gum Bases for Forensic Purposes," *Journal of Chromatography*, vol. 101, 1974.

Lukens, *et al.*: "Forensic Nuclear Activation of Paper," USAEC Report GA-10113, Gulf Energy & Environmental Systems, 1970.

Lundquist, Frank: *Methods of Forensic Science*, vol. 1, Interscience Publishers, New York, 1962.

MacDonell, Herbert and Lorraine Bialousz: *Flight Characteristics and Stain Patterns of Human Blood*, U.S.G.P.O., Washington, D.C. 1971.

McCrone, W. C., and G. C. Woodard: "The Vinland Map: Genuine or Forged?" *Physics in Technology*, January 1975, p. 18.

Moenssens, Andre E.: *Fingerprint Techniques*, Chilton, Philadelphia, 1971.

Murray, Raymond C. and C. F. Tedrow: *Forensic Geology*, Rutgers University Press, New Brunswick, NJ, 1975.

Myre, Daniel C.: *Death Investigation*, International Association of Chiefs of Police, Washington, D.C., 1974.

O'Brien, Kevin P. and Robert C. Sullivan: *Criminalistics Theory and Practice*, 2d ed., Holbrook Press, Boston, 1972.

O'Hara, Charles E. and James W. Osterburg: *An Introduction to Criminalistics*, Indiana University Press, Bloomington, ID, 1972.

"Oil Spill Identification System," Document ADA 00380/LK, National Technical Information Service, Springfield, VA.

"Out of the Ashes: The Examination of Burned or Charred Evidence," *FBI Law Enforcement Bulletin*, December 1955.

"Penned: The Role of Handwriting in Law Enforcement," *FBI Law Enforcement Bulletin*, March 1959.

Penrose, L. S.: "Dermatoglyphics," *Scientific American*, December 1969.

Pillay, K. K. S., S. H. Levine, and W. A. Jester: "Radionuclear Forensic Investigation," Pennsylvania State University, Department of Nuclear Engineering, Breazeale Nuclear Reactor, University Park, PA., Oct. 1974.

"Preserving Prints of Shoes and Tires on Hard Surfaces," *FBI Law Enforcement Bulletin,* June 1961, revised April 1974.

"Properties of Glasses and Glass Ceramics," a Corning Glass publication, Corning, NY, August 1973.

Reid, John and Fred Inbau: *Truth and Deception: The Polygraph Technique,* Williams & Wilkins, Baltimore, 1966.

Rodgers, P. G., et al.: "The Classification of Automotive Paint by Diamond Window Infrared Spectrophotometry, Part III, Case Histories," *Canadian Society of Forensic Science Journal,* vol. 9, No. 3, 1976.

Ryder, Michael: *Hair,* Crane, Russak & Co., 1973.

Sansone, J. J.: *Modern Photographs for Police and Fireman,* W. H. Anderson, Cincinnati, 1972.

Savage, George: *Glass,* Putnam, New York, 1965.

The Science of Fingerprints, U.S. Government Printing Office, Washington, D.C., 1971.

Soderman, Harry and John J. O'Connell: *Modern Criminal Investigation,* 5th ed., Funk & Wagnalls, New York, 1962.

"Some Historical Aspects of Document Examination," *FBI Law Enforcement Bulletin,* April 1965.

Sussman, Leon: *Blood Grouping Tests: Medicolegal Uses,* Charles C. Thomas, Springfield, IL, 1968.

Svensson, Arne: *Techniques of Crime Scene Investigation,* 2d ed., American Elsevier, New York, 1965.

"They Write Their Own Sentences," *FBI Law Enforcement Bulletin,* September 1953.

"Tips on Making Cast of Shoe and Tire Prints," *FBI Law Enforcement Bulletin,* October 1963.

Townshend, David G.: "Photographing and Casting Toolmarks," *FBI Law Enforcement Bulletin,* April 1976.

Turner, William W.: *Criminalistics,* Bancroft and Whitney, San Francisco, 1964.

"Typewriter Examination," *FBI Law Enforcement Bulletin,* May 1967.

"Use of Voiceprint in Court Proceedings Creates Legal Debate," *Wall Street Journal,* March 13, 1972, p. 1.

Vanderbosch, Charles G.: *Criminal Investigation,* International Association of Chiefs of Police, Washington, D.C., 1968.

"Visual Presentations Assist Investigation and Prosecution," *FBI Law Enforcement Bulletin,* May 1963.

Voice Identification Research, U.S. Justice Dept. publication PR 72-1, U.S. Government Printing Office, February 1972.

Walls, H. J.: *Forensic Science,* Praeger, New York, 1968.

"Writing Standards Must Be Admissable for Court Testimony," *FBI Law Enforcement Bulletin,* October 1960.

Index